ENGLISH CHURCH
FITTINGS FURNITURE
AND ACCESSORIES

Fig. 1. ASTBURY, CHESHIRE.

ENGLISH CHURCH FITTINGS FURNITURE AND ACCESSORIES

By

J. CHARLES COX
LL.D., F.S.A.

AUTHOR OF "THE ENGLISH PARISH CHURCH,"
"CHURCHWARDENS' ACCOUNTS," &c., &c.

WITH AN INTRODUCTION BY
AYMER VALLANCE

This edition digitally re-mastered and
published by JM Classic Editions © 2008
Original text © J Charles Cox 1923

ISBN 978-1-905217-93-9

All rights reserved. No part of this book subject
to copyright may be reproduced in any form or
by any means without prior permission in writing
from the publisher.

PREFACE

THE idea of this book grew out of its predecessor, *The English Parish Church*, which was published by Messrs. Batsford about the close of 1914. That comprehensive but compendious volume received such unexpected praise from all classes of authors, architects, ecclesiological experts, as well as men of letters at large, that I felt inclined to listen to the suggestion made by several friends, well versed in such matters and backed by my publishers, that I should undertake a sequel or supplementary volume dealing solely with the interiors and surroundings of our churches, such as the churchyard and those details which group themselves under the precise term of "fittings," and form no part of the actual fabric.

In short, the notion of these pages is to expand the last, curtly brief, chapter of the first book, to which the name was given of "What to note *in* an old Parish Church." To such a supplemental book it seemed only reasonable to assign as a distinctive label the title of *English Church Fittings, Furniture and Accessories*.

An obstacle at once suggested itself to my mind in the issuing of these pages. I had been the joint author, in conjunction with Dr. Henry Harvey, of a book on somewhat similar lines, styled *English Church Furniture*, published in 1907 by Messrs. Methuen & Co. It will be found, however, that the former work, of which a third amended and enlarged edition will shortly be issued, is projected on quite different lines. It aims at producing long and complete lists, county by county, of such matters as fonts, pulpits, screens, etc., a notion which is quite alien to the plan of the present book. Moreover, this is in no sense a mere repetition or abridgment of its predecessor, and fully half of this book is of absolutely novel details which are not even alluded to in the "Furniture" work.

Another distinctive feature is the wealth of new illustrations. As I have said on another occasion, I feel it to be mere justice to remark that if this book meets with any degree of success or appreciation, it will be at least as much due to the beautiful pictures, chiefly from unhackneyed sources, as to the nature of the letterpress.

Under these circumstances, Messrs. Methuen have had the courtesy to waive the objection which they might have technically raised to its publication.

The pleasant task remains to me—always, I conceive, a real joy to the conscientious book-writer—of giving brief but genuine thanks to the chief of many kind helpers. To my publishers, the late Mr. Herbert and Mr. Harry Batsford, I owe much, for not only have our business relationships been cordial, but their advice and help have been so frequent that I regard them as coadjutors. Foremost amongst old and eminently capable friends I must mention those well-known antiquaries, the late Rev. R. M. Sergeantson, rector of St. Peter's, Northampton, and my cousin, Mr. Aymer Vallance. Among the clergy who have given me particular help or special information I desire to remember with gratitude the aid of the Rev. J. Clare Hudson, vicar of Thornton, near Horncastle, of the Rev. G. E. Jeans, vicar of Shorwell, Isle of Wight, the Rev. T. B. Brocklehurst, vicar of Giggleswick, the Rev. Canon Fowler, of Durham, the Rev. R. G. Norris, vicar of Wedmore, Wells, the Rev. G. W. Saunders, vicar of Curry Rivel, Taunton, the Rev. A. P. Howes, vicar of Rye; and not a few others who have been privately thanked. Several gentlemen, cleric and lay, to whom I am indebted for illustrations, are thanked in the subsequent note of acknowledgment.

For the painstaking and helpful "reading" of the book, both in typescript and in print, I owe much to my daughter, V. M. M. Cox.

The church cannot be approached without passing through the churchyard, and as it received its own special consecration, and has many interesting associations, it certainly deserves greater attention than is usually bestowed upon it by ecclesiologists, and especially by the ordinary run of those who take some real interest in old churches. It is, therefore, only fitting that it should herein receive primary attention, under various sub-headings, ere the interior of the church is reached.

But most of these pages are concerned with the chief features of the church's interior, and they have been put together in the hope that they may prove useful and helpful to the many students of our old parish churches who lack the time to make acquaintance with the various books and treatises that have been penned upon most of the items pertaining to the expression of their inner ritual and worship. It has been rightly said of the actual fabric of an ancient Christian church, that "Every stone that we look upon in this repository of past ages is both an entertainment and a monitor." And if this is the case even with their exterior, still deeper should be the thoughts associated with the inner craftsmanship and beauty produced by successive generations of our pious forefathers, for all the skill that they consecrated to God in brightening His sanctuary was thus used in order

> "to rouse the heart and lead the will
> By a bright ladder to the world above."

J. CHARLES COX.

NOTE.

My late uncle, Herbert Batsford, commissioned the Rev. Dr. Cox to prepare this book on the same lines as his *English Parish Church* but to deal with Interior Fitments, Furniture and other Accessories. Dr. Cox was engaged on the compilation of the book for a number of years and at the time of his lamented death, a year or two ago, he had finished it, without an introduction, and had also partially arranged for the illustrations. Since then it has been found advisable to revise and extend it in view of fresh developments and also thoroughly to remodel and largely increase the illustrations, in the endeavour to illustrate briefly, but not inadequately, the chief types and variations of each feature, especially as regards both early and later periods, and the distinctive local work of different districts. Even exercising the utmost economy in both text and pictures it was evident that the scope and extent of the book rendered it imperative to publish it in a somewhat more ample form and larger size than *The English Parish Church.*

Mr. Aymer Vallance, M.A., F.S.A., whose friendship with Dr. Cox extended over many years, has kindly consented to write a full illustrated introduction to the book, and every effort has been made to furnish a concise but clear account of the numerous features of interest in a typical English Parish Church.

HARRY BATSFORD

March, 1923.

NOTE OF ACKNOWLEDGMENT

IN addition to the acknowledgments in the Preface, we are indebted in many ways for drawings and photographs. Especially we have to express our gratitude for many of the pictures reproduced to Mr. Fred. H. Crossley's incomparable series of fine photographs of Church features and fittings. The numbers of these are as follows: 1, 3, 4, 6, 11, 14-6, 18, 20, 22-3, 25, 27, 37-45, 49-51, 61-3, 73-8, 80-1, 84-7, 89, 90, 92-7, 100-2, 104-5, 108, 111-5, 121-2, 127-130, 133-4, 136-9, 141-2, 144-7, 150, 152-5, 159, 161-4, 167, 169-70, 175, 177, 179, 182, 186, 193-8, 202, 216-7, 224-7, 232-3, 235, 239, 243-4, 251, 254-7, 259-261. We owe thanks also to the series of photographs taken respectively by Dr. G. Granville Buckley, for Figs. 72, 79, 98, 103, 116-7, 131-2, 135, 242, 245-8; the Rev. F. Sumner, Figs. 17, 109, 125-6, 156, 223; the Rev. F. R. P. Sumner, Figs. 91, 207, 263; and Miss L. A. P. Sumner, Fig. 48. A number of Renaissance woodwork subjects are from a special series by Walshams Ltd., taken under the direction of the late Herbert Batsford. Messrs. Frith have contributed from their extensive series of English Church views Figs. 2, 21, 30-1, 88, 119, 140, 143, 168, 176, 178, 184, 249, and we have to thank Mr. W. Marriott Dodson for Figs. 5, 252, 258; the late Mr. W. Galsworthy Davie, Figs. 26, 28, 165, 208-9, 228; Mr. Goulding of Beverley, Figs. 68-9; Mr. Horace Dan, Fig. 234; Messrs. J. Welch & Son of Portsmouth, Fig. 185; Mr. S. A. Driver, Figs. 46-7; and Messrs. W. H. Smith & Son, for Fig. 118. In addition, the Surrey Archæological Society has kindly supplied the Serpent, Fig. 220; Mr. Call of Monmouth, Fig. 149; Mr. Tyndall, of Ely, Fig. 151; Messrs. Park & Son, Fig. 272; Mr. F. Mair, Fig. 273; Mr. Boak of Bridlington, Fig. 203, and Mr. R. N. Heyworth, of Knighton, the Radnor Organ, Fig. 215. We must acknowledge the kindness of Mr. Allen L. Belcher for Figs. 55-8, from "Kentish Brasses" by W. D. Belcher, and Mr. Percy G. Stone for the painting at Shorwell, Fig. 204, from his "Antiquities of the Isle of Wight." Mr. F. E. Howard has supplied the Embroidery from Gt. Bircham, Figs. 267-8, and the Maidens' Garlands, at Ilam, Staffordshire, Fig. 274, was taken by the late Sir Benjamin Stone, and is included by permission of his sons. The British Museum has kindly permitted the reproduction of Stained Glass drawings from the Warrington Collection, as well as Figs. 123-4, 187-190, 211-3, and to the Victoria and Albert Museum (Board of Education) we owe Figs. 181, 240, 253. For Figs. 24 and 238 we must thank the Derbyshire Archæological Society, and Mr. Aymer Vallance has kindly supplied Figs. 7-9 and 13. Mr. J. C. Wall has drawn for the book Figs. 33, 65-7, 110, 116: Fig. 221 is by Miss G. Cox, and Figs. 199-201 are from Mr. N. H. J. Westlake's work on "Mural Paintings."

Fig. 166 is from "Notes on the Parish Church of Lymington" by the Rev. C. Bostock; Fig. 172 from a paper on "Hatchments" by Christopher A. Markham, F.S.A., in the Proceedings of the Archæological Society of Northampton; Fig. 173 from the Rev. R. M. Sergeantson's "History of the Church of St. Peter, Northampton," and Fig. 237 from Mr. E. A. Jones' "Church Plate of the Diocese of Bangor;" several subjects have been derived from the issues of "The Reliquary"; to all of these thanks are due.

Should an acknowledgment of any photograph or drawing have been inadvertently omitted, we trust that it will be understood that it has only occurred owing to the death of the author at the time when the book was in the midst of preparation.

ERRATA

Page 56, Fig. 42, for Ardine read *Arderne*.

Page 83, Fig. 62, for Lancashire read *Lincolnshire*.

Page 103, 6th line from bottom, for "stole" read *"stone."*

Page 104, line 36, for 14th Century read 13*th Century*.

Page 109, line 29, for 1400 read 1500.

Page 119, Fig. 110, for 14th Century read 15*th Century*.

Page 122, line 19, for "Western" read *"Eastern."*

Page 129, Fig. 122, for St. Mary read *St. Mary the Virgin*.

Page 130, Fig. 124, for Romsey, Hampshire read *Ramsey, Huntingdonshire*.

Page 186, Fig. 179, for 15th Century read 14*th Century*.

Page 207, Fig. 191, for "Worcestershire" read *"Warwickshire."*

Page 264, Fig. 244, for "Norman" read *"Transitional."*

Page 267, line 21, for "Norman" read *"Transitional."*

Page 295, line 28, for "15th" read *"13th."*

Page 296, line 31, for "Chipping Camden in Gloucestershire" read *"Steeple Aston, Oxon."*

Page 296, line 40, for "13th Century" read *"late 15th Century."*

CONTENTS

CHAP.		PAGE
	INTRODUCTION	1
I.	THE CHURCHYARD	24
II.	MONUMENTS WITHIN THE CHURCH	47
III.	THE TOWER AND BELLS	76
IV.	FONTS AND FONT COVERS	87
V.	THE SEATING OF CHURCHES	103
VI.	PULPITS AND LECTERNS	121
VII.	SCREENS AND LOFTS	133
VIII.	IRON-WORK	154
IX.	ARMOUR, ROYAL ARMS, HATCHMENTS	164
X.	CLOCKS AND SAND GLASSES	181
XI.	CHAINED BOOKS AND CHURCH LIBRARIES	193
XII.	PAINTED GLASS	199
XIII.	MURAL PAINTINGS	212
XIV.	CANDELABRA AND CRESSET STONES	224
XV.	ORGANS AND OTHER MUSICAL INSTRUMENTS	233
XVI.	ALTARS, REREDOSES, ALTAR RAILS, PLATE, ETC.	245
XVII.	PISCINÆ, SEDILIA, EASTER SEPULCHRES	265
XVIII.	ALMERIES, BREAD CUPBOARDS, COFFERS, ALMS-BOXES	274
XIX.	ENCAUSTIC TILES	287
XX.	VARIA: Dog Tongs, Embroidery, Acoustic Jars, Confessionals and Low Side Windows, Biers and Coffins, Maidens' Funeral Garlands	294
	INDEX	307

"But wouldst thou know the beauty of holiness?—go alone on some week-day, borrowing the keys of good Master Sexton, traverse the cool aisles of some country church: think of the piety that has kneeled there—the congregations, old and young, that have found consolation there—the meek pastor—the docile parishioner. With no disturbing emotions, no cross conflicting comparisons, drink in the tranquillity of the place, till thou thyself become as fixed and motionless as the marble effigies that kneel and weep around thee."

—*Charles Lamb.*

Fig. 1A. Interior of a Church as Depicted by an Eighteenth Century Artist.

From a Drawing by F. Wright, 1790.

INTRODUCTION.

CENTURIES and centuries ago, when the city of Rome was yet young, or ever Julius Cæsar was, nay, or ever Consuls were, while Rome was Rome of the Kings, it befel that Lucius Tarquin the Second was wearer of the purple. And, seeking audience of him, there came a mysterious aged woman, who, being admitted into his presence, produced nine volumes, filled from cover to cover with the script of ancient Runes, which she desired Tarquin to buy from her. The price she named was enormous—a king's ransom, no less. Tarquin declined to pay the sum asked, and the woman went away; but, having burned three volumes, came back again and, to his amazement, offered him the remaining six books for the same price she had asked for the original number. Once more the king refused, and again the woman went away; but presently returned with only three volumes left, which she offered once again, and that for the same price she had named at the beginning. Thereat the king was troubled and took counsel of his soothsayers and advisers what he should do. Their rede was that the books of prophecies must be secured at all costs; and so the king did, and thus obtained for himself and his country the great treasure of the Sibylline Books. Which things are an allegory. Though that which is plentiful be dear, that which is scarce is, on that very account, of immensely enhanced value. And when to the factor of rarity be added that of antiquity also, the value becomes inestimable. For once that which is old has perished, no power on earth can re-create it.

Hence it is impossible to over-estimate the importance of systematic study of the priceless and ever-diminishing treasures of the past. For to study is to acquire appreciation; and to appreciate is to realise the paramount obligation of preserving with most scrupulous care that which has come down to us, in order to hand on this precious heritage intact to posterity.

Foremost among repositories of antiquity are the fabrics and fittings of our historic parish churches, venerable and lovely still in spite of the many devastating changes that have swept over them. Instances, of course, unhappily abound in which the olden church fabric has been pulled down and rebuilt or has been robbed of its proper characteristics by the drastic hand of the " restorer." In every case of the kind the edifice belongs to the category of modern buildings, and as such alone can it be appraised. On the other hand, it is not too much to say that no ancient church, however plain and humble its structure and ornament (provided it shall have escaped recent reconstruction and refitting), can be totally destitute of features of archæological interest or artistic value.

It must be borne in mind that, while the chancel was the rector's, who, as such, was responsible for its maintenance and repair, on the other hand the nave was the part that belonged to the parishioners, who, in their turn, as responsible for its upkeep, took a personal interest in adorning and maintaining their portion of the sacred fabric. This being the case the nave of the parish church was apt to be put to a variety of uses. It was, remarks J. C. Jeafferson, " by turns, or simultaneously, a public hall, a theatre, a warehouse, a market, a court of justice." In the absence of other public buildings the parish nave would become " a hall for the poor," as also " it was a museum of sculpture and painting, an academy of music," while "running through all these arrangements there was a current of salutary religious influence."*

For this secularisation, if one must apply the term, was due not to any irreligious spirit, but to the guileless, happy confidence of children who felt themselves quite at home in their heavenly Father's house. It was only when the morose and sombre Puritanism of the 16th and 17th centuries drove men to dread Almighty God rather than to love Him, that they began to feel shy and ill at ease in church —a feeling mistaken for reverence—and that they learned to draw hard and fast distinctions between sacred and profane.

The intimate and necessary association then of the town or village church with the common life of every parish community, as that life's centre and focus, in daily, nay hourly, requisition, could not but cause the mediæval church to occupy a far more prominent position in former times than it does at the present day, when its doors are practically closed to any purpose except actual services, and these, for the most part, frequented only on one day in the week.

A certain index of the people's passionate love for and pride in their parish church in Mediæval England is afforded by the study of ancient wills, which illustrate more convincingly than any other class of documents the widespread solicitude which unfailingly provided for all that pertained to the worship of Almighty God and to the

* Walter Johnson, *Byways in British Archæology*.

FIG. 2. THAXTED, ESSEX.

Fig. 3. CHARLTON-ON-OTMOOR, OXON: SCREEN. EARLY 16TH CENTURY.

Fig. 4. GRUNDISBURGH, SUFFOLK: Chancel Screen. East Anglian Type, 15th Century.

Fig. 5. PATRICIO, BRECONSHIRE: A Typical Welsh Rood Screen. Late 15th or early 16th Century.

Fig. 6. MARWOOD, DEVON: Detail of Screen. Late 15th or early 16th Century.

beautifying of His hallowed sanctuary. Compare these olden testamentary bequests with those of modern times, and the difference in the attitude of the people then and now towards the maintenance of their religion is sufficiently startling. " True," it is sometimes objected, " but mediæval layfolk were both unlettered and priest-ridden, and when the time came for one of them to make his will, he would have no choice but to call in the only man in the place who could write, and that man being the priest, would naturally, by judicious pressure, contrive to wring from the poor dying wretch whatever clerical avarice might require." But such a view of the case is both shallow and ill-founded. The exact contrary is the truth. These are spontaneous dispositions of persons entirely free in their choice, whether to give or to withhold, free and unfettered as air—of persons whose lavish bequests, so far from being wrung from them in the hour of dissolution through craven fear of threatened hell with all its torments, are couched in the language of sturdy independence. Only men dealing with others on terms of perfect equality would be in a position to speak as they do. Nay, rather, their wills are suggestive and characteristic of persons having the upper hand, imposing conditions upon servants in their pay. Again and again they stipulate that the priest who accepts the responsibility of carrying out their bequests must be *honestus*, one, that is, of upright and reputable behaviour. Let there be no mistake nor misunderstanding on the subject. Requirements of this nature express the layman's, not the cleric's, point of view. Loyalty to his own caste would alone prevent the priest from sanctioning the passing of such reflections on the part of a layman upon members of the sacerdotal body. No, the supposition is not feasible. The generous bequests in mediæval wills were not made under any sort of pressure, but voluntarily, and proceed from the layman's inherent affection for and pride in the parish church, as an institution and property peculiarly his own. Not infrequently these factors expressed themselves in healthy rivalry, neighbouring parishes vying with one another in the effort to produce a surpassingly rich and handsome display in their respective church fabrics.

And yet the æsthetic value of old English church fittings, as distinct from their symbolic or ecclesiastical significance, is a study which, if it has already met with a certain amount of appreciation in the 20th, was, strange to say, largely neglected in the 19th century. The achievements, however, of our forefathers in wood, stone, metal work, decorative painting and embroidery, all contributing to the magnificent ensemble of the mediæval interior, were remarkable and deserving of the highest admiration, as may be gathered from such isolated remains as are to be found in our ancient churches from one end of the country to another, or in a more complete form in the rarer instances which happily yet occur, here and there, in such superbly equipped parish churches as those of Astbury, Cheshire (Fig. 1); Ewelme, Oxon (Fig. 16); Mere, Wilts; Long Melford, Suffolk; Ranworth, Norfolk; or Thaxted, Essex (Fig. 2), for example. Hundreds of these specimens might be named, which are worthy of the most attentive study, not only from the purely archæological and ecclesiological standpoint, but also for the valuable object lessons which they furnish in the history and processes of the various handicrafts of our native land.

It may be claimed, without vaingloriousness, that the standard of the workmanship of our country's craftsmen, and the versatility of their design, beautiful in itself as well as being perfectly adapted to its purpose, will bear favourable comparison with the artistic products of the European continent, which through becoming better known to students have on that account attracted to themselves a larger share of admiration.

It is of no little interest to observe the growth and correlation of the various arts of this country, to watch how they acted and reacted upon one another; or to trace the rise and expansion of some among them, while others may be said to have lagged behind the rest, if not to have stood still. The first to develop was the mason's craft, and naturally and rightly so, for the subordinate and applied arts require first to be provided with a roof over them, or, at any rate, some sort of fixed home to attach themselves to, before they have any motive or justification for existing. Incidentally it may be observed that, so long as the *soi-disant* Royal Academy of Arts devotes its energy almost exclusively to the excellent, but secondary and accessory, arts of painting and sculpture, to the virtual neglect of architecture, it is neglecting its primary function, and can never hope to direct the taste of the nation into the paths of artistic sanity and progress. For architecture is the one all-important and paramount art of arts, the parent and sovereign of them all. In the Middle Ages the progression of architecture was steady and always in advance of that of the other arts, so that it afforded them a definite and conspicuous standard, in whose train they ranged themselves, reflecting in their several ways the norm or current style of the great mother art. Contemporaneously with the early stages of the advance of the mason's art, the virile craft of the ironsmith attained to a specially remarkable proficiency; but towards the close of the Middle Ages smithing exhibited perhaps the least amount of vitality and imaginativeness of all the arts. It is only necessary to contrast, for example, the rich and varied design

FIG. 7. LALESTON, GLAMORGANSHIRE: 15TH CENTURY CHURCHYARD CROSS.

Fig. 9. WYCHLING, KENT: Saxon Lead Font, early 13th Century.
(*The enclosing arcade is modern.*)

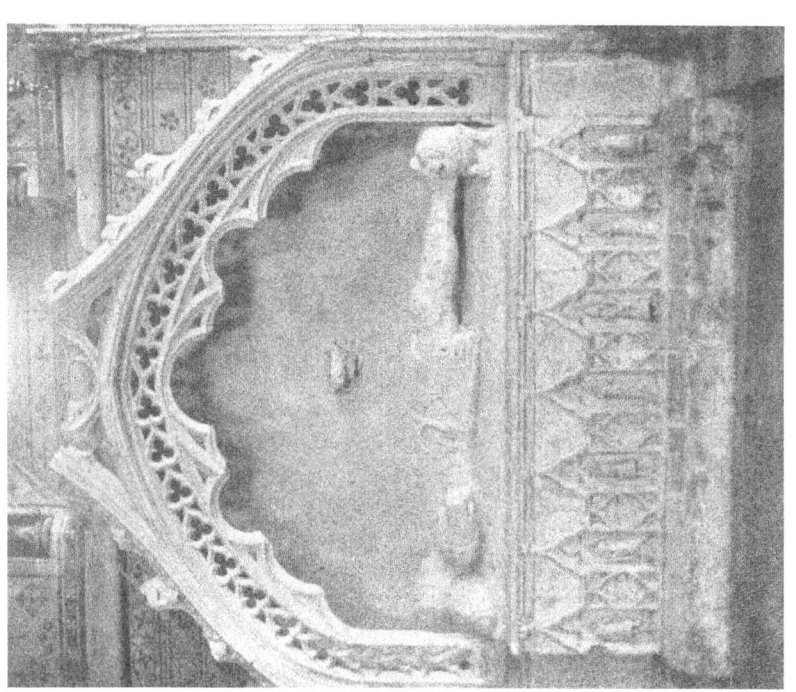

Fig. 8. FOLKESTONE, KENT: Tomb of Sir John de Segrave. 1349.

FIG. 11. HULL, HOLY TRINITY CHURCH:
14TH CENTURY FONT.

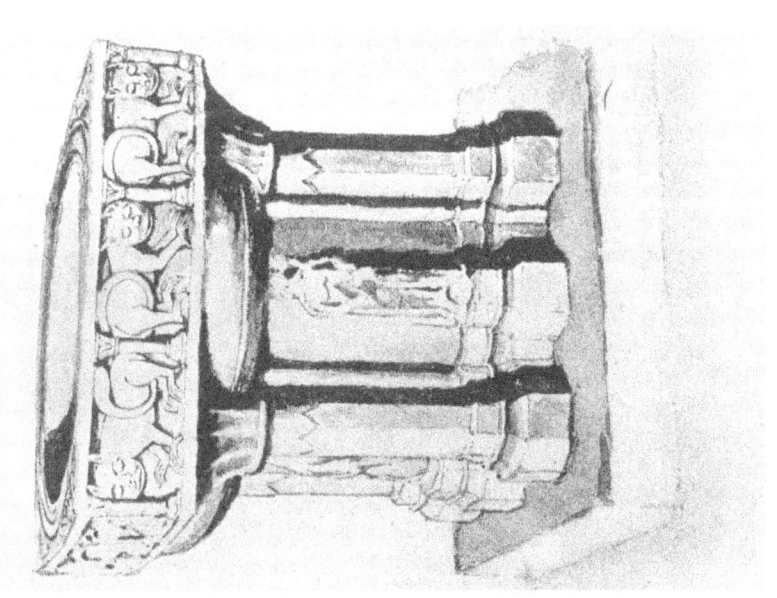

FIG. 10. ST. PETER, IPSWICH:
TOURNAI FONT, LATE 13TH CENTURY.

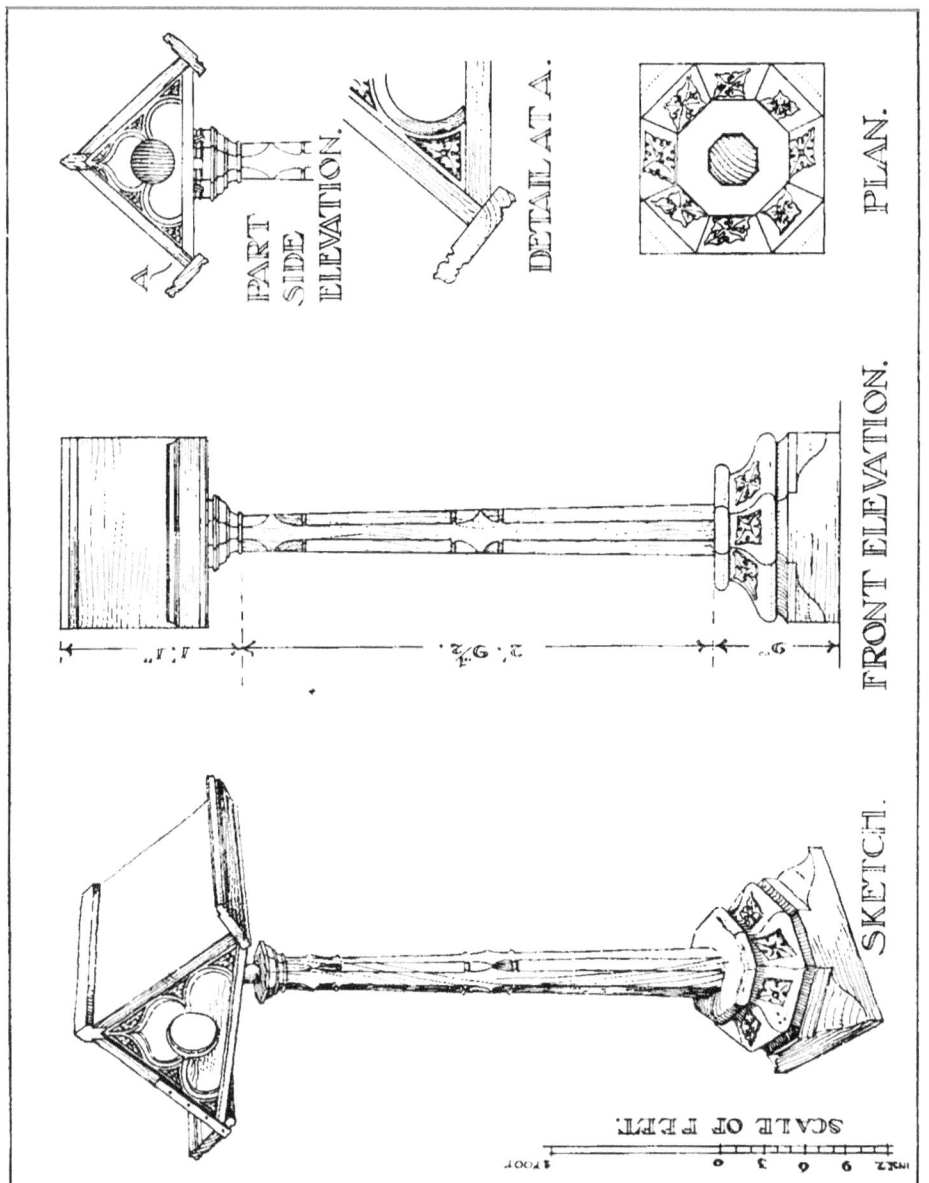

FIG. 12. HAWSTEAD, SUFFOLK: 15TH CENTURY OAK LECTERN.

of 13th century door-furniture and its magnificent scroll-foliage work, spreading over the whole surface of a door, with the unresourceful monotony of the straight strap hinges, typical of the 15th century, to realise the immense difference between the products of the respective periods. As to woodwork, its advance might have been measured in proportion as the carpenter and carver learned to emancipate themselves from the fetters of the earlier stone forms, and to elicit the inherent properties and capacities of their material. Compare, for example, the turned shafts and other features, directly derived from stonework, of the screen at Stanton Harcourt, Oxfordshire, with the vigorous maturity of other screens in the same county, e.g., Handborough or Charlton-on-Otmoor (Fig. 3), works wholly characteristic of wood construction and ornament. Or again, in the case of the art of the glass-painter, compare the crude colours and light-excluding effects of early 13th century glass, e.g., in the apse of Canterbury Cathedral, with the brilliance of the windows of the mid 15th century, flooding the interior with light and splendour, as in the ante chapel at All Souls' College, Oxford (effects largely due to the perfecting of the resources of yellow stain), and it will be realised that both woodwork and glasswork, having attained their highest development subsequently to ironwork, retained that pre-eminence so long as Gothic art itself flourished.

A significant factor is the prevalence of well-defined, divergent local types, a subject which it would be both interesting and profitable to follow out in detail. A few points only may be enumerated here. Take, for example, the western counties of Devonshire and Cornwall, having for the chief church of the diocese the squatly statured Cathedral of Exeter. The lowness of proportion of the mother church gives the keynote to the churches of the district, and is in striking contrast to the dignified and soaring dimensions of the typical churches of East Anglia, and the lofty openwork of the screens in which they conspicuously excel. A middle course between the two extremes would seem to have been followed in the Midlands, as in the churches of Derbyshire and Nottinghamshire, for example, which though sane and normal are less distinguished than those of East Anglia (Fig. 4); while the Welsh type, again, resembles that of the Devonshire churches, the decoration in Wales (Fig. 5) and Devonshire (Figs. 6, 127, 128), alike, especially the latter, inclining to a florid character, overloaded and lacking in boldness and the sense of restfulness, which reserve in ornament, with plenty of plain spaces to relieve and set off the richer elaboration, assuredly provides.

The author's plan is to draw the attention of his readers first to external features among the immediate surroundings of our old parish churches; and next, passing through the church door, to treat in turn of the many objects of interest within the building. And here it should be noted that notice is by no means confined to pre-Reformation features only. It may well cause surprise to find to what late dates are attributed most of the existing examples of lychgates. The use of lychgates of course dates back to pre-Reformation days, but of extant lychgates, though traditional in shape and construction, the author questions whether any are actually of mediæval date. The local occurrence of certain features is well exemplified at the outset; for if the county of Kent is second to none in respect of the number of lychgates it contains—that at Beckenham (Fig. 19) being of conspicuous merit—the said county is conspicuous for the total absence of any complete example of a churchyard cross, and even of all but the scantiest fragments of such crosses. The ancient churchyard cross steps survive at Folkestone and Teynham; and there is a fragment of a (probably 14th century) cross-head in the museum at Maidstone; but beyond these there is practically nothing to show in the whole county. One of the chief causes for this remarkable dearth may be the lack of suitable native freestone. Hence it is likely enough that the majority of the old crosses in Kent were constructed of timber, which has now vanished, as much on account of the perishable nature of the material as from any direct action of fanaticism.

At Laleston, in Glamorganshire (Fig. 7), is a strikingly handsome churchyard cross of 15th century work, which differs from any of those described in " Old Crosses and Lychgates,"* unless it be the demolished High Cross of Chester, though the resemblance is not really anything but remote. The Laleston cross belongs to the shaft-on-steps type, and its head at first sight looks not unlike the cross at Derwen in North Wales, but the peculiar feature of the Laleston cross-head, of tabernacle work and imagery, is that it consists of two tiers or stages, so that it might almost be described as a two-storeyed Eleanor, or spire-cross, mounted on a tall shaft. This motif may well have been of more frequent occurrence in former days than surviving crosses would lead one to suppose; for it is possible that some cross-heads which now consist of a single tier may originally have had an upper storey which has now perished, completely altering the contour of the top portion of the monument.

Among churchyard memorials may be cited a very fine table-tomb, with an engrailed cross at the head and foot, in the churchyard of Teynham, Kent. This example, which appears hitherto to have escaped notice, is illustrated in the latest (the 35th) volume of *Archæologia Cantiana*.

* *Old Crosses and Lychgates*, by Aymer Vallance, M.A., F.S.A. (Batsford, 1920).

Fig. 13. Harty Church, Sheppey, Kent: Carved Oak Coffer, late 14th Century.

Fig. 14. EYE, SUFFOLK.

Fig. 15. WESTHALL, SUFFOLK.

PAINTED DECORATION ON SCREENS, LATE 15TH CENTURY.

In respect of post-Reformation tombstones the author mentions the excellence of the lettering, in many cases even of a comparatively recent date. Such marked characteristics may be observed in various districts as to suggest the existence of traditional schools of monumental masons. Thus, in the church and churchyard of Dewsbury and of other neighbouring parishes, in the West Riding of Yorkshire, may be noted some admirably lettered inscriptions belonging to the 17th and 18th centuries.

A propos of the author's remarks on the survival of cock-fighting, one may cite the example of a cockpit in the green not far from the west end of Chislehurst Church in Kent.

After noticing the monuments without the church's walls it is natural to turn to those within. Of these monuments there is an immense variety. A fine example of a 14th century canopied tomb, believed to be that of Sir John de Segrave, *obit.* 1349, stands in a recess on the north side of the chancel at Folkestone Church. In the south arm of the transept at Minster Lovell, Oxfordshire, is an exquisite example of a stone table-tomb, with statuettes along the sides and ends. Of wooden tombs and effigies, chiefly no doubt on account of the less durable nature of the material, a comparatively small proportion has survived. Perhaps the most complete in existence is a monument with three recumbent effigies in Thornhill Church, Yorkshire, representing, it is believed, Sir John Saville with his successive wives, Alice and Elizabeth. The whole was surmounted by a tester, like a four-post bed, but the posts have unfortunately been sawn through and the canopy has vanished.

Although ironsmithing passed through a state bordering on stagnation in the 15th century, it was too virile an art not to revive, which is what it did before the close of the 16th century. To this period and later belongs a number of admirable specimens of wrought iron railings surrounding tombs, e.g., the tomb (1611) of the second founder, Thomas Sutton, in the chapel of the Charterhouse, London. It stands against the north wall, close to the altar. Again there is excellent ironwork in the finials of a tomb at the south extremity of the south arm of the transept at Ashford Church, Kent. The type of design in question is a peculiarly native product. It is not, indeed, Gothic, but is lineally descended from a Gothic ancestry, exhibiting forms evolved solely from the workmanlike treatment of the material itself. As such it is deserving of attentive consideration. There are, however, not a few lamentable instances in which these beautiful works have been broken up, or cast out of the churches to which they belong. Thus, at Boughton Malherbe, Kent, portions of railings removed from a tomb are now misused to form a fence outside the west door of the building. And, worse still, the railings which originally protected a tomb in Hawstead Church, Suffolk, have been set up in an open space in the parish to surround a tree planted in honour of the Coronation of Edward VII.

Among the evidences of the defensive use of churches may be cited a singular feature at Faversham, Kent, where, in the west wall of the north arm of the transept is a cross-shaped loophole for the use of a cross-bowman. It is not maintained that the said loophole is necessarily *in situ*, but its presence is sufficiently extraordinary to be worth noting in the above connection.

Ancient stone altars were without ornament, for the simple reason that when uncovered, as once a year they had to be according to the solemn ritual of Good Friday, they must then present a perfectly plain and bare appearance, else the stripping would lose its significance. The stone altar consisted of two parts, viz., a solid rectangular sub-structure of ashlar, and the *mensa*, or slab, fixed horizontally upon the top. The *mensa* would be in one piece, and was usually chamfered along its under edges, where it overhung the substructure. The *mensa* was distinguished on its upper surface by five incised crosses, requisite for the ceremonial anointing which invariably took place at the consecration of every altar. In addition there was generally a cavity in the front of the *mensa* to form a receptacle for relics, a tradition originating in the days of persecution, when the tombs of early Christian martyrs, interred in the catacombs, served for altars. In any event, whether there were relics or not, the five crosses were indispensable. At the change of religion in England in the 16th century the rage of the Reformers vented itself with peculiar animosity upon the stone altars of the old faith. Their stonework was demolished and the slabs themselves dismantled and profaned in various ways, either by being smashed to pieces, by being misappropriated for the gravestones of private individuals, or by being laid on the floor of the church porch or just within the entrance, in such a position that they could not avoid being spurned and trodden underfoot by every person who passed in or out of the building. Many altar-slabs survive in this situation, and if raised might be identified by the chamfering of their under edges, though the incised crosses on the top shall have become obliterated by wilful violence, or by the wear and tear of foot-traffic.

In regard to leaden fonts, a pure accident, in 1921, led to the discovery of an additional specimen, the existence of which had not previously been recorded nor even suspected—viz., at Lower Halstow, not far from Sittingbourne, Kent. Here the lead font had been completely hidden by a composite casing of brick and rubble work, the font itself resembling merely a lead lining within the masonry basin. At Eythorne, in the same county, is an interesting specimen of the 17th century, showing how late the tradition of making lead fonts continued, though the mediæval period had long passed away. Another Kentish example, little known owing to its remote situation, and obscured by a modern arcading, stands on a modern base in Wychling Church, Kent (Fig. 9). The ornament is so slight and simple that it is difficult to be sure of the date, but it appears to belong to the first half of the 13th century. There exists a curious class of fonts, commonly known as "Tournai Fonts," of black marble, or "touch," wrought abroad in the district of Tournai. Specimens of these remain chiefly in the larger or cathedral churches, but there is a remarkably fine example, its sides sculptured with lions, in the parish church of St. Peter, Ipswich (Fig. 10). Then, again, there is a certain number of fonts which are provided with an extra drain at one side, a remarkably perfect instance of which peculiarity may be seen at St. Martin's, Exeter.

Among 14th century fonts may be enumerated the very graceful examples at Holy Trinity, Hull (Fig. 11), and at St. Mary Magdalen's, Oxford. These have a tracery ornament only, while the fonts of about the same date at Ware, Herts, and St. Stephen's Church, St. Albans, are surrounded by standing imagery. The sole Kentish example of a "seven sacraments font" occurs at Farningham Church, but this is only a very poor and rude imitation of East Anglian work, with which indeed it is not worthy of being named in the same breath.

The incidence of font covers further illustrates the local distribution, or rather limitation, of church fittings. One very fine pinnacle cover exists at Fingringhoe, Essex ; and one other each at two parish churches in Canterbury, viz., St. Dunstan's and at Holy Cross.

Lecterns are much more frequently made of latten than anything else, but there is a certain small number of specimens in wood ; among which may be cited the lectern at Hawstead, Suffolk (Fig. 12), and two Kentish examples, viz., at Detling, near Maidstone (14th century), and at Lenham (15th or early 16th century).

It is possible that sedilia of wood existed in the majority of cases where there is no sign of stone sedilia, though wood has rarely survived. Not to mention cathedral and conventual churches, beautiful examples exist in the two neighbouring Kentish churches of Doddington and Rodmersham. In both these cases the sedilia are integrally one structure with parclose screens, and could not have been demolished without involving the destruction of the latter, which since the adjoining south chapels had become appropriated to private individuals, it did not suit the owners, jealous of their rights, to permit.

As to the "piscina," the late Sir William St. John Hope used to object to the term as incorrect, on the grounds, first, that it literally means a fish-pond, and, secondly, that the mediæval name for it was "sacrarium," or lavatory. The drain, however, is called *piscine* in France, whence perhaps it may be that the word was introduced into the terminology of our own country.

A remarkable specimen of a coffer of 14th century workmanship, of the type known to our forefathers as a "Flanders kist," because, no doubt, imported from the Low Countries, is yet preserved in Harty Church (Fig. 13) in the Isle of Sheppey. It is the only one of its kind possessed by any parish church in this country.

Of ancient alms-boxes may be mentioned a 16th century example, which takes the shape of a moulded post, at Eastchurch in the Isle of Sheppey.

Of pre-Reformation embroideries a remarkably beautiful cope of the 14th century, with scenes from Scripture and the martyrdoms of the Apostles, etc., on a white ground, cut up at the change of religion to form a hanging, belongs to the church of Steeple Aston, in Oxfordshire. It was for some time on view at the Victoria and Albert Museum, having been loaned by a recent rector. Of post-Reformation embroideries, surely the communion-table cloth of purple velvet, with applied sprays of flowers and fruits, wrought by the ladies Culpeper during the triste days of the Commonwealth, and now preserved at Hollingbourne Church, Kent, is as magnificent an example as one would wish to see. Among mediæval chalices, one of the most interesting is that, of late Gothic workmanship, which disappeared at the Reformation upheaval, but bearing the inscription "Restore me to Leyland," Lancashire, whence it originally came, has now found its way to the Catholic church of that place.

In conclusion, it will be seen that the ground traversed in these pages is vast, the objects encountered on the way both many and varied. And yet not a tithe survives of all that once made our old parish churches the pride and delight of the people of our own land, and the admiration of visitors from overseas. So scattered now are their artistic treasures that no single church, in its present day condition, affords the satisfying splendour and loveliness which ennobled it in the past. It is only by comparison and by piecing together from far and near the special features of many different parish churches that any adequate conception of their vanished glories can be obtained—here a rood loft, as at Flamborough (Fig. 142) in the East Riding, or Llanwrst in Wales; here an image, as at Cawston, Norfolk, or Breadsall, Derbyshire; here a painted screen, as at Attleborough or Ranworth in Norfolk, Eye (Fig. 14), and Westhall (Fig. 15)

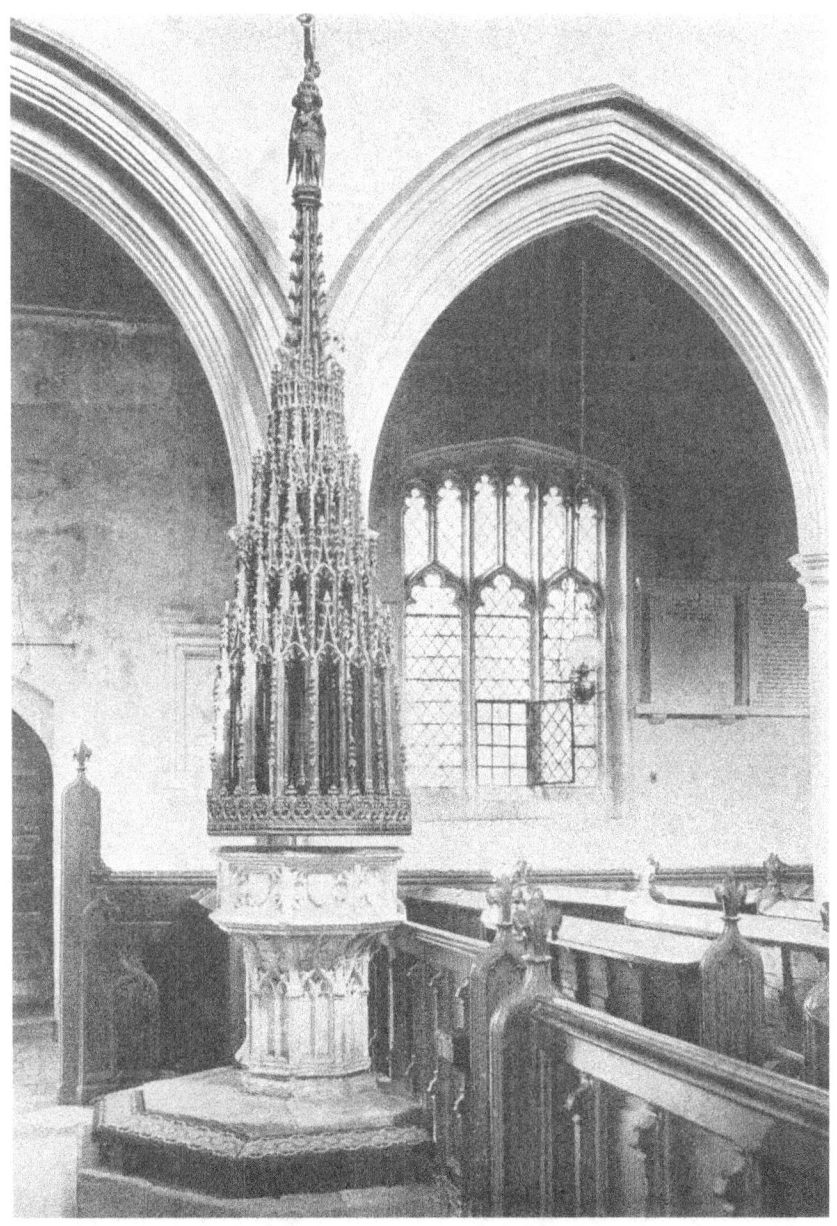

Fig. 16. EWELME, OXON; 15TH CENTURY FONT.
(*The cover is much restored.*)

Fig. 17. NORTHWOLD, NORFOLK. EASTER SEPULCHRE, 15TH CENTURY.

in Suffolk, or at Ashton in Devonshire ; here a soaring font cover, as at North Walsham, Norfolk, or at Ewelme, Oxfordshire (Fig. 16) ; here a perfect range of stall-work, as at Lancaster, or at Higham Ferrers, Northants ; here sedilia or Easter Sepulchre, as at Hawton, Nottinghamshire (Fig. 252), and Northwold, Norfolk (Fig. 17) ; a mural painting, as at Brook in Kent ; or painted glass windows, as at St. Martin's, York, or at Thornhill or Woolley in the West Riding. If we can picture a church containing not merely a single feature of this number, but each of them gathered together under one and the same roof, then we shall be able to realise that which once was, but has now been lost beyond recall. And then the legend of the " Sibylline Books " will surely come home to us with its timely warnings, its poignant lessons, and we shall understand how and why it is that every item of the art of our fathers which is yet preserved must, like the undestroyed Sibylline books, be cherished at all hazards, and that not because what has perished was of little or no account, but because what remains is priceless. And who is there so utterly devoid of imagination and romance that, gazing upon some ancient church, with its grey and hallowed walls, or listening to the mellow cadence of its wistful bells, does not seek to conjure up before his mental vision the picture of all that which it once represented, and sigh for the vanished glory of it, while, at the same time, devoutly rendering thanks to the Giver of all mercies for the decimated relics of those ancient splendours which decay and pillage, ignorance and bigotry, have suffered still to survive ?

September 1922.   AYMER VALLANCE.

CHAPTER I

THE CHURCHYARD

IN the very early days of Christianity there is no evidence of the burial of the dead in the outer court of the church, but instances occur as soon as the 4th century. Such a custom became general, however, after the 6th century; it is said that Cuthbert, Archbishop of Canterbury (745-756), caused this habit to be universally adopted throughout England. The first recorded instance of the formal consecration of a churchyard is mentioned by Gregory of Tours, the 6th century historian of the French church.

Entrance to the fenced-off consecrated area of the churchyard was usually gained through the lychgate, or gate of the dead, from *lic*, Anglo-Saxon for a corpse, sometimes known as the corpse-gate. This wide gateway is occasionally provided, as in Cornwall, with a raised stone slab in the centre, on which to rest the corpse or coffin, but it is usually protected by a broad outstanding gabled roof, so as to afford shelter to the bearers whilst awaiting the arrival of the priest to say the introductory sentences of the burial office. Such gateways undoubtedly prevailed in pre-Reformation days, and there is recorded evidence of them at least as early as the 14th century. It is, however, doubtful if any large number of those lychgates now in use as the entrances to country churchyards retain any work of mediæval date, either in wood or stone. There are several which appear to date from the 17th century. The gateway on the south of Kellington churchyard, W.R., Yorks, is dated 1698. Some of the timberwork of the two old Middlesex lychgates of Hayes and Heston seems clearly to date from the first half of the 17th century. These two lychgates have quaint pulley arrangements for opening and closing; the former is still in working order. Heston gateway was well illustrated by lithographed drawings, including transverse and longitudinal sections, in the Dictionary issued by the Architectural Publication Society in March, 1862. At the same time good drawings to scale were also produced of the picturesque roadside lychgate of the parish church of Beckenham, Kent (Fig. 19), about which Hone chatted pleasantly in his *Year Book* so long ago as 1827. This old church (St. George) was

THE CHURCHYARD

entirely rebuilt in 1886, but happily the lychgate, which originally was roofed with shingles, was spared.

At least half a dozen of these venerable gateways have disappeared, well within the writer's recollection, in the county of Kent alone, which even now is probably still richer in lychgates than any other English county, ancient examples remaining at Beckenham, West Wickham, Lenham, Staple and Boughton Monchelsea. The old lychgate of South Weald, Essex, mentioned by Buckler in 1856, which we have several times admired, has been, in comparatively recent years, "improved away." The delightful lychgate of timber, with a stone-tiled roof, of Clun, Salop (Fig. 18), though apparently far older, was only erected in 1733; it is scarcely to be credited that the so-called churchwardens sold it in 1839 to a man who wanted it for a summer-house! Happily it was repurchased by a curate of Clun and replaced at the west end of the church in a useless position. There it remained until 1899, when it was restored to its original position. At Oswestry, in the same county, there is a lychgate dated 1631, well known as the "Griddlegate."

Nor ought we to omit to mention the fine old lychgate of the parish church of Garsington, Oxon.

If space permitted, a large number of quotations could be made from early wardens' books as to the lychgate; suffice it here to quote from the invaluable parish accounts of St. Edmund's, Salisbury. In this case the church was surrounded by a large churchyard, usually spoken of as the Litten, the main entrance to which, on the south, was the lychgate, sometimes termed the stile. The main gate had a lock, and was kept fastened except for funerals; by the side was a whirligig or turnstile for those on foot.

1462-3.—*Et pro ii capit mearemii pro le lychegate et impositionem ejusitem*, viiid.
1477-8.—Amendyng of the church style, xii*d*.; repares to the same, vj*d*.; a laborer to helpe make, ii*d*.; a pese of Tymber to the whirlegogge, ii*d*.
1648.—Ordered to wall up the place where the great gate stood that the Carte come in & out at, & only leave a dore convenient to bring the Corps in.

The habit of holding fairs and markets within churchyards was a scandal of fairly common occurrence, in spite of the censures of the Church and the action of the more energetic of the bishops. Finally Parliament stepped in, and, in 1285, an Act prohibited them being held in such places. Nevertheless this unseemly use of churchyards continued from time to time in isolated cases; and so late as the days of Henry VI another Act proscribed the holding of fairs in churchyards on Sundays. The wardens' accounts of St. Edmund's,

Salisbury, show that in the 15th century and early in the 16th century a regular source of income was the letting of standings for stalls, both within and without the wall of the Litten, during the fair of St. Edmund, to fruiterers and to general artificers. The accounts of St. Andrew Hubbard, of the City of London, contain such entries as the following :

1457-8.—Of Margaret the fruiteer for standynge at the churche dore, vi*d*.
1458-9.—Of Margarete Kene for sittinge at the Churche dore, vi*d*.
1466-8.—Of Margarete Kene for occupynge the bench under the chirche wall for ii yeres, iiis.
1476-7.—Of Margarete Kene for hir standynge at the Chirch dore for an hole yere, iis.

Here and there throughout England, but chiefly in the south-east, the main approach to the churchyard is made beneath an ancient house, and the lychgate is hung beneath. Hartfield, Sussex, is a notable instance of this, where the adjacent half-timber house is dated 1520. Of Kent examples, the village approach to Penshurst church on the south side is a well-known case. Like instances occur at Chalfont St. Giles, Bucks, and Bray, in Berkshire. South of the church of Bray is a passage to the churchyard under a timber-framed house of two chambers, connected with a charitable bequest. At Bickington, Devon, there is an old "church house" built over the lychgate; whilst at Throwleigh, in the same county, a "church house" of the 15th century stands immediately to one side of the churchyard entrance.

In Cornwall the stone piers of a former covered gateway often remain, as at St. Winnow, but at St. Leven the lychgate remains, with stone seats and corpse stone.

Churchyard Crosses

The upstanding cross, as an ensign of Christianity, is known to have been commonly erected by the graves of the departed at least as early as the middle of the 5th century. In the later pre-Norman days there was always a central cross erected in the churchyard to remind the people of the reverence due to the sacred spot. Sometimes such a cross marked the site where a Christian missionary first preached the Faith before ever a church was built. These old churchyard memorials are naturally to be looked for chiefly where stone abounded; in other parts they doubtless were of wood and have naturally perished. There are about sixty inscribed stone crosses to individuals in ancient churchyards, dating from the 7th to the 11th century, still extant; they are chiefly met with in Cumberland, Durham, Northumberland, Yorkshire and Cornwall, but two examples occur, in Lancashire and in London, and single instances in Essex,

Fig. 19. BECKENHAM, KENT: LYCHGATE.

Fig. 18. CLUN, SHROPSHIRE: LYCHGATE.

Fig. 21. BISHOP'S LYDEARD, SOMERSETSHIRE: Churchyard Cross, 15th Century.

Fig. 20. TILSTON, CHESHIRE: Sundial in Churchyard, 15th Century.

Kent and Hampshire. About 250 uninscribed pre-Norman sculptural stones, mostly of upstanding cross form, or parts of cross shafts, also remain in churchyards or have been removed to churches for preservation—they are scattered throughout England. They are frequent in the northern counties, in Yorkshire and in Cornwall. Derbyshire stands high on the list, having over a score of examples, mostly of much interest; the churchyard instances of Eyam, Bakewell, Hope, Blackwell, Bradbourne, Norbury and St. Alkmund, Derby, are all well described and pictured in vol. xxxi of *The Reliquary and Illustrated Archæologist*.

The finest of all these pre-Norman crosses is that which still stands in its original position on the south side of the church of Eyam. It is almost entire, though much weatherworn. The fine cross-limbed head is perfect, having a height of 2 feet 6 inches whilst the width of the arms from north to south is 3 feet 3 inches. The total present height is 9 feet 4 inches, but about two feet of the top of the shaft are missing. About the beginning of last century the head was found half buried in a corner of the churchyard and replaced. On the west and end faces of the head are four angels, the centre one, at the intersection of the arms, is surrounded by a plain circular moulding; there are also angels on the ends of the arms. The shaft on the west side, here illustrated, has in the lower part three circles of elaborate knotwork, whilst above them are two sculptured figure subjects, the one the Virgin and Child and the other a seated figure with a horn. On the east face of the shaft is carved throughout a kind of vine trail in five convolutions or spiral coils, like similar work on the crosses of Bakewell and Bradbourne. Both of the narrow north and south sides are covered with an interlaced pattern derived from a six-cord plait. The late Mr. Romilly Allen, the best authority on such subjects, considered that this noble example of Saxon sculpture dated from the 8th century.

Lancashire has a variety of highly interesting pre-Norman crosses, notably at Whalley, Heysham and Lancaster. The churchyard cross of Halton is of exceptional value. Certain iconoclasts destroyed portions of it to construct a base for a sundial, but in 1890 the late Rev. W. S. Calverley secured its careful restoration, replacing the missing portions by plain stonework. He considered the sculptured figures to be of momentous interest as demonstrating the mingling of pagan and Christian ideas, and pointing to the triumph of the latter over the Viking deities. On the one side are the emblems of the Four Evangelists with figures of saints below them, whilst on the other side are weird figures believed to represent scenes from the Sigurd legends.

Somersetshire is famous for the numerous and fine examples of churchyard crosses. In two churchyards, Rowberrow and Kelston, there are fragments of 9th century Saxon crosses, at Harptree one of the 12th century, and at Chilton Trinity, Dunster, and Broadfield of the 13th century. But those of the 14th and 15th centuries are quite numerous. Of these there are some instances, amongst many others, more or less perfect, at Alford, Barton St. David, Broadway, Chelvey, Chewton Mendip, Crowcombe, Doulting, Hassington, Luccombe, Rimpton, Spaxton, Stringston, Sutton Bingham, Timberscombe, Wedmore, Wiveliscombe and Wraxall. But the best of these mediæval Somersetshire examples remains to be mentioned, namely, the 14th century churchyard cross of Bishop's Lydeard, near Taunton (Fig. 21). It has the figure of St. John Baptist in a small niche projecting from the lower part of the shaft; the cross is raised on three tiers of octagonal steps, whilst each face of the octagonal socket or base stone has sculptured figures in relief. The eastern face has Our Lord seated and a winged lion; a second one has the Resurrection, whilst each of the remaining six have two of the Apostles. A remarkable feature of this example is that there is a cavity or hollow in the second step, 1 foot 4 inches wide and 8 inches deep; it was probably intended as a receptacle for offerings on special occasions. The cross at the head of the shaft is a poorly conceived modern copy of the original.

In not a few churchyards the shaft of the ancient cross has been utilized as the pedestal for a sundial, as is the case with the 15th century shaft at Tilston, Cheshire (Fig. 20).

It is a mistake to imagine, as many people do, that our churchyards are destitute of mediæval remains, with the exception of the ancient cross. The falsity of such a notion is disproved by the facts set forth in the following section, which it would have been quite easy to have made at least four times as long by including examples from other counties.

Churchyard Memorials

The small church of Loversall, W.R., Yorks, is of little architectural interest, but on the south side of the graveyard is a table-tomb (Figs. 22 and 23) having on the top a cross fleury and a sword, whilst the sides of the tombs have arcades of tracery, undoubtedly belonging to the early part of the 14th century. On the north side of the churchyard of Saxton, in the same Riding, is a table-tomb to Lord Dacre, who was slain at the battle of Towton Field in 1461. This highly interesting table-tomb has always stood in its present position outside the church; it has heraldic ornaments at the sides and end, and a marginal inscription round the top. In the north-east corner of Kellington churchyard, in the same Riding, there is an ancient monument with a human effigy and a dragon or serpent, of which Dodsworth tells a wonderful legend as to a shepherd named Birde who was killed by a serpent; but the unknown effigy is most probably intended for a woman. There is a 15th century table-tomb on the south side of the churchyard of Buckland, Gloucestershire; and at Newland, in the same county, the graveyard has a highly interesting table-tomb, bearing the effigy of John Wyrall, 1457, a forester-of-fee, or hereditary forester of Dean Forest, said to have been ejected from the church.* There is also in this churchyard a slab incised with the effigy of a forester (*temp*. James I) holding a bow in one hand and an arrow in the other. In the Lincolnshire graveyard of Torksey there is (or was) a remarkable tomb with the effigy of a prioress of the small Cistercian nunnery of Fosse in this parish.†

As to early effigies cast out from the churches during heedless repairs and restorations, and now lying weather-worn and decaying in country churchyards, a list of at least a hundred might be readily compiled, though several have of late years been rescued. A single instance shall be cited. On the south of the churchyard of Aldbrough, a small West Riding village abounding in Roman remains, there is a large ejected grave slab, with a mediæval bust within a circle at the upper end. When visiting Aldbrough in the 'eighties of last century, in company with two other antiquaries, we were gravely assured by the old woman in charge of the church that this was the most remarkable monument in all England, for it was that of Queen Boadicea, who was slain by the Romans on this very spot! To our credit be it recorded that we all three retained our gravity.

There are to be found numerous so-called coffin-lids, or rather flat sepulchral slabs, often of an early date and extending to the 13th century, especially in such counties as Durham, Northumberland, Yorkshire, Northamptonshire and Derbyshire. They should be looked for as serving in part, or perfectly, for coping-stones to old churchyard walls,

* For full description and two engravings of this memorable tomb see Dr. Cox's *Royal Forests of England* (1905), pp. 66-7.

† Bloxam, writing in 1866, records in his *Companion to Gothic Architecture* instances of 14th and 15th century monuments, mostly table-tombs, then standing in churchyards: Sutton Courtney, Berks; Astbury, Cheshire; Ampney Crucis, Fairford, and Leckhampton, Gloucestershire; Godshill, and Silchester, Hants; Great Bowden, Leicestershire; St. Giles, Oxford, Lewknor and Combe, Oxon; Corby and Thrapston, Northants; Ayston, Rutland; Brimpton, Cossington, Glastonbury, Martock, Mitchingley and Weston-in-Gordano, Somerset; and Brailes and Stoneleigh, Warwickshire.

as at Maxey, Northants; Elton, Rutland and other churchyards in the neighbourhood of the once renowned quarries of Barnack. Instances occur in the graveyard of St. Oswald, Durham, and one of the 14th century at Wootton, Beds. As is well known and elsewhere instanced, these slabs are of frequent occurrence in the wallings of old churches, especially in Perpendicular towers and clerestories.

Although a large majority of our old churchyards have no headstones or other monuments earlier than those of 18th century date, one sometimes finds late 16th and 17th century monuments which are well worth studying. Thus, in the cemetery of Darley Dale church, Derbyshire, near to the south transept, are several large 17th century table-tombs of much merit; they number nine in all, and are vigorously sculptured. The most remarkable of these is to the memory of a weaver, and the sides are carved with figures of the old handloom, shuttle, etc. (Fig. 24). A second example, dated 1632, is surmounted with several different symbols, including a chalice. A third, dated 1640, has its sides and ends covered with bold tracery mouldings, apparently a century older than the date on the upper slab.

Headstones of the 17th century were far commoner in some churchyards than is generally supposed, for in Buckinghamshire they occur at Datchet, Hitcham, Horton, Iver, Twyford, Westbury and Winslow, varying in date from 1608 to 1680. In the churchyards of Middlezoy (1614), of Oddicombe (1626), and of Burnham (1637), all in Somerset, there are good table-tombs, the sides of which are panelled after a debased Gothic fashion. There is also a remarkable table-tomb in the churchyard of Dorchester, Oxon, the trefoiled sides of which are distinctly Gothic, although the inscription, in a sunk squared panel at one end, gives the date of 1634. The churchyard of Swinbrook, in the same county, has also a large number of good 17th century tombs; a group of these is shown in Fig. 27.

The headstones of the 18th and early 19th centuries are generally well designed. The most usual ornamental motifs are the winged cherub heads—good examples of which may be seen in the headstones at Holme, Norfolk (Fig. 26), and St. Mary-the-Less, Cambridge (1809), (Fig. 29); the classic urn and foliage, as exemplified in Fig. 28, from Godmanchester churchyard (1789), and the skull and hour glass emblems, which are scarcely as pleasing to modern taste. The lettering is almost invariably worthy of study, being plain, legible and dignified.

The quiet beauty of many a country churchyard is sometimes marred by coarse and heavily executed iron railings which surround some graves and monuments, yet one may often come across iron

Fig. 22. LOVERSALL, YORKSHIRE : 14th Century Table Tomb.

Fig. 23. LOVERSALL, YORKSHIRE : 14th Century Table Tomb.

Fig. 24. ST. HELEN'S, DARLEY DALE, DERBYSHIRE:
The Weaver's Tomb, 17th Century.

Fig. 25. NORTH CRAWLEY, BUCKINGHAMSHIRE:
Wooden Headstone, early 19th Century.

railings of good design showing the classic influence of the 18th century.

The wooden "bed-head" or grave-boards of Surrey, Sussex and Kent (just occasionally met with in other counties), with its simple moulded terminal posts and latitudinal-shaped inscription board between them, though a cheap substitute for a headstone, is somewhat picturesque, and deserves mention as it is rapidly passing out of use. Mr. P. M. Johnston says of these grave-boards that "they probably have a very ancient pedigree, and must have been the rule rather than the exception in many churches of the Home Counties, and in a wooded country they have a special appropriateness." We have noticed a few as old as the first half of the 18th century, and one as late as 1893; they naturally perish somewhat rapidly, especially if fixed under trees. There is an interesting variety of these bed-heads in the churchyard of Horley, Surrey.

The instance depicted (Fig. 25) is from the churchyard of North Crawley, Bucks; it serves as the memorial of Sarah, wife of George Brandon, 1835.

Trees in Churchyards

The beauty and antiquity of the trees in many an English country churchyard is one of its most attractive features. By a Provincial Constitution, cited in *Lynchwood*, anyone felling or grubbing up any churchyard trees was to incur sentence of the greater excommunication, and to remain shut out of the communion of the Church until such time as he shall make amends. Nor can the parson himself cut down such trees unless they are required for the repair of the chancel. This is the ancient Common Law of the Realm, and therefore the protective Statute of 1707, forbidding the felling of churchyard trees —*ne Rector arbores in cemeterio prosternet*—is but declarative of that law under which offending rectors have from time to time been heavily fined.

Hence it comes to pass that various churchyards are celebrated for the luxuriant growth and antiquity of their timber. On the south of the church of Croughton, Northants, there is a singularly fine elm tree, having a girth of 22 feet. Within Tortworth churchyard, Gloucestershire, is a celebrated Spanish chestnut tree, which had at one time, it is said, the vast girth of 50 feet; but the old tree has now almost entirely decayed, though four stems are growing up around the ancient stump. There is also a fine chestnut tree in the churchyard of Thursley, Surrey, and another in the churchyard of Rodmell, Sussex. In the churchyard of Butterwick, Lincs., there is a remarkably big sycamore tree, said to have been planted in 1653. Plumpton churchyard, Sussex, also boasts a like tree of exceptional size. The glory of the churchyard at Boldre, Hants, on the verge of the New Forest, is a fine maple tree, confidently proclaimed to be the largest tree of its kind in England. The churchyard of Westmeston, Sussex, has much local fame for the size of its oak tree. Several of our country churchyards are favoured with a fine growth of walnut trees, such as can be seen around the Surrey churches of Mitcham and Great Bookham, and at Great Coates, Lincolnshire. These walnut trees are of later growth and are not indigenous.

Not a few churchyards are encircled by a belt of trees, as at Addlethorpe, Lincolnshire; Embledon, Northumberland; and North Cray, Kent. Some hundreds are well planted throughout the area of Lincolnshire, wherein Harrington, Raithby, Revesby, Somerby, and Theddlethorpe All Saints may be cited as examples. In Nottinghamshire occur the well-wooded churchyards of Babworth, Granly, Rampton, and Widmerpool. Amongst a multiplicity in Somerset, those of Combe Florey, Holford, Oare, Selworthy, Stogumber, and Winsford are notable instances. Also in Kent there are many, amongst which may be named Chiddingstone, Lamorbey, Otford, and Sutton-at-Hone. Perhaps the groups of trees in and around the comparatively treeless county of Cornwall are the most striking. In several parishes the only trees are those around the church, and the following may be named out of many others: Braddock, Davidstow, St. Clement, St. Enoder, St. Just-in-Roseland, Lanivet, Lanhydrock, Lewanick, Linkinhorne, Mawgan, Michaelstow, St. Mellion, Penzance, Perryhill, Ruan Major, Sancreed, Veryan, and Wadebridge.

The yew stands out alone as the pre-eminent tree of the English churchyard. The popular notion is that the churchyard yew was specially grown in a sacred place to provide bows for the famed English archers. There is a certain element of truth in this surmise. Thus at Ashburton, Devon, the churchwardens received iiis. iiii*d*. " for lopping the yew tree," and they paid xiis. to " the bowyer for makyng of bowes." As late as 1633 the parish constable of North Wingfield, Derbyshire, arrested a vagrant for cutting branches for bows from the churchyard yews. But the far more prevalent use of yew in England was for the decking of the church with its twigs and boughs at Eastertide, as the special emblem of immortality. Indeed, this significant custom prevailed very widely to the midst of the 19th century throughout Herefordshire and in the adjacent parts of Worcestershire, as well as in West Somerset.* Yew was also used occasionally

* The present writer has seen the screens of Little Malvern and of Monksilver, Somerset, profusely garnished with yew at Easter during the fifties of last century.

as a substitute for the eastern palm on Palm Sunday. The wardens' accounts of the later pre-Reformation days of several City churches testify to providing the churches with willow catkins, box, and yew for the Sunday before Easter. In Caxton's *Directions for keeping Feasts*, the following occurs relative to Palm Sunday : " Wherefore Holy Church this day makyth solemn processyon . . . and because that we have nowe olyve that beareth grene leaf, we take ewe instede of palm and olyve and bearen about in processyon." There seems to be not a shadow of doubt that the persistent care of yew trees throughout English churchyards had its origin and continuance from its general acceptance, as a bright and hardy evergreen, which served in the burial-ground of Christians as a fit symbol of the immortality of the soul.

The superb yew tree of Darley Dale, Derbyshire, is still the glory of its churchyard. Since I wrote at length about it, after several visits paid in 1875-6, it has suffered much, having lost three considerable branches, including the well-known antler-like summit, 17 feet of which were twisted off by a tremendous north-west gale in December, 1894. There are two, possibly three, churchyard yews in England with slightly larger girth measurement, but they are far more of wrecks than the Derbyshire champion, even in its present condition. It is 32 feet in girth a few feet from the ground, where it divides into two huge limbs. There are finer yews of a less age with a greater spread of branches, of which the two Hampshire examples at Corhampton and Brockenhurst are about the best. But, taking all in all, considering age, size, and comparative vigour, there is not the least doubt that the Darley yew is *facile princeps*.*

Derbyshire has many other fine churchyard yews, the second best of which is at Dovebridge, having a girth of 23 feet and a spread of branches of 212 feet. Other notable examples occur in the churchyards of Mugginton, Etwall, Sudbury, Beeley, and Mayfield, but Hampshire stands first in the growth and frequency of the yew both within and without churchyards. The Selborne yew has a girth of $25\frac{1}{2}$ feet 4 feet from the ground ; Woodcote a girth of 27 feet 6 inches, and Faringdon about 30 feet, but these two last trees are in a ruinous condition. Grand Hants examples are also to be seen in the churchyards of Hurstbourne Priors, Breamore, Crawley, Hambledon, South Hayling, Hound, and Warblington. In Twyford churchyard there is by far the largest

---

* See *Derbyshire Architectural Journal*, vol. xxvii, 1905. In vol. ii there is an admirable and critical article on this yew by the late Mr. Greaves, K.C., wherein he advances the opinion that it was not at that time more than 700 years old.

and oldest trimmed yew tree in existence; it is 15 feet in circumference 5 feet from the ground, and is kept closely trimmed in a pyramidal form.

Far more curious than this are the two big yew trees in Bedfont churchyard, Middlesex; they were clipped in 1704 to assume the form of the initials of the respective wardens, whilst their tops are imitative peacocks!

Surrey has several grand churchyard yews, but only two or three can be mentioned here. At the west end of Tandridge is one of the finest in all England, but very seldom visited. It has a circumference of $32\frac{1}{4}$ feet at $3\frac{1}{2}$ feet from the ground; it is hollow, and spreads out into four main limbs at a height of 4 feet. Yet it is in full vigour, and has a spread of 80 feet from north to south. At Crowhurst, on the Kent border, is a more celebrated but much mutilated churchyard yew (Fig. 31). The hollow of the trunk was foolishly enlarged in 1820, when it was made to hold a round table, capable of seating a dozen people; at the same time a doorway was fitted into the opening. This barbarously vulgarized tree is said to have a girth of $32\frac{1}{2}$ feet, but this is partly artificial; it has been repaired with several large pieces of tin or iron.

Curiously enough there is another Crowhurst, in the adjacent county of Sussex, which is also famed for its great ancient churchyard yew; according to Mr. Brabant's *Little Guide* it is $37\frac{3}{4}$ feet in girth at the base, but base measurements form no certain criterion.*

The quaintest conceit in churchyard yews occurs at Painswick, Gloucestershire, famous for its great army of yew trees trimmed after a circular fashion (Fig. 30). They number ninety-nine, and the story goes that all attempts to complete the hundred fail, for the newcomer always dies.

Church Marks

A curious custom used to prevail, in early post-Reformation days, among several parishes in the Weald of Sussex, which still survives here and there, of surrounding the churchyard with posts and rails. In the 14th volume of the *Sussex Archæological Society Collections* (1862), it is thus explained under Chiddingly: " The surrounding churchyard is amply stored with memorials of the departed, and encompassed by wooden rails, which are kept in repair by the tenants of the respective farms, a certain portion being supported by each. The respective rails are marked with the initials of the tenants, and

* It is only fair to state that in Mr. Johnson's section on yews in his *Byeways of British Archæology* the circumference of the yew at South Hayling is given as 33 feet, and that of Tisbury, Wilts, as 37 feet.

Fig. 26. HOLME, NORFOLK: Headstones, 18th Century.

Fig. 27. SWINBROOK, OXFORDSHIRE: 17th Century Tombs.

Fig. 28. GODMANCHESTER, HUNTINGDONSHIRE: Headstone, 18th Century.

Fig. 29. St. Mary-the-Less, Cambridge: Headstone, early 19th Century.

are, in consequence, denominated *Church Marks*. This primitive custom, though not confined to the parish, is peculiar to this part of the country." A document is cited, transcribed in 1772, "from ancient records," which sets forth the number of churchyard marks with the names of the farms or lands, and in most cases the names of the tenants or owners. The number is 56, and the part of fencing for which they are held responsible varies from 45 feet to 3 feet. The churchyard of the pretty Down village of Berwick used to be thus surrounded. At Cowfold the initials are deeply incised. In the 19th volume of the *Sussex Collections* (1867) a register of church marks is given, dated 1636, showing that the fence round the graveyard was kept in repair by 81 tenants. We have also seen the original records of such "marks" in the Weald churches of Ardingly and West Hoathly, Sussex.

Games and Sports in Churchyards

As a broad rule, the sanctity of the consecrated churchyards of England was generally respected throughout the mediæval period. The hallowed feelings attached to the burial grounds of Christians were enhanced by the sanctuary rights which pertained to every churchyard, as well as to every church, throughout Christendom, from the middle of the 5th century downwards. Every shedder of blood and every fugitive from justice was just as safe, for a certain period, within the cemetery as within the fabric of the church. The sternest punishments of the Church, supported by the civil law, were imposed upon the violators of these cemetery rights, as can be abundantly proved by numerous instances recorded from the 11th to the 16th century. Henry VIII narrowly limited all sanctuary rights, and they were entirely swept away in 1623.

It must, however, be remembered that the modern ideas as to the strictly limited uses of all parts of the parish church were alien to our forefathers, to whom the Church was the common house of the people. Its precincts were consequently used for a variety of secular purposes, which may nowadays appear irreverent. The churchyard then was a more or less open space, encumbered with but few memorials to the departed, whereas large village greens were of quite exceptional occurrence and " recreation grounds " were unknown. Hence came about the use of churchyards for the practice of archery. In the days of the Plantagenets, before butts were established, Edward III enjoined the use of the long-bow in two precepts to county sheriffs, in 1363 and 1365, and an Act of Richard II compelled all servants to shoot with it on Sundays and Holydays. In an Inquisition of Proof of Age, in the case of Edward Tregey, of West Grinstead, Sussex, in 1399, who was born and baptized on St. George's Day, 1378, one William Wyling testified that on that day Giles Parker shot an arrow through his leg in the churchyard when practising. A like accident occurred in a Staffordshire churchyard in the same reign during archery practice on a Sunday, only in this case the victim was struck with an arrow in the right arm. In much later times, under Queen Elizabeth, the games that were licensed to be played on such days were "The shotinge with the standard, the shotinge with the brode arrow, the shotinge at the twelve skore prick, the shotinge at the Turke," etc.

In King James' "Book of Sports" is the following paragraph :—

> And as for our good people's lawfull recreation our pleasure likewise is, that after the end of Devine Service our good people be not disturbed, tolled or discouraged from any lawful recreation, such as dancing either men or women, archerie for men, etc.

There is no doubt whatever that the chief site chosen for archery practice was, in the 14th century, and often at far later periods, the consecrated ground immediately around the parish church. One of the commonest proofs of this is the occurrence throughout all parts of England and Wales of grooves made on suitable stones in church walls, particularly near the porch, and now and again in ancient churchyard walls, by the sharpening of arrows on them. In fact, wherever there was a suitable freestone in the walls of a church, or in its immediate vicinity, it became a whetstone for arrows. Both in Somerset and in Wales, we have noticed these arrow grooves on the pedestals and steps of the churchyard cross, and it is even said that the Montgomeryshire fonts of Mochdre and Llanerfyl are thus marked.

At Dolgelley it was the custom to play ball against the church, and the rector used to watch, and would not allow absentees from church during morning prayer to play. Extracts are given from the wardens' accounts of Bryn Eglwys, Denbighshire, 1677, from Llanelidan, 1683, in the same county, and from Kerry, Montgomeryshire, 1750, as to money spent in making arbours or booths, and in providing seats for the spectators of these rural games. The parson was in the habit of acting as scorer in these important matches of fives, and the scores were kept by scratches on the church walls, or even on the tombstones.

Within a couple of feet of the ground on the north walls of rural churches in Wales a red line or a deep scratch may still be noticed, beneath which the ball would not be in play, as at Llansilin, near Oswestry.

Instances or traces of game playing in churchyards are quite exceptional in England, with the exception of some of the small churches of Cumberland. The churches and chapels of that county took a long time to recover from the neglect of Elizabethan and Stuart days, and from the gross abuses under the Commonwealth. It was not until the episcopacy of William Nicholson (1712-1718) that any real effort was made to bring about even common decency in the great majority of the church fabrics of Cumberland. Bishop Nicholson's visitation diaries show an appalling state of affairs. In sixteen churches the chancels were actually used as day-schools. No wonder that the graveyards were the common playgrounds of the youngsters.

The strangest use of all, to which not a few of the Welsh churchyards lent themselves, was for the purpose of cock-fighting,* that wretched form of sport to which the Welsh remained devoted even to the early dawn of the 19th century. Writing in 1896 the late Revd. Elias Owen, with whom I had some acquaintance, claimed to have talked with aged people who had witnessed churchyard cock-fighting after service was over. He also gave plans of the cockpits still remaining in the graveyards of two Montgomeryshire churches; the one to the north of the church of Pennant Melangell, about 24 feet in diameter, and the other in the churchyard of Llanfechan, 27 feet in diameter, with a slightly elevated mound for spectators.

That cock-fighting took place in consecrated ground elsewhere than in Wales is well established. Not long ago, in company with a well-known antiquary of the district, the present writer took notes and measurements of the old cockpit within the churchyard of Chapel-en-le-Frith, Derbyshire. The local traditions about the cockpit closely adjoining the chapel of Alsop-en-le-Dale, in the same county, were strong and circumstantial. Immediately to the north of the Hereford-shire church of Cradwell are the traces of a cockpit.

Amongst the excesses brought to light in Archbishop Laud's days, during the visitation tour of his vicar-general, Sir Nathaniel Brent, in 1634 and the following years, throughout the various dioceses of the southern province, evidence was forthcoming of cock-fighting and wagering, on Shrove Tuesday, 1637, actually within the chancel of Knotting Church, Beds—the scandal being all the viler because of the presence of the rector and churchwardens.

* As to cock-fighting, a favourite sport of Edward III, Henry VIII, and James I, see my edition of Strutt's *Sports and Pastimes* (1903) 224-227. The practice was made illegal in 1849, but was still illicitly practised by wealthy patrons, and apparently winked at by the authorities. I am ashamed to say that I once, in 1862, witnessed a bout of cock-fighting in a gentleman's (?) grounds near Oxford.

On the subject of churchyard games, since the above was written I have received from Mrs. Connor, the wife of the Revd. W. F. Connor, rector of King's Nympton, Devon, more than one communication as to the conflicting stories current about the former use of an enlargement of the parish churchyard immediately to the west of the west tower. This parallelogram, measuring 153 feet by 123 feet, begins about 100 feet distant from the tower, and it is separated from the old churchyard by a row of fine old yew trees. It is surrounded on the three other sides by banks of well grown trees; on the south side by seven grand old beech trees. This piece of ground usually goes by the name of the Bowling Green, but others speak of it as the Play Ground. It has been suggested that the latter title is a corruption of Plague Ground, and that the space was an enlargement of the cemetery during a visitation of this character. A former rector, when engaged in the removal of earth from this site, came across a considerable deposit of human bones, a find which obviously supports this view. Moreover, I am assured that the parish registers, which begin in 1538, also support the plague theory. But the whole matter, as represented to me, obviously requires more investigation.

Fig. 31. CROWHURST, SURREY: Yew in Churchyard.

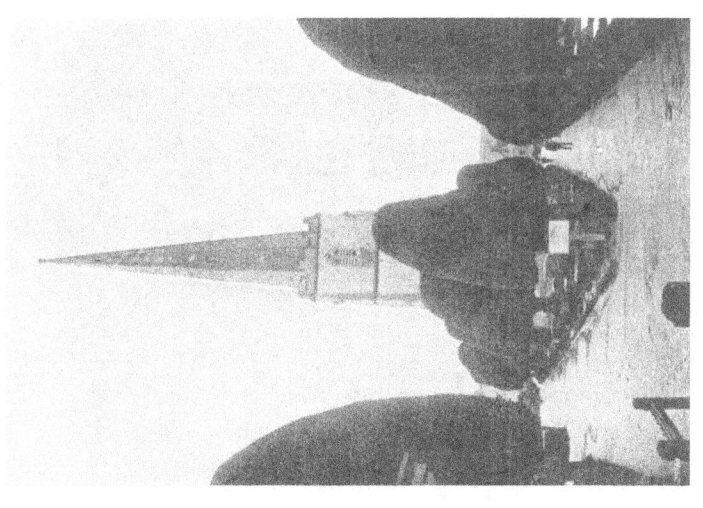

Fig. 30. PAINSWICK, GLOUCESTERSHIRE: Yews in Churchyard.

Fig. 32. BAKEWELL, DERBYSHIRE: ANGLO-SAXON COPED COFFIN LID.

Fig. 33. WIRKSWORTH, DERBYSHIRE: ANGLO-SAXON COPED TOMB.

CHAPTER II

MONUMENTS WITHIN THE CHURCH

Saxon

THE monumental remains yet extant in many of our old churches speak, with more or less vigour, of the diverse arts and crafts brought into play to preserve from decay the memory of those who once worshipped within these walls during successive generations.

The Romans erected many a sculptured headstone or monument to the deceased during the four centuries of their occupation, but on that we are silent, for no Romano-British burials, sarcophagi, or sepulchral monuments can be shown to be Christian. The advent of Christianity brought about the introduction of the cross, the standard of the Faith, together with rude saintly figures, though it was not until the Saxon days from the 8th to the 11th century that they were generally introduced. The Normans destroyed much of the monumental work of their predecessors, as is shown by the discovery of Saxon remains used as building material in several Norman churches.

By far the most interesting Saxon monument within a church now in use is the early Christian coped tomb, fixed against the wall of the north aisle, of Wirksworth, Derbyshire (Fig. 33). We may take it that a church of some size was certainly erected here as early as the 7th century, for Wirksworth was at that time the centre of an active industry in lead mining. This ancient piece of sculpture came to light in 1821, when it was found face downwards, immediately below the chancel pavement, directly in front of the altar over a stone-built vault grave containing a large male skeleton. The slab, measuring 5 feet by 2 feet 10 inches, was ingeniously described in the *Gentleman's Magazine* of that date after a fairly correct fashion. The subjects represented in this remarkable piece of sculpture are: The washing of the Apostles' feet—The Agnus Dei on the cross, in the place, through restrained reverence, of the Divine Victim, together with the four Evangelistic symbols—The Carrying to the Tomb—the figure below the bier typical of the triumph over Death, and the heads in a circle above suggestive of the watching soldiers—The Resurrection—and the Ascension, with a group of disciples returning to Jerusalem. We believe with confidence that this was the slightly coped tomb (not an altar-piece, as at one time supposed), raised to some little height, over the burial-place of the founder of the first church at Wirksworth, and that it dates from early in the 8th century, or possibly towards the close of the 7th century.*

Why was this once-prized stone found in such a position in 1821 ? Because it was the habit of the conquering Normans to do all in their power to disassociate the names and memories of revered members of the Saxon church from the minds of those whom they had conquered. Hence the builders of the proud Norman church of the days of Henry I reversed this slab, and buried it beneath the pavement that they had raised.

Another pre-Norman but much later coped tomb, which used to stand within a church, was brought to light in Derbyshire, during the extensive repairs and rebuilding of the great church of Bakewell, *c*. 1841, when a vast quantity of old memorial slabs and headstones were discovered, a considerable number of which are stored within the porch. This small coped tomb only measures 3 feet 4 inches in length and 15 inches in breadth, and probably was placed on the coffin-lid of a much larger size than itself, after the manner of the tomb of William II at Winchester. Both sides of the quaintly capricious carvings are shown in the illustrations (Fig. 32).

Incised Slabs

To mark the interment of Christians within churches incised slabs of infinite variety were in use in late pre-Norman days, and onwards for several centuries. They were marked with more or less simple crosses and were usually nameless; the simplest forms being often of Saxon date. By degrees they assumed more elaborate designs, the cross rising from outlined steps, usually termed a "calvary," and the head of the cross becoming floriated. On one or both sides of the shaft of the cross symbols were introduced to mark the profession or occupation of the deceased. These exist in amazing variety, and include swords, shields, and various weapons for men-at-arms; bows, arrows, and horns for foresters; axes for woodwards; pastoral staffs, chalices, patens, or missals for ecclesiastics; shears, gloves, fish, pincers, carpenters' squares, etc., etc., for different trades, and keys

* The numerous reasons for assigning this early date are carefully set forth by the present writer, together with a much longer description of the sculpture, in *Byegone Derbyshire* (1892), pp. 19-32. Dr. James, the learned Provost of Eton, has suggested that the whole subject represents the legendary burial of the B.V.M., with which surmise, for a variety of reasons, we do not agree.

MONUMENTS WITHIN THE CHURCH

for officials. The square-ended shears seem to denote a woolstapler, and are of frequent occurrence. At one time they were said to mark a female interment, a far too hasty opinion adopted from two double slabs, the one at Byliffe, Northumberland, and the other, much later, at Dale, Derbyshire. But there are numerous instances to upset this theory, such as the not infrequent occurrence of sword and shears by the side of the shaft of the cross on the same slab. Most probably the pointed shears or scissors denoted a clothier. A large example of the blunt-ended shears is given from St. Oswald's, Durham (Fig. 35). At this church nearly thirty mediæval grave-covers from this date down to the 13th century, have been of the stairway on the south side of the tower ... ample of an incised slab from the Chapel of the Castle, Newcastle, shows a sword and a knife (Fig. 34).

At one time it was supposed that these slabs had originally served in all cases as covers to stone coffins, hence the erroneous name of " coffin-lids " was usually assigned to them.

A striking proof occurred of the falsity of this title in October, 1884, when a finely executed sepulchral slab was found on the south side of the nave of Kedleston church, Derbyshire, about 6 inches below the then floor level. It had evidently been originally fixed on the old pavement level. The slab was carefully moved, and the ground below minutely examined. There was no stone or other coffin, and the corpse had at most been buried in a leathern shroud. The skull and other bones were found in the soil 2 feet 6 inches below the slab. This massive grey stone, about 9 inches thick, is neatly bevelled at the edges, and the stem of the cross has a boss near the top, like those of processional crosses. The design of the floriated head is simple but singularly effective, being formed by four interrupted circles, with a quatrefoil within the diamond formed by their conjunction, and each circle making a slipped trefoil. The plain cross is hardly ever found among slabs, whether incised or in relief. It is said that the plain Latin cross was regarded as the Cross of Shame, and it is almost unknown in architecture or illumination of the best periods. The floriated cross was the Cross of Glory, pointing to the triumph of the Crucified One over death ; it is in fact a cross adorned with garlands. This particular slab was placed with its foot to the east, and the interment below corresponded in position. The rule of those days was to bury a layman with his face to the altar, but a cleric with his face to the people. It has elsewhere been shown that this slab was in all probability over the grave of Thomas de Curzon, fourth lord of Kedleston of that name ; he was living in 1226, and the exact date of his death is not known, but it occurred before 1245.

Derbyshire affords an infinite variety of incised grave-covers. There is hardly a single old church or chapel throughout the county which has not yielded many instances of these early sepulchral memorials built up into the fabric. Our church-repairing ancestors of the 13th and 14th centuries appear to have been utterly unscrupulous in appropriating these unlettered memorials of the departed during rebuilding, and still more so in the Perpendicular work of the 15th century, particularly in the construction of towers. Whenever a flat slab was required for a foundation stone, for the jamb of a doorway, and more especially for a lintel, these flat grave-stones came in handy for the purpose.

Vast stores of such remains of Saxon and later dates came to light in the forties of last century, when the large church of Bakewell underwent considerable reconstruction. A great number of these are preserved in the south porch, whilst a still larger number were purloined by Mr. Bateman for his Lomberdale collection. An exceptional number can still be seen *in situ* within the fine tower of North Wingfield.

When the grievous and absolutely wanton destruction of the chancel of Hope, Derbyshire, took place in the summer of 1881, two grave-covers were discovered in the foundations, of a somewhat later date, probably of the reign of Richard I or John. The heads of the crosses of this period have a floriated design within a circle, the cross being thrown into relief by cutting away the remaining part of the stone within the circle to the depth of about quarter or half an inch, the stem of the cross and other symbols being simply produced by ordinary incised lines. Both of these slabs had obviously been constructed to cover the remains of foresters-of-fee, or hereditary foresters of the great Forest of the Peak. The symbols incised comprise a cross-hilted sword, a bugle with baldric, and a broad-headed arrow.*

At Coxwold, N.R., Yorks, there is a good example of a grave-cover with a short-handled axe, the token of a woodward. Yorkshire affords an immense number of these incised slabs. The careful investigations of Mr. J. E. Morris have shown that they exist in upwards of seventy old churches in the North Riding, sixty in the West Riding, and forty in the East Riding. Mr. Hodgkin has also catalogued forty-one Co. Durham churches where they occur.

There are several instances in Yorkshire of grave-covers partly incised and partly in relief; a noteworthy example is at Thornton-in-Lonsdale.

It is quite impossible in this limited space to mention a tithe of the varieties of incised grave slabs which could be noted. Up to the

* The writer was present when these two slabs were removed; see the 4th vol. (1882) of the *Derbyshire Archæological Journal*.

51

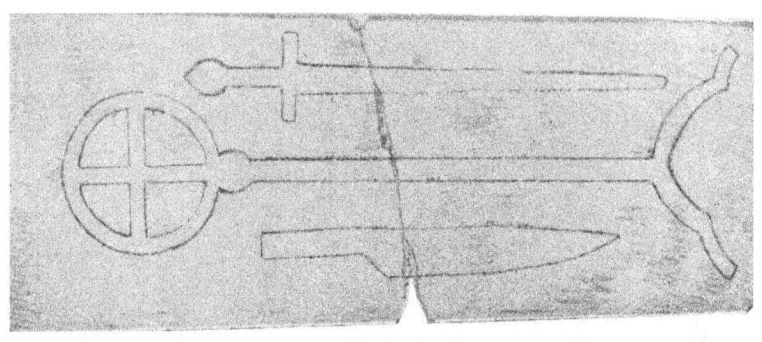

Fig. 34. NEWCASTLE: From the Castle Chapel. Fig. 35. ST. OSWALD'S, DURHAM: Fig. 36. SHOULDHAM, NORFOLK:

INCISED SLABS.

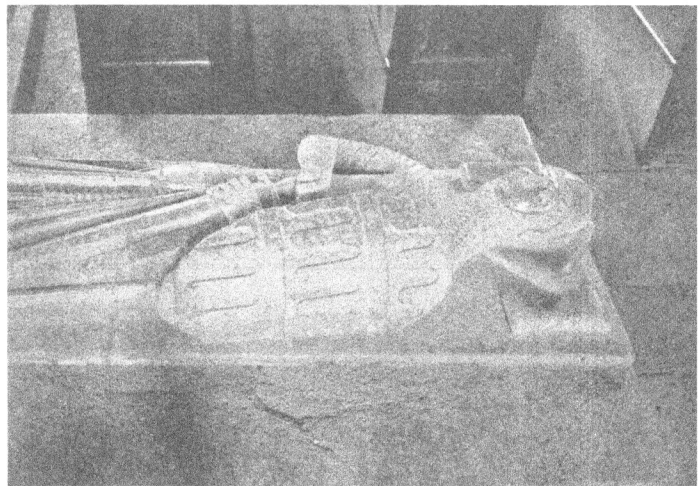

FIG. 37. DODFORD, NORTHAMPTONSHIRE: Sir Robert de Keynes, 1305, Effigy in Purbeck Marble showing "Banded" Mail.

FIG. 38. STOWE-NINE-CHURCHES, NORTHAMPTONSHIRE: Effigy of Sir Gerard de Insula, 1285, showing 13th Century Armour.

present the student has to fall back upon the old manuals of Cutts and Boutell. There are also some excellent papers by the late Revd. G. Rowe, the York Secretary of the *Associated Societies*, in their reports during the seventies of last century. Reference, however, must not be omitted to the curious embellishment of the cross shaft on many of these slabs ; it has usually been styled the " Double Omega " from its likeness to a reversed pair of the last letter of the Greek alphabet. A large number of conjectures have been offered as to the origin and meaning of this embellishment, but it is still a puzzle. Possibly, if this grave-cross represents the cross carried in front of a funeral procession, it may be intended for appendages or ribands to steady the upright cross. Sometimes, as at Shouldham (Fig. 36) and Sempringham, Norfolk, there is a rod ending in *fleur-de-lis* inserted between the two " omegas." There are at least forty churches where this strange ornament has been found on old grave-covers, chiefly in the counties of Norfolk, Northampton, Nottingham, Cambridge, and Huntingdon.

In the 13th century it became usual to carve the cross of the sepulchral slab in relief. These crosses were often beautifully embellished by foliage springing from the shaft. A simple example of this kind of work must suffice ; it is a slab now in an upright position beneath the tower of Blyth, Notts.

Incised Effigies

A method of commemorating the departed which was adopted with some frequency during the 15th century, especially in Derbyshire and the adjacent counties of Staffordshire and Nottinghamshire, was that of utilizing slabs of Chellaston alabaster (which could then be readily obtained in large blocks), and incising them with effigies. The lines were filled with pitch, which rendered the design very distinct. There was usually a marginal description. These slabs were for the most part laid even with the floor ; they had the advantage of not encumbering the space of the church after the fashion of table-tombs, and the disadvantage of being speedily defaced under footwear. Great numbers of these slabs have become hopelessly defaced, and the alabaster has been frequently re-used in modern times for the construction of reredoses, altar steps, etc.

One of the finest examples of this kind of workmanship is an incised slab, now against the wall of the north transept of Darley Dale church, Derbyshire, whereon are depicted the full length effigies of John Rollesley, 1513, and Agnes his wife. The man wears a long civilian's fur-lined gown and has a double-linked chain about his neck ; the woman has the diamond-shaped head-dress with falling lappets, and an embroidered girdle to her close-fitting gown. Between their heads is a shield with the impaled arms of Rollesley and Cheney, which has originally been filled up with pigments of the right tinctures. Below the parents are the small effigies of eight sons and four daughters.

Next to Derbyshire, Staffordshire has the best and largest number of these incised effigies; they number about fifty, and vary in date from 1433 to 1593, the best of these is the slab to Hugh and Cecile Erdeswike, 1473, in the church of Sandon.

Semi-effigial Slabs

There are three varieties of the semi-effigial monuments, each representing a different way of portraying a partial effigy: (*a*) Those parts of the figure which were presented were sunk below the surface of the stone, and made to appear as if they were disclosed to view through apertures formed for that purpose; (*b*) in the second variety, the partial development of the effigy was produced by entirely cutting away the adjacent parts of the stone; (*c*) in the third variety, the head, bust, or half figure appears to have been placed upon the stone. The earliest and most numerous instances of these different sorts of semi-effigies occur in Lincolnshire, Yorkshire, Derbyshire, and Nottinghamshire, and may be assigned generally to the 13th century.

Effigies of Purbeck Marble.

The Purbeck marble of Dorsetshire, used for architectural purposes even by the Roman conquerors, served from the 12th century onward for sepulchral slabs of fonts, as well as for other structural purposes within our churches. Purbeck in early Gothic days was an important centre of the mason's art, and it was shown more especially in the sculpture of the first effigies. These dark marble Purbeck effigies chiefly prevailed from 1150 to 1300. Their shape and general construction were ere long followed in cheaper freestone, and the trade in this material rapidly fell off so soon as the easily wrought alabaster was introduced at the dawn of the 14th century. Henceforth alabaster took its place in the best of effigies and table-tombs. The period of the stone effigy ran partly concurrently with that of Purbeck, and prevailed, in round figures, from 1250 to 1360.

The Purbeck effigies were usually of low relief, and formed part as it were of the slab or grave-cover on which they rested. They are chiefly of bishops, and are naturally to be found in cathedral churches; but some are of knights in armour, and are to be seen in parish churches up and down the country in districts to which water carriage was accessible. One of the latest instances is to be found at Dodford, Northants (Fig. 37). It is the effigy of Sir Robert de Keynes, 1305, sculptured on a slab of Purbeck marble, and slightly raised on five

Fig. 39. SPRATTON, NORTHAMPTONSHIRE: Sir John Swynford, 1371, showing 14th Century Armour, Plate and Chain Mail together.

Fig. 40. SPILSBY, LINCOLNSHIRE: John, 3rd Baron Willoughby, 1372. Alabaster Effigy clad almost entirely in Plate Armour.

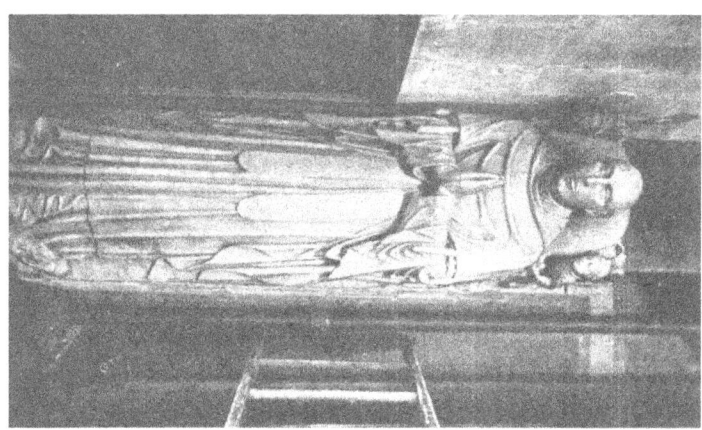

Fig. 41. ST. MARY REDCLIFFE, BRISTOL: Tomb of William Canynge the Younger, 1474.

Fig. 42. ELFORD, STAFFORDSHIRE: Sir Thomas Ardine and Wife Matilda. Alabaster, late 14th Century.

blocks of the like material. The knight has a close-fitting coif of mail with a ridged head-piece over it, and wears a hauberk of mail with a quilted gambason over it. On the left shoulder is a heart-shaped shield (a curious survival for this date) with the arms of Keynes; but the remarkable feature about this effigy is that all the mail which is visible is of that rare kind called " banded " as opposed to the ordinary ringed mail. There are only four other instances of this form of mail, namely at Kirkstead chapel, Tollard Royal, Tewkesbury, and Newton Solney.

MILITARY EFFIGIES.

The 13th century, an eminently warlike period, was the time of the general use of mail armour, that is, of steel rings so interwoven as to produce a continuous fabric. As the century developed, additional defences were added to the mail, such as metal plates to guard both knees and elbows. By the middle of the century, when knightly effigies of stone began to multiply in our churches, the *chausses*, or mail defences of the legs, appear quilted with thews or *cuisses*. Then came the *plastron de fer*, worn either under or over the mail hauberk, to protect the breast. Over the hauberk was worn the long flowing sleeveless surcoat of some rich material, secured round the waist by a narrow belt, a shoulder belt securing the heart-shaped shield to the left side. The *coif de mailles* covered the head, secured by a fillet, whilst the mail extended over both hands and feet. All this is shown in the oldest of our brasses at Stoke D'Abernon to Sire Johan d'Abernoun, dated 1277; or at Stow-Nine-Churches, Northants, in the stone effigy of Sir Gerard de Insula, who died in 1283, as here illustrated (Fig. 38).

With the dawn of the 14th century there came about a distinct change in the armour, and the whole century is usually spoken of as the period of mixed armour. Fresh additional defences, in the form of plate armour, continued to be added to the foundation of mail. Early in the century, the mail coif disappears, and is replaced by a *basinet* or close-fitting steel helmet, from which the *camail*, or tippet of mail, depends, covering the shoulders. The shield grows smaller, and the surcoat gives way to the *cyclas*, a minor garment cut short in front, but worn long behind. As the century advances, the shield is no longer worn, the basinet grows tall and pointed, the plate armour increases, the hauberk is often covered by a *jupon* emblazoned with arms, the sword belt is much enriched and is buckled straight across the hips, and the sword is narrower and longer than before with a perfectly straight cross-guard. Effigies of this date usually show the head resting upon the crested helm.

A fine example of a later 14th century effigy is that of Sir John Swynford, who died in 1371, at Spratton, Northants (Fig. 39). It is beautifully wrought in alabaster and stands in the north chancel aisle of Spratton on a low embattled table-tomb; it is enclosed on the south side with coeval iron rails, with prickets for tapers.

At Spilsby, Lincolnshire, there is a remarkable and exclusive assemblage of Willoughby effigies. An illustration is given of the elaborate heraldic tomb on which rests the alabaster effigy of John, the third Baron Willoughby (Fig. 40). He fought gallantly at Poictiers in 1356, and died in 1372. The effigy is almost entirely in plate armour, with feet on a lion, and head resting on a crested helm. Round the edge of the slab are carved diminutive figures of monks with rosaries, etc.

Elford, Staffordshire, has a magnificent alabaster table-tomb of the close of the century (Fig. 42). On the sides of the tomb are twenty-two statuettes. The effigies are those of Sir Thomas Arderne, 1391, and his wife Matilda (Stafford), 1400. On the front of the knight's basinet are the words " Jesu Maria "; a ponderous *camail* falls over his shoulders, but plate armour elsewhere. The ungloved right hands of the knight and his lady are interclasped; the pretty conceit is occasionally met with elsewhere, but this is the first example of it. The lady wears an ornamented bodice, flowing robes and a super-mantle. Both effigies have their heads supported by angels. Both also wear the Lancastrian collar of SS, founded by Henry IV, long before his accession, in 1399.

The 15th century is essentially the period of plate armour at its best. The change to complete armour of this character dates from the time of Henry V, 1420. A *cuirass* of this period, formed of front and back plates, covers the body of the knight, whilst a number of overlapping narrow plates, termed *tasses*, are dependent from the waist. A *gorget* of plate protects the throat and joins the globular shaped basinet. At the shoulders are *roundles*. All these and many other details mark a change which was developing, *c.* 1450, after a fashion that we cannot here elaborate. At Dennington, Suffolk, there is a very fine tomb in St. Margaret's Chapel, at the east end of the south aisle, with the striking alabaster effigies of Sir William Phelipp, K.G., Lord Bardolph, 1439, and his lady, 1445. The knight wears the collar of SS, and the garter on the left leg; his wife has the horned head-dress, with rich nets and a coronet. These effigies bear traces of colouring and gilding.

One of the several beautiful alabaster tombs of Norbury, Derbyshire, bears the effigies of Sir Ralph Fitzherbert, eleventh Lord of Norbury, who died in 1483, and his wife, Elizabeth (Marshall). The knight is bareheaded in late plate armour, and his feet rest on a lion, whilst round his neck is the collar of Suns and Roses, founded by Edward IV. The lady wears a close-fitting bodice and gown, with a mantle; the hair is arranged in a pointed reticulated head-dress; the neck is encircled by a chain, with a pendant of the Virgin and Child; two small dogs are at the foot of her robe; and the head-pillow is supported by two angels.

The great church of St. Mary, Redcliff, the pride of Bristol, has two unknown effigies of a priest and a lady in the south transept, of the close of the 15th century. In its present form, the church owes its grandeur largely to the two William Canynges, father and son, who each held the mayoralty several times. The effigy of the younger, who died in 1474, is in an ecclesiastical garb (Fig. 41). This is in accordance with what is said of him on an old wooden inscription. He was " ye Richest Merchant of ye towne of Bristow. Afterwards chosen 3 times Mayor of ye said towne for ye good of ye Common Wealth of ye same. He was in order of Priesthood 7 years and afterwards Deane of Westburgh, and died ye 7th of November, 1474." On a table-tomb, beneath a handsome recessed arch is the comely effigy of his wife Joan, though this is disputed by some. It is needless to add that he did not take orders until after his wife's death.

The best church in which to study the survival of the wearing of armour from Elizabethan days right through the 17th century is that of Swinbrook, Oxfordshire (Fig. 50). It was during all that period the chief seat of the great landed family of Fettiplace, who moved here from Childrey, Berkshire, about 1550. On the north side of the chancel are two lofty monuments, arranged in triple tiers or shelves, on which recline the effigies of six representatives of the family. In the three compartments of the oldest of these lie three effigies, each bareheaded with moustache, beard and long curled hair, and a ruff round the neck, but clad in debased padded armour; reclining sideways, supported by the right arm and elbow; they are dated, respectively, 1504, 1562 and 1613. The other three, as shown in the illustration, adopt an easier attitude, for though still wearing quasi-armour and adopting a recumbent sideways attitude, each has the left knee raised and grasped by the left hand (Fig. 50). These effigies are supposed to represent John Fettiplace, Esquire, who died in 1657; Sir John Fettiplace, Bart, 1672; and Sir Edmund Fettiplace, Bart., who erected this monument, in 1686, in memory of his uncle, his father and himself.

In the church of Winestead, near Patrington, E.R., Yorks., is a recumbent effigy of Sir Christopher Hilyard (1602). The figure is wearing plate armour, and the sides of the tomb are enriched with attractive early Renaissance ornament (Fig. 44).

A good example of the survival of plate armour in the days of James I occurs in the chancel of Framlingham, Suffolk. The very fine monument to Henry Howard, Earl of Surrey, and his countess (Fig. 45) shows the effigy of the earlier robes of state worn over his armour; as he was beheaded in 1547, his coronet lies by his side; but the tomb was not erected until 1614, and both armour and costume are of that date.

Shrouded Effigies

In the 15th century the ghastly and repulsive custom grew up of depicting the departed in their shrouds, chiefly in the case of brasses. The shroud was usually partly open in front so as to display the face and part of the body. This idea had its origin in the vein of morbidness which was an accompaniment of the "new learning," when paganism regained much of its lost strength, and the doctrine of the Resurrection waned in the enfeebled Faith. From 1500 to the death of Henry VIII brass engravers multiplied these representations with great frequency. At Oddington, Oxon, an additional horror is added to the shrouded effigy of a priest, by the presence of worms covering the body.* Occasionally this shrouded notion is carried out in stone or marble. There is a notable instance of this at Fenny Bentley, Derbyshire, where the recumbent effigies of Thomas Beresford, 1473, and of his wife, Agnes (Hassall), 1467, are placed on an alabaster table-tomb, tied up in shrouds, fastened round the heads and ankles, so that no portion of the human frame is visible. The effect is at once ghastly and ludicrous. The monument was probably erected some time after their death, and the form was possibly adopted to conceal the lack of skill in the sculptor. Shrouded representations of sixteen sons and five daughters, mere shapeless bags, are also shown on the south side and east end of the tomb.

Canopied Tombs

Towards the end of the 13th century a canopy over-arching the table-tomb came into fashion, and was used with striking effect in some of our cathedral and larger churches. The canopy multiplied in the next century, and became more and more enriched as time went on, whether over a detached table-tomb or over a slab or effigy in a wall recess. The favourite position for the canopied table-tomb, where the chancel had aisles, was beneath an archway between an aisle and the chancel; perhaps the finest effect is produced by the monumental canopies of the 15th century in this position.

* Macklin's *Brasses of England*, 210-215.

Fig. 43. Gt. Brington, Northamptonshire: Tomb of Sir John Spencer, 1522, and Isabella Graunt.

FIG. 44. WINESTEAD, EAST RIDING, YORKSHIRE: Tomb of Sir Christopher Hilyard, 1602.

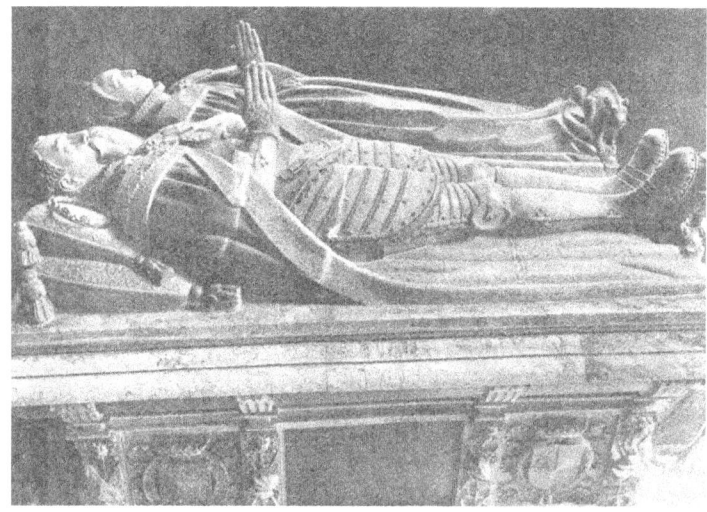

FIG. 45. FRAMLINGHAM, SUFFOLK: Tomb of Henry Howard, Earl of Surrey, 1614.

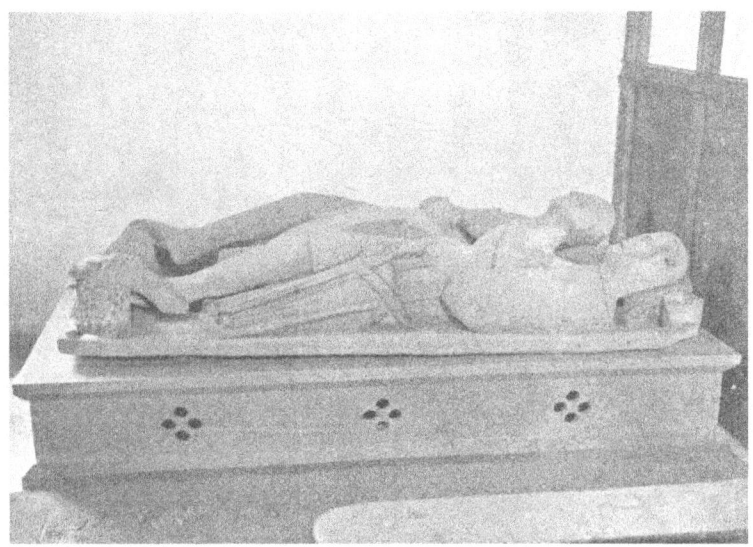

Fig. 46. WORMINGFORD CHURCH, ESSEX: Wooden Effigies.

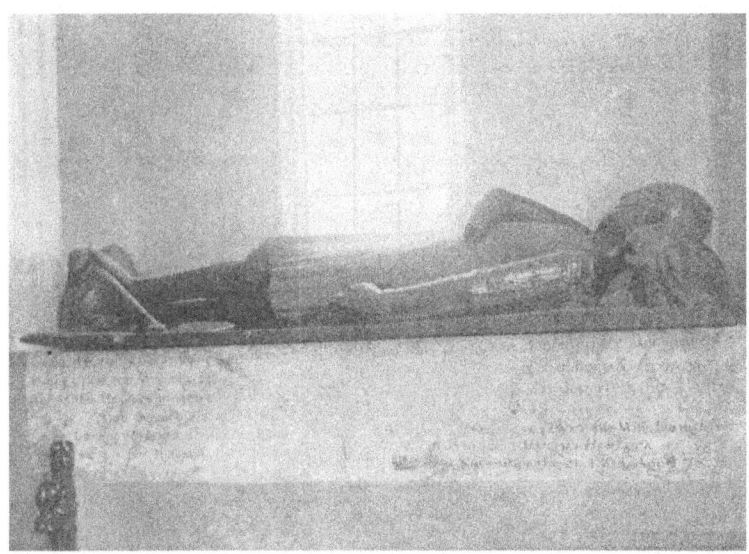

Fig. 47. ELMSTEAD OLD CHURCH, ESSEX: Wooden Effigy.

Fig. 48. ARUNDEL, SUSSEX: A Howard Tomb showing Iron Herse.

Fig. 49. STOWE-NINE-CHURCHES, NORTHAMPTONSHIRE: Lady Elizabeth Carey, 1617. Effigy by Nicholas Stone.

A very good example, c. 1430, when Perpendicular was at its best, occurs in the interesting church of Minehead, Somerset, between the chancel and a north chapel. But the effigy of a priest in Eucharistic vestments beneath it, holding in his hands the remains of a chalice, seems to be a good deal earlier.

Another remarkable and highly enriched example of a canopied tomb, of a totally different character, is the sumptuous memorial to Alice, Duchess of Suffolk, in Ewelme Church, Oxfordshire. She lived on here after her husband's murder, and died in 1475. The effigy shows her wearing the *Garter* round her left arm. In a screened recess below the monument proper the Duchess is represented in her shroud. The repulsive habit of carving the *cadaver* of the deceased is a discredit to the sculpture of this century, but the architectural ornament of this tomb, with its panelled sides with statuettes of angels, is exceedingly beautiful.

In the north chapel of the church at Brington, Northants, is a series of monuments to the Spencer family, which has been connected with Brington from mediæval times to the present day. The earliest is the magnificent canopied tomb of Sir John Spencer (*obit*. 1522), and his lady, Isabella, heiress of the Graunts (Fig. 43). The knight is wearing elaborate plate armour with mail skirt, whilst the lady has an heraldic mantle quartering the arms of Graunt and Ruding (her maternal grandfather's family). She also wears the contemporary reticulated head-dress with lappets. The sides of the tomb are enriched with armorial shields within quatrefoils. The beautiful canopy of freestone is carved and moulded, the spandrils containing shields, whilst the frieze is carved with rosettes and shields within quatrefoils above a band of carven Gothic foliage. In the centre of the frieze appear the arms of Spencer, ancient, with helm and mantling. The supporting piers terminate in turrets of stone tabernacle work; and the soffit of the canopy is beautifully panelled, and supports in the centre an angel bearing arms.

Herse.

Effigies of bronze are almost unknown in England and are only to be found in Westminster Abbey, Canterbury Cathedral and at Warwick. But an interesting feature in connection with table-tombs is the metal hearse which served for the protection of the effigy and for providing prickets for candles. The word *hearse* or *herse* has been for some time exclusively used for a funeral car, but its original English meaning was a frame for holding candles. This framework, usually of wood, was placed over the shrouded or coffined body when it was brought into the church. Over it was spread the pall or hearse cover, whilst on the top were various candles or tapers lighted at the obit and at anniversaries, when permanent hearses of iron were provided for persons of distinction.* There is a hearse of iron round the tomb of John Marmion and his wife, 1366, in Tanfield Church, N.R., Yorks, which was used for supporting a pall, with sconces for holding seven candles, two on each side and three on the ridge. The best-known example is the hearse of brass over the effigy of Richard Beauchamp, Earl of Warwick, 1439, in the celebrated Warwick Chapel of St. Mary's, Warwick. There is another instance at Spratton, Northants, where there are iron rails and candle prickets on the south side of the effigy of Sir John Swynford, 1371. There is also an iron hearse at Bedale, N.R., Yorks.

A fine iron screen surrounds the tomb of the Earl of Arundel, at Arundel, formed of embattled rails and ten buttressed standards terminating in prickets (Fig. 48). The finest sepulchral ironwork with which we are acquainted, outside those of Westminster Abbey and the Cathedrals of Canterbury and Salisbury, is the elaborate work surrounding the tombs of Sir Thomas Hungerford, 1398, and his wife, Joan, 1412, at Farleigh-Hungerford, Somerset; the elaborate and beautiful terminals to the rails show no trace of prickets, but there used to be wooden sconces attached for candles. A portion of a beautiful iron hearse, cast out some time ago from the Lincolnshire church of Snarford, has found a home in the Victoria and Albert Museum, South Kensington.

Wooden Effigies

There are about ninety wooden effigies now extant in our churches. Twenty-four of these are of women, but almost all the remainder are of men in armour. They are chiefly of 13th and 14th century date, but rarely occur after the Black Death of 1348-9. There is an interesting and exceptional one of a late 15th century canon at All Saints, Derby. Essex stands first of the counties in the number of these oak effigies, being a county practically deficient in stone. There is a priest at Little Leighs, three knights at Danbury, a lady at Little Hockesley, a civilian and a lady at Little Baddow, a knight and a lady at Wormingford (Fig. 46), a knight at Elmstead (Fig. 47). The wooden effigy of a knight at Messing was burnt as firewood " by order of a late vicar."

* On the evolution of the word Hearse, see a learned chapter by Mr. Peacock in Andrews' *Church Gleanings* (1895). Hearses in the original sense, frequently occur in old parish books, see Dr. Cox's *Early Churchwarden Accounts*, 57, 170-172, and illustrations in *English Church Monuments* by F. H. Crossley, F.S.A. (Batsford, 1921.)

Evidence has been discovered of the destruction of these wooden memorials in at least a score of cases in comparatively modern days. It is probably fair to assume that at least as many as those now existing have perished. There was a tragic end to the oak effigy of Stephen de Radcliffe, 1245, which stood in a founder's recess in the old church of Radcliffe-on-Trent, Notts. The loyal inhabitants dressed up this wooden effigy, on the occasion of celebrating one of the Peninsula victories, to represent Buonaparte, and, after carrying it in procession through the village, committed it to the flames of a bonfire!

Attitudes of Effigies

When once the custom of depicting the departed Christian in a humble recumbent attitude, with the hands folded in prayer, was abandoned during the Reformation upheaval, a variety of undevotional attitudes were adopted, of which perhaps the favourite one was that of lolling on the elbow, as shown in the armed effigies of the Fettiplaces at Swinbrook (Fig. 50). We quite grant that now and again a skilled sculptor produced a work of art in connection with such an attitude, as is illustrated in the case of the beautiful portrait in marble of Lady Mary Mordaunt, daughter of Henry, Earl of Peterborough, whose first husband was Henry, Seventh Duke of Norfolk. This monument stands in a chapel of Lowick Church, Northants; the lady died in 1705. But the whole conception is strangely out of place within a church. Even in so celebrated a monument as that of Lady Elizabeth Carey, 1617, at Stow-Nine-Churches, Northants (Fig. 49), supposed to be the work of Nicholas Stone, the master-mason of Charles I, of white marble recumbent on a slab of black, the contrast with the reverential attitude of the best mediæval work affords a painful contrast. In this instance her ladyship is portrayed reclining on a rich cushion with one hand on her breast and the other lying by her side, but wearing the then fashionable stiffened and embroidered stays. The attitude may be natural, but it is without a spark of devotion.

There is, however, one post-Reformation attitude quite unobjectionable in monumental sculpture, which prevailed widely up and down England during the 17th century, though it originated in the days of Elizabeth, namely that of kneeling. The most striking example of this attitude with which we are acquainted is in the Suffolk church of Helmingham, where the south side of the nave is occupied by so large and costly a naval monument that the roof had to be displaced for its reception. Helmingham has been occupied by the ancient family of Tollemache since the 15th century. The Hall, a venerable brick mansion of the early days of Henry VIII, was visited by Queen Elizabeth for five days when she was entertained by Sir Lionel Tollemache. The monument in question contains the kneeling effigies within separate niches of the four first Tollemaches, each named Lionel, who resided at Helmingham.

It is hardly possible for a standing effigy to be anything but offensively self-assertive, and to be more or less alien to the reverential and humble ideas which ought to cling to a consecrated church. Nevertheless there is something attractive about the niched upright figure of Peregrine Bertie, 1610, the Eleventh Lord Willoughby, in Spilsby Church, Lincolnshire (Fig. 51).

One of the most ostentatious monuments of a standing figure that was ever designed for a Christian church is the huge white marble memorial to Sir Robert Clayton, Knight, 1707, and his lady, Dame Martha, 1705, which dominates and disfigures the church of Bletchingly, Surrey. The knight and his lady stand forth in gorgeous array between great Corinthian pillars, flanked by weeping cherubs. The only touch of frail humanity about it is the small reclining effigy of their only son at the feet of his parents. Sir Robert was once Lord Mayor of London, in 1680, and is represented in his official robes, with long flowing wig. The grandiloquent epitaph to this pompous person states that: "He fixt the seat of his family at Marden, where he left a remarkable instance of the potency of his genius, and how free Nature may be improved by man." Of the showy house erected by this City knight at Marden, a manor of the adjacent parish of Godstone, only the stables are now standing. It is scarcely to be credited that this vainglorious monument was put up in the knight's lifetime, and that for a twelvemonth he attended Sunday service with this enormous affair ministering to his vanity.

Another example of a single standing figure, wherein the departed is represented as looking round in full vigour, and in his best official garb, stands within the picturesque Devonshire church of the beautifully situated village of Shute, overshadowed by an enormous yew tree. It is peculiarly unsuited to the quiet solemnity of a village or even a town church. This sacred place is rendered absolutely repulsive to any man of refined taste and sentiment by the prominent upstanding statue in white marble of Sir William Pole, who died in 1741, a Master of the Household to Queen Anne.

LEDGER STONES

Memorial ledger stones have been curiously neglected by the many writers on the monumental memorials of our English churches. But

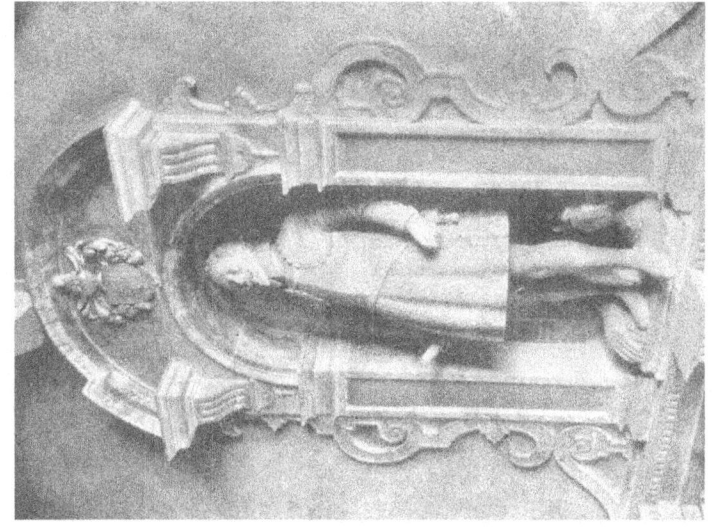

Fig. 51. SPILSBY, LINCOLNSHIRE: PEREGRINE BERTIE, LORD WILLOUGHBY, 1610.

Fig. 50. SWINBROOK, OXFORDSHIRE: FETTIPLACE MONUMENT.

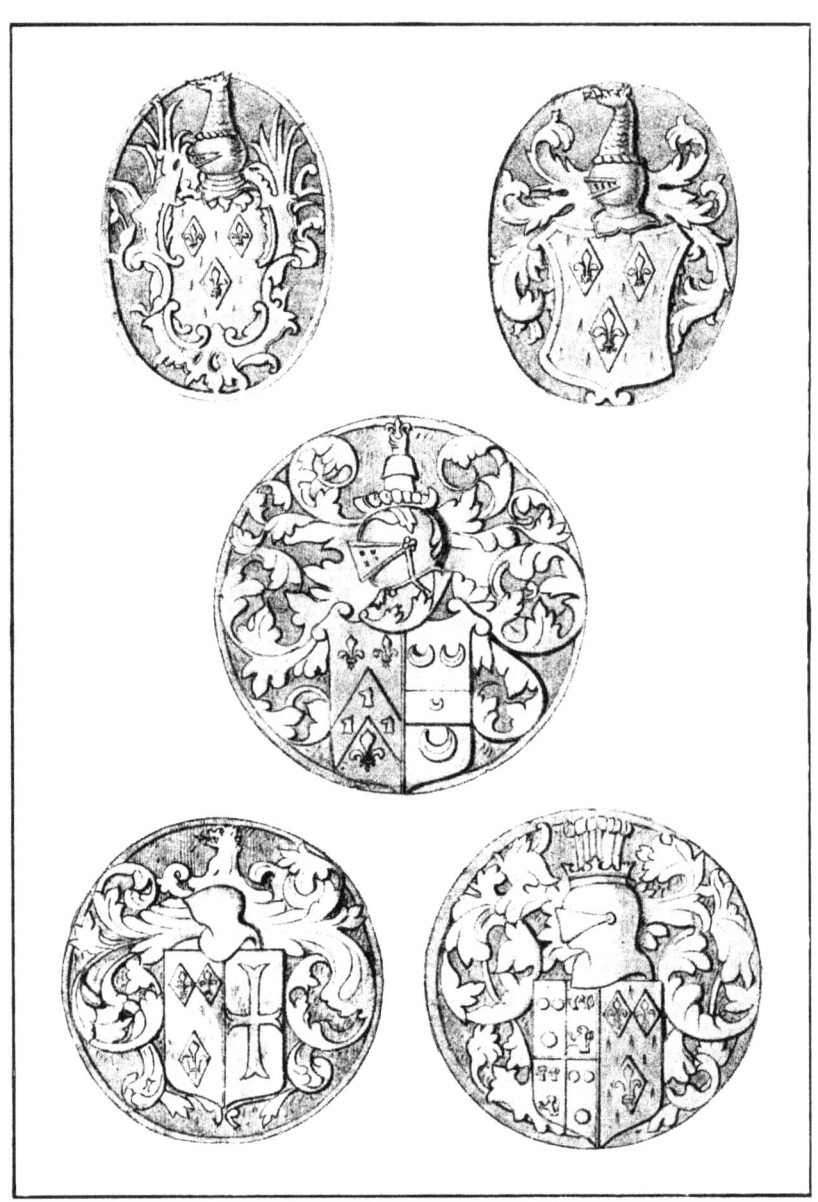

FIG. 52. HOLY TRINITY, HULL, YORKSHIRE: ARMORIAL LEDGER STONES.

Fig. 54. Cheam, Surrey: Wall Tablet.

Fig. 53. Great St. Mary's, Cambridge: Wall Tablet.

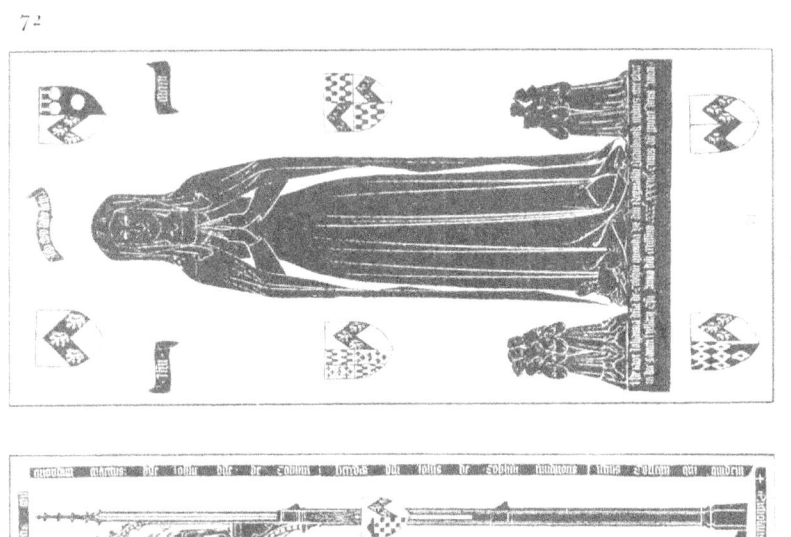
Fig. 58. Joan, Lady de Cobham, 1433.

Fig. 57. Sir Nicholas Hawberk, 1407.

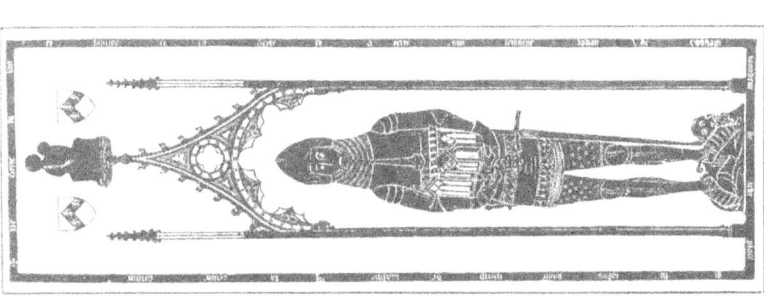
Fig. 56. Sir John de Cobham, 1354.

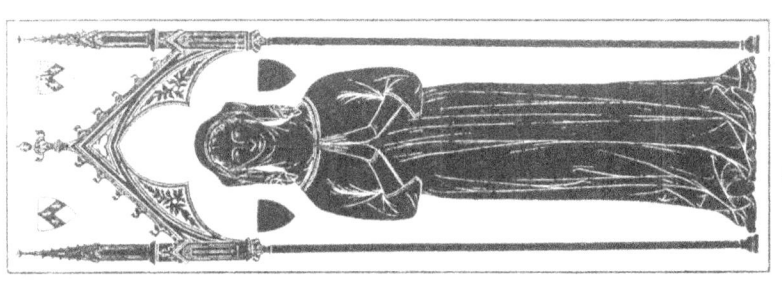
Fig. 55. Jone de Kobeham, 1298.

COBHAM, KENT: MONUMENTAL BRASSES.

these massive floor slabs, which largely prevailed in several districts throughout the 17th century and early in the succeeding century, are by no means destitute of artistic merit, and are often invaluable to the student of genealogy and heraldry. During the period they were in use " a school of heraldic sculptors of no mean proficiency must have been in existence; the beauty and variety of treatment of the mouldings and accessories of the shields which the ledger stones display being a witness of their skill." (*See* Fig. 52.) The material of these stones usually employed was a hard stone of a bluish-grey colour, whilst the armorial carving at the head of the slab and the inscription below was executed in low relief and offered no impediment to the feet of the passers-by. The date of the earliest of these stones in the spacious church of Hull is early in the 17th century; they are about twenty in number, half of which pertain to that century and half to the first part of the 18th century. In the *Reliquary N.S.*, vol. ii (1888), p. 131, Mr. D. Alleyne Walker contributed five valuable illustrated articles to this magazine on the ledger stones of Holy Trinity, Hull, during the time that the present writer was the editor. The present illustrations (Fig. 36) are reproduced from these articles.

Cartouche Tablets

In the 17th century the custom prevailed of decking the walls of our churches with memorial tablets of the kind generally termed *cartouche*. It is usually of marble, and may be compared to a sheet of paper with the corners or ends curled up; the centre was reserved for the inscription, and it was commonly surmounted by arms, helm, crest and mantling. Of these cartouches, often highly ornamental, two characteristic illustrations are given. The one is an elaborately carved piece of sculpture at the east end of the south wall of Cheam, Surrey, to James Bovey, 1695, and to his wife, Margaret, 1714; the three cherub faces are introduced after a most pleasing fashion (Fig. 54). The other one occurring at Great St. Mary's Cambridge (Fig. 53), is a good deal later and is stiffer in style; it is to the memory of Thomas Daye, 1745.

Brasses

In the brief consideration given to the subject of monumental brasses, which are to be found all over England but chiefly in the counties of Kent and Essex, it should be remarked that they are of two types. The Flemish type, which are but few in number, consisted of rectangular metal plates of considerable thickness, made to cover the whole of the stone slabs to which they were affixed, and were engraved all over. The best examples of this type are at King's Lynn (two), Newark and Newcastle.

In Brasses of the English type the several parts of the design were cut out in separate pieces of thin metal, and let into matrices or indents cut to receive them, so that they lay flush with the face of the slab. Brasses of this description are said to have been introduced towards the end of the 12th century, but the earliest extant examples are of the following century. The oldest brass is the effigy of an armed knight in mail, Sir John D'Aubernoun, in the church of Stoke D'Abernon, Surrey; he died in 1277.

These brass effigies exhibit every possible variety of detail in knightly armour and in ecclesiastical vestment, as well as in civilian costume of both sexes, during the prolonged period through which they prevailed, namely, through parts of the 13th and 17th centuries, and through the whole of the intervening dates.

It would be obviously idle to attempt to give illustrations or to describe a tithe of the characteristic styles that did service from the reign of Edward I to that of William III. Should any reader desire to become fascinated with the study of memorial brasses, he is strongly advised to give at least a day to the inspection of the attractive church of Cobham, Kent. He will there find the most splendid collection of memorial brasses in the whole of England if not of Christendom. There are fourteen fine brass effigies to the ancient and stately family who took their name from the manor over which they were lords, and, in addition, there are five brasses to members of the collegiate church, consisting of a master and four chaplains, which was founded here in 1362 by Sir John de Cobham. They extend in date from 1298 to 1498, and were carefully arranged and relined in 1841, but happily they escaped any kind of "restoration," by means of which several of our best brasses have lost all historic interest.

A special feature of these large Cobham brasses of the 14th century is the beauty and grace of the canopies, of which there are six ogee-headed examples. In each case the canopies have side shafts and pinnacles between which and the central finials are placed two shields of arms. All the finials are delicately foliated, and in two cases—those of John the founder and Dame Margaret—they terminate in small figures of the Holy Mother and Child. Another charm is the interesting character of the French inscriptions on narrow marginal fillets. Thus, the first John de Cobham is described as *le cortays viaundour*, or the courteous host, and the second, John as *foundeur de ceste place*. The character of the knightly armour and the draperies of the ladies throughout this century, and in the dawn of the 15th century, lent itself with singularly good effect to its treatment in the engraving of these outline brasses, when this craftsmanship was at its best. It will be well to give plates and brief descriptions of four of the most striking

MONUMENTS WITHIN THE CHURCH

of these memorials to two knights and two dames of this wonderful Cobham group* (Figs. 39-42).

Fig. 55.—Jone de Kobeham, *ob.* 1298, but the brass was not laid down until 1320. She was the daughter of Sir Robert Septvans, of Chartham. This is not one of the earliest known examples of a canopy, but there is only one brass of a lady of earlier date.

Fig. 56.—Sir John de Cobham, third Baron, *ob.* 1407. The brass, however, was laid down upwards of forty years before his death. He founded the college in 1362, and beautified and restored the original parish church. He holds in his hands the model of a Decorated church. As to the armour, it should be noted that the hauberk of mail has shrunk to the proportions of a vest, and is only seen at the lower edge ; on the head is a pointed steel basinet, to which is laced a camail or tippet of mail protecting the neck and shoulders ; a broad belt or bawdrie is worn across the hips, with sword attached on the left side, and misericorde dagger on the right ; the body is encased in plate armour, but the thighs in leather cuisses studded with small plates of steel.

Fig. 58.—Joan, Lady de Cobham, *ob.* 1433. Costume that of a widow, but without the barbe ; six sons on her right and four daughters on her left. She married (1) Sir Robert Heminhale, (2) Sir Reginald Braybrooke, (3) Sir Nicholas Hawberk, (4) Sir John Oldcastle, the Lollard, and (5) Sir John Harpendon.

Fig. 57.—Sir Nicholas Hawberk, *ob.* 1407, third husband of Lady Joan. At foot on a pedestal stands the figure of his son John. This is considered the finest military brass of the period ; the knight's head rests on his tilting helm. The triple canopy contains the figures of the Holy Trinity, the Virgin and Child, and St. George and the Dragon.

---

* See Mr. W. D. Belcher's *Kentish Brasses* (1888), vol. i, 43, 44 ; also Dr. Cox's *Rambles in Kent* (1913), 194-197. The writer carefully examined and took rubbings of the whole of the Cobham brasses as long ago as 1872. There are various manuals on Brasses, but in our opinion by far the best and most useful is *English Brasses*, by the late Rev. Herbert Macklin, originally published in 1907, but now in a 3rd edition.

CHAPTER III

THE TOWER AND BELLS

THE tower is often well worthy of a careful inspection, especially from the interior. In the upper stage, which has been in many cases rebuilt, portions of incised slabs, perhaps pre-Norman, or marked with curious emblems, may be detected, or stones with Saxon zig-zag tooling may be found, or remnants of Norman mouldings, whilst all the rest of the church may be of later dates.

Then, too, it must be remembered that church towers, which were obviously used occasionally for defensive purposes, are by no means confined to border counties such as Cumberland, Northumberland, Durham or Hereford. Such notable instances of this as the vaulted towers, and iron-bound doors opening only into the nave, as at Burgh-on-Sands, Newton Arlosh and Great Salkeld are not only to be found in the border counties, where the visits of the marauding Scots were very frequent; but they may be looked for much farther afield. The Scotch invasions penetrated far into England. There are many instances of grim fortified church towers in the North Riding of Yorkshire; four of the towers of that district, namely Bedale, Masham, Middleham and Thornton Watlass, are provided with upper chambers, in each instance having a fireplace; the newel stairway of the first of these used to be protected by a portcullis. Manfield and Melsonby, in the same Riding, have also been evidently planned with a view to defence or as a refuge during raids.

It has elsewhere been pointed out how abundant are the proofs of towers being used as domiciles from Saxon days onwards, and mention was made of six Norfolk towers with fireplaces and flues; * but many more could be named, such as the early church of Studland in the Isle of Purbeck. That careful observer, Mr. J. E. Morris, has pointed out that Wadsworth, W.R., Yorks, had formerly two chambers on the roofs of the aisle, one on each side of the west tower, and approached therefrom, " stupidly destroyed at some so-called restoration,"† but the traces of them still remain.

A good example of a fortified church tower may be noted at the highly interesting church of St. Stephen, Old Radnor, near the

* *English Parish Church*, pp. 111-125.
† *Little Guide to West Riding*, p. 6.

Welsh border. It is very strongly built, and has three large windows on the south side, also one on the west and two on the north. The turret on the north-east corner was used for a beacon light—part of the iron cradle was there fifty years ago, although no trace of it can now be found. Access to this turret must have been obtained by a ladder. At each of the other three corners a small stone platform was let into the wall, about 4 or 5 feet from the landing roof, on which a man could stand to look out for approaching danger. The battlemented top has also slits for archers. For this information concerning Old Radnor Church Tower, the author is indebted to the excellent little guide by Mrs. Lloyd, wife of the incumbent.

Then, too, care should be taken to see if there are any remains of the serving window, a small window or opening in some upper chamber of the tower, whence the sexton could see the action of the Mass, and ring the bell at the appropriate moments, in the days when the use of the low-side window for that purpose had been given up, and in churches where there was not any serving bell-cote on the gable. There are several such windows in the Lincolnshire churches, and they are to be noted as far south as Shorwell in the Isle of Wight, and as far north as St. Oswald's, Durham.

Right in the centre of England, the 14th century tower of Rugby shows by its exceptional construction, that the idea of defence was in the mind of its builders. This lofty tower is without a single sustaining buttress. The lower windows are far from the ground, and so narrow as to be little more than loopholes, whilst the only entrance is from the body of the church. It has also a fireplace, the smoke shaft of which is carried up through the thickness of the wall to the battlements. These peculiarities were pointed out many years ago by the late Mr. Bloxam, who stood in the very front rank of the antiquaries and ecclesiologists of the last generation. But in commenting on this and other defensive towers, the essence of which seems to have been to provide places of refuge for the villagers in case of any sudden raid or disturbance, in addition to serving as a campanile and adding general dignity to the fabric assigned to the worship of God, Mr. Bloxam made a curious mistake. He definitely asserts that the use of towers for such purpose did not continue after the 14th century. This statement is quite wrong. There is abundant evidence that the fear and the actuality of Scotch raiding, involving heavy loss of cattle and of human life, lasted in the north of England up to the days of the accession of James I. Thus the accounts of the Earl of Northumberland for 1450 show that in that year his steward contributed sixty-six shillings to the chapel of North Charton, in

Ellingham parish, towards the expense of building a tower at the west end for the protection of the villagers during Scotch raids.

Again, as late as 1573, an elaborate return was drawn up of the great number of horses, kine, oxen and sheep that had been raided from a score or so of Northumberland parishes, together with the names of the tenants who had been thus despoiled.* At a still later date, in Elizabeth's reign, the inhabitants of several parishes were warned to keep their church towers in repair, notably in the case of Long Houghton, as a protection against sudden forays.

It should also be remembered that many a church tower used to serve as a beacon, more especially on the borders of both Scotland and Wales. The only case in which the cresset for the beacon fire remains on a church tower is said to be that of Hadley, on the borders of Middlesex and Herts; this cresset was lighted as recently as the Jacobite rising of 1745.

BELLS.†

But after all, however adaptable a church tower might be for a residential or defensive purpose, its main and original purpose, so far as England was concerned, was to serve as a campanile or bell tower, whence the summons should ring out far and wide calling folk to the house of Divine worship.

Although bells can undoubtedly be traced to a period far earlier than the beginning of the Christian era, they appear to have been in use in connection with churches as early as the 5th century, when the true Faith was openly recognized by the Empire. That bells were in use by the Anglo-Saxon Christians is first made clear by Bede's vivid account of the church of St. Hilda, at Whitby, in 680. Church bells are also mentioned in the Excerpts of Archbishop Egbert, in 750, and in the Canons by King Edgar, in 960. One of the fascinating illustrations to the *Benedictional* of St. Athelwold, *c.* 970, contains the representation of a campanile with bells hanging in it. There is abundant evidence of the increase of bells and bell-towers after the Norman Conquest. Though there are several bells still hanging in one tower of presumably earlier date, the oldest dated example is preserved in the church of St. Chad, Claughton, Lancashire; the Latin inscription round the shoulder, in ordinary Roman type, reveals the date as 1296. At Cold Ashby, Northants, is a bell dated 1317.

* See vol. ii, pp. 248-250 of the *Victoria Counties History of Northumberland*.

† For fuller information see the excellent work of the late Rev. Dr. Raven, *The Bells of England*, 1906 (Methuen), and Mr. H. B. Walton's *Church Bells of England*, in the Church Art Series; also the older writings of Ellacombe on the *Bells of the Church*, and Fowler's *Bells and Bell Ringing*.

It is quite impossible to dilate on the variety of the old bell inscriptions throughout the kingdom, and of the change in the nature of the lettering and ornaments as time advanced. And this is wholly unnecessary, for the large majority of the counties are now provided with admirable monographs on the subject. Suffice it to say that the details of the letters attained to their greatest beauty and finish in the first half of the 15th century. Certain bells, which cannot in this respect be surpassed, were probably issued from some unknown foundry in North Lincolnshire. There are eleven of these bells, with exceptionally noble lettering, in Lincolnshire, and one in Notts, at Carlton-in-Lindrick. In three instances these particular bells are dated. There are three of them in the fine Marshland church of South Somercotes; two of these are dated 1423, and the third one is possibly a little earlier. Of the three bells of Somerby, one from this foundry is dated 1431, and was the gift of Sir Thomas Cumberworth. A double sheet of capital letters from these three dated bells was issued in 1867, by Mr. W. A. Tyssen Daniel Amhurst, excellently engraved by Mr. Orlando Jewitt, from which our illustrations are taken* (Fig. 59). The most notable of these letters is the capital M, which is of much force; the figure on one side of the main stem is an armed knight, whilst on the other side is a lady, presumably his wife. Another striking letter is an O, in the centre of which is an episcopal head, clean-shaven, and of determined expression. It is very possibly intended to represent Bishop Fleming, who ruled this diocese from 1420 to 1431. It is not difficult to imagine that those are the resolute features of this prelate who made so spirited an appearance at the Council of Siena against the Lollard opinions. He was the founder of Lincoln College, Oxford. Another of the letters, D, shows a beautifully modelled St. George and Dragon; it requires much talent to produce so striking a figure on such a small scale.

The church of Wool, near Wareham, Dorset, has a ring of six bells, including four old inscribed bells. These are dated and lettered as follows:

    I.   "Love God, 1606." Diameter, 25¾ in.; weight, 3 cwt. 2 qrs.

    II.   "Searve God, W. 1606." Diameter, 31½ in.; weight, 6 cwt. 2 qrs.

    III.   "C.W. T.B. Anno Domini 1659." Diameter, 36 in.; weight, 8 cwt. 2 qrs.

    IV.   "John Hayte C.W. Anno Domini 1738. W.K.B.F." Diameter, 28¾ in.; weight, 4 cwts.

* We are much indebted to the Rev. Percival Johnson, the rector of South Somercotes, for the gift of this sheet.

In 1907 these bells were made into a ring of six by the addition of a new tenor and treble. They were then all hung in a modern steel and iron frame. Fig. 60 is reproduced from a photograph taken about that time. A local tradition, mentioned in Hutchin's *History of Dorset*, states that when Bindon Abbey was surrendered at the Dissolution, the bells were stolen by the parishes of Wool, Coombe Keynes and Fordington.

Our strong advice to the church student is to be sure to ascend to the actual bell-chamber. Even if he possesses a volume giving the exact and illustrated descriptions of each bell, he will find it far more interesting to puzzle them out for himself, and possibly, to take his own rubbings or casts. The writer's own recollections of visits in the seventies to every belfry in his own county are amongst the most pleasant and lasting of his reminiscences.

Then, too, it is well worth while to study and to understand the look of the cage or frame wherein the bells hang. Comparatively few know anything of the mere outline of the present, gradually developed, process of bell-ringing. The ropes hang through holes in the floor of the bell-chamber into the belfry or ringing-room below. These ropes are fastened in a groove round a wooden wheel for leverage. No little skill is required in handling the rope, and it can only be learnt by experience. The first half pull " drops " the bell; the second " nets " it; then it swings up to the slur-bar, or to a clever contrivance called the " stay and slide," which prevents the bell from falling over, and keeps it stationary till the next change is called, when it swings down and up to the other side, the clapper striking as it begins to ascend. The accompanying photograph (Fig. 61) of the old bell-frame for the six bells of Clun, Shropshire, taken when the bells were in action, shows two of the bells staying momentarily with their mouths in the air, and one in the act of swinging downwards.

As to the general shape and parts of a church bell, an example is given of the single bell of the early English chapel of Kirkstead, Lincolnshire (Fig. 62). It was photographed during recent repairs, but it is destitute of any inscription.

The bell-ringing stage of the tower or the basement of the tower used often to be adorned with Ringer's Rhymes, of a local but moral and instructive nature, painted on wooden tablets or sometimes on the walls themselves. Several of these quaint but interesting rhymes have, to our knowledge, disappeared during recent years, both in West Somersetshire and Yorkshire, during the mania for indiscriminate " restoration."

By far the oldest of such inscriptions is to be found in quaint Elizabethan lettering, painted in red and black over the doorway

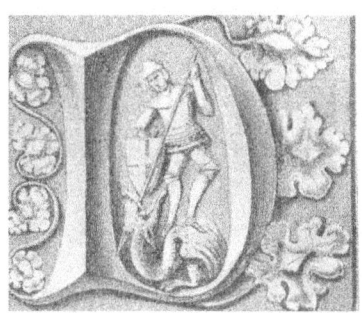

FIG. 59. SOMERBY AND SOUTH SOMERCOTES, LINCOLNSHIRE:
LETTERING FROM BELLS.

Fig. 60. WOOL, DORSETSHIRE: Set of Bells.

Fig. 61. CLUN, SHROPSHIRE: Bell-frame, showing Bells in Course of Ringing.

Fig. 62. KIRKSTEAD CHAPEL, LANCASHIRE.

Fig. 63. KELMSCOTT, OXFORDSHIRE:
Bell Turret.

Fig. 64. BELL TURRETS.

up to the belfry in the basement of the tower of Sutton, Lincolnshire. The following is a correct transcript :

> You ringers All who heare doe fall
> And doe cast over a bell, doe forfeit
> to the Clerke theirfore A
> Groate I doe you tell. And if you
> thinck it ys to little and beare a valliante
> Minde, Y' more you give unto him then
> You prove to him more kinde.

There are a number of such rhymes in the county of Cornwall. We have copied them in eight church towers. At St. Winnow and Lanlivery they are respectively dated 1810 and 1811, but they mostly appear to be fairly early 18th century date. At St. Endellion the rhymes are surmounted by figures of six bells and below them six ringers in red and black small clothes. The St. Merryn board also shows five ringers in black small clothes; whilst over the rhymes of Fowey appears a section of the tower, displaying ringers, ropes, and bells. There are also four ringers depicted with the Lanreath rhymes, c.1750. Other rhymes are at the churches of St. Austell and Wareham. Perhaps the best of these sets of rhymed caution to ringers is that which is found under the tower of St. Endellion :

> We ring the Quick to Church, and dead to Grave,
> Good is our use, such usage let us have,
> Who here therefore doth Damn, or Curse or Swear,
> Or strike in Quarrel though no Blood appear,
> Who wears a Hatt or Spurr, or turns a Bell,
> Or by unskilful handling spoils a Peal,
> Shall Sixpence pay for every single Crime,
> 'Twill make him careful against another time.
> Let's all in love and friendship hither come
> Whilst the shrill treble calls to Thundering tom,
> And since bells are our modest recreation
> Let's rise betimes and fall to Admiration.

In all these Cornish ringer's rhymes, as well as in others, we have noted in bygone days in Devonshire, Derbyshire and Yorkshire, there is one point in common, namely an invariable fine for wearing either hat or spur. Perhaps in the former case it implied due reverence for the consecrated building, and in the other the danger likely to be incurred if the rope caught the spur.

Penalties for these two offences likewise appear in the belfry rhymes of Culmington, Salop, 1663; St. John's, Chester, 1687; Tong, Salop, 1694; Dummer, Hants, c.1700; All Saints', Hastings, 1756; Shilvington, Dorset, 1767; Bowdon, Cheshire; Bowden Magna, Leicestershire; and Rye, Sussex.

To the knowledge of all ringers and amateur ringers, and to most campanologists, there is many a ringing chamber emblazoned with records of far greater interest than the mere jingle of penalty rhymes, namely, inscriptions as to changes successfully rung within a given time on the bells of that tower such as Bob Major, Treble Bob and Grandiose Tripples. Change-ringing, an art peculiar to England, has a literature of its own which cannot be treated of in these pages. The scientific art of change-ringing requires an octave of bells and was unknown until the 17th century. St. Margaret's, Lynn, had eight bells in 1663, and St. Peter's, Mancroft, Norwich, in 1670, and Horsham, Sussex, in 1673. But societies were formed for the more elementary exercise of change-ringing at a much earlier date. A bell-ringing society, called the "Scholars of Cheapside," was founded in 1612; and in 1637 was founded the "Ancient Society of College Youths," so called because they practised on the six bells of St. Martin's, College Hill, a church destroyed in the Great Fire. Towards the end of this century a third society was formed, known as the "Society of London Scholars," a title altered in 1746 to the "Cumberland Youths," in honour of the victor of Culloden.

Of late years considerable attention has been devoted to the subject of church bells, and there is not a belfry in the kingdom which has not been visited by keen campanologists, nor a single inscribed bell left whose lettering or ornaments have not been rubbed or had casts taken. At the present moment every bell inscription has been satisfactorily dealt with throughout the counties of Bedford, Berks, Cambridge, Cornwall, Devon, Essex, Gloucester, Hertford, Kent, Leicester, Lincoln, Northampton, Rutland, Shropshire, Stafford, Somerset, Suffolk, Surrey, Sussex, Warwick and Worcester; also those of London, Holderness and York. Several others have been partially treated or are now in progress.*

In the smaller village churches, where there was often no tower or belfry accommodation, the bells were swung in turrets of brick or stone or timber above the western gable. A variety of these village bell-cotes is shown in Figs. 63 and 64; the elaborate and beautiful example from Preston, Gloucester, is well worth notice. This turret is raised over the chancel arch, the place generally occupied in later mediæval days by the sanctus bell-cote: a small turret containing a single bell, which was rung at certain intervals during the celebration of Mass. The Preston bell-cote, however, apparently contained more than one bell. The sanctus bell-cote was usually more or less plain in shape, like the turret from Emneth, Norfolk, illustrated in Fig. 64.

* The inscriptions on the bells of all the old churches of Derbyshire are given by the writer, who has taken rubbings of them all, in his four volumes of *Churches of Derbyshire*. It had been arranged with the late Mr. Llewellyn Jewett to bring out a completely illustrated volume, but on his death the arrangement fell through.

CHAPTER IV

FONTS AND COVERS

Fonts

NEXT to the details of the porch, which have been noticed, the font is the first thing within a church to attract attention, for, according to the invariable custom of mediæval days, it was placed near to the main entrance. Contrary to the usual and oft repeated opinion, it has recently been proved beyond possible dispute, that baptism by affusion and not by immersion was the nearly universal custom in primitive days.*

Baptisms in buildings, apart from the general fabric of the church, were unknown in England. It is somewhat singular that so few examples of pre-Conquest fonts remain in this country. In the two cases of Little Billing, Northants, and Potterne, Wilts, their Saxon date is proved by the pre-Norman lettering of their respective inscriptions. Probably half-a-dozen other examples are extant and exhaust the list of undoubtedly early fonts ; but it should be remembered that several have been constructed in later days out of such materials as Roman altars and Anglo-Saxon sculptured stones ; instances of the former being at Wroxeter, Salop, and West Mersea, Essex ; and of the latter at Wilne, Derbyshire (Fig. 66), and at Melbury Bubb, Dorset.

The use of metal for fonts was not unknown in England, but it is of very rare occurrence used save in lead. There are about thirty old English fonts made of lead, belonging to different periods, varying

---

* See the Rev. Clement F. Rogers' scholarly and exhaustive treatise on *Baptism and Christian Archæology* (1903), profusely illustrated. On the highly interesting subject of Fonts, Cox and Harvey's *English Church Furniture* should be studied, wherein many pages are devoted to the great number of font inscriptions, whilst the Fonts of each county and their characteristics are described in detail. See also Cox's *Early Churchwardens' Accounts*, pp. 149-159, etc. ; and *Fonts and Font Covers* of Church Art series, rich in illustrations, and the chapter on Fonts and Covers in Messrs. Howard and Crossley's *English Church Woodwork*. (Batsford, 1917.)

from Norman times down to the end of the 17th century. About half of them are Norman; of these three are circular and beautifully wrought, with full length figures under round-headed arches. There are twenty such figures at Ashover, Derbyshire (Fig. 65), eleven at Dorchester, Oxon, and six at Walton-on-the-Hill, Surrey. The last of these (Fig. 71) is a very fine specimen of late Norman; it is of small dimensions, the bowl having a diameter of 20 inches and a depth of $13\frac{3}{4}$ inches. The figures are of divers patterns, each being twice repeated. The first has the right hand raised in benediction, whilst the left holds a book to the breast; the second has the right hand in like position, but the left rests the book on the knee; and the third has the right hand on one knee, whilst the left rests the book on the other knee.

A very considerable number of our early fonts are of Norman date; in many an old church the substantial font is the only piece of Norman work remaining; the two usual shapes are circular or cylindrical, and square or cubical. There are also two other designs later in the period, the one chalice or cup-shape, consisting of base, shaft and bowl, the other having a bowl supported on shafts, usually a central one and four at the angles. The cubical shape predominated in the south and west; out of ninety-five Norman fonts in Devon only fifteen are circular. In Yorkshire, both in the North and East Ridings, the contrary is the case; there are hardly any square examples in the East Riding, whilst out of forty Norman fonts among the small churches of the North Riding the whole are plainly cylindrical.

Derbyshire is a county very rich in Norman fonts. In addition to the highly interesting font at Ashover, previously mentioned, there are good Norman fonts at Chesterfield, Church Broughton, Mellor, Tissington and many other churches. We illustrate the Norman font of Winster in this county (Fig. 67), of curious shape and carved with quaint figures.

The two examples of these different shapes are both taken from the East Riding. The exceptionally good font at Reighton (Fig. 69), is square or cubical, with a shaft at each angle surmounted by a scalloped capital, whilst the panels are filled with various forms of diaper work. The round tub-shaped font of Ruston Parva (Fig. 68) has a cable moulding running round the top, and below it is a narrow band of carving in a zig-zag arrangement. St. Kea, Cornwall, is a good example (Fig. 70) of the late Norman five-shafted variety.

One of the most beautiful and bold font designs of the Early English period occurs at Eaton Bray, Bedfordshire (Fig. 72) At

89

Fig. 65. ASHOVER, DERBYSHIRE: Lead Font, Norman.

Fig. 66. WILNE, DERBYSHIRE: Saxon Font.

Fig. 67. WINSTER, DERBYSHIRE: Norman Font.

Fig. 69. REIGHTON, EAST RIDING, YORKSHIRE. NORMAN FONT.

Fig. 68. RUSTON PARVA, YORKSHIRE: CYLINDRICAL NORMAN FONT.

Fig. 71. WALTON-ON-THE-HILL, SURREY: Lead Font, Late Norman.

Fig. 70. ST. KEA, CORNWALL: Norman Font.

Fig. 73. PATRINGTON, EAST RIDING, YORKSHIRE: 14TH CENTURY FONT.

Fig. 72. EATON BRAY, BEDFORDSHIRE: 13TH CENTURY FONT.

Fig. 74. WALSOKEN, NORFOLK: 15TH CENTURY FONT.

Fig. 75. LAXFIELD, SUFFOLK: 15TH CENTURY FONT.

FONTS—SEVEN SACRAMENTS TYPE.

Fig. 76.
UFFORD, SUFFOLK:
Font Cover.
15th Century.

Fig. 78. BURGH, LINCOLNSHIRE:
Detail of Font Cover, 17th Century.

Fig. 77. UFFORD, SUFFOLK:
Detail of Font Cover.

95

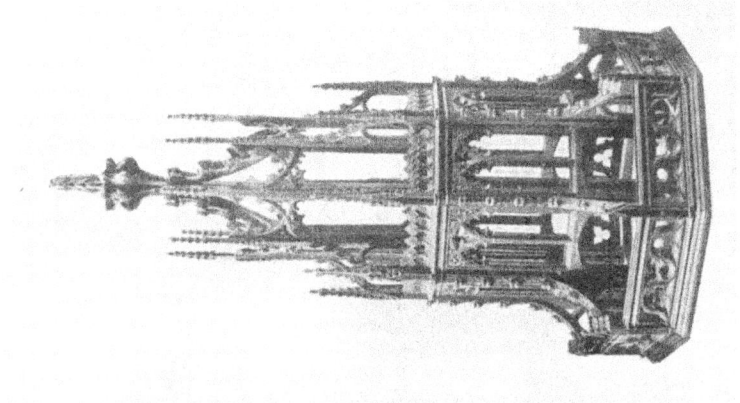

Fig. 79. FINNINGHAM, SUFFOLK: Fig. 80. COPDOCK, SUFFOLK:
FONT COVERS, 15TH CENTURY.

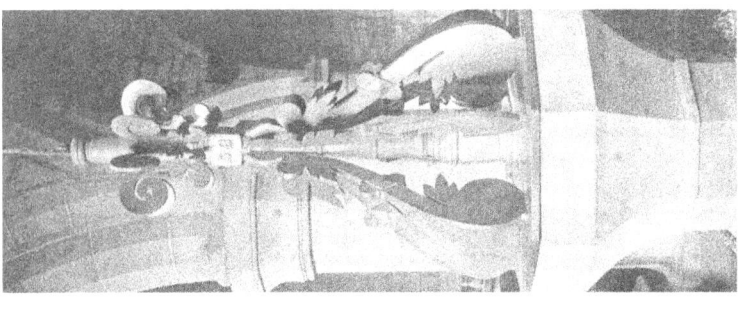

Fig. 81.
ARKSEY, YORKSHIRE: 1662.

Fig. 82.
ST. BOTOLPH, CAMBRIDGE.

RENAISSANCE FONT COVERS.

Fig. 83.
ST. JAMES, GARLICKHYTHE.

Keysoe, in the same county, likewise of the 13th century, is the only Norman-French font inscription:

> *Trestui ke par hici passerui*
> *Pur le alme Warel prieu*
> *Ke Deu par sa grace*
> *Verrey merci li face. Am.*
> (Pause, whoever passes by this spot, and pray for the soul of
>   Warel that God by His grace may grant him true mercy. Amen.)

Fonts of octagonal shape came into use in a few cases of late Norman or Transitional date, and this form is also occasionally found in Early English examples. Fonts subsequent to the time of Henry III are octagonal with but few exceptions.

Fonts of the Decorated period are exceptional; the beautiful font of the famous East Riding church of Patrington is a good example of 14th century workmanship (Fig. 73).

About the middle of the 15th century, when the carving of the fonts was becoming more elaborate, especially throughout East Anglia, the idea came in of utilizing the eight faces for the representation of the Seven Sacraments of the Church, usually reserving the eighth face for a carving of the Rood. There are thirty-two of these sacrament fonts, nineteen in Norfolk, eleven in Suffolk, and one each in Kent and Somerset. One of the finest of these is at Walsoken, Norfolk (Fig. 74), a noteworthy piece of late Perpendicular sculpture. The bowl is delicately carved with groups typifying the Seven Sacraments, whilst the eighth side depicts the Rood or Crucifixion. The shaft has figures of saints under groined canopies. Round the base is the inscription: " Remember the souls of S. Hoynter and Margaret his wife, and John Beforth, chaplain, 1544."

Another good example of a sacrament font is that of Laxfield, Suffolk, of 15th century date (Fig. 75). This font has good groups of figures under rich canopies, but loses in dignity through the almost complete absence of shaft. The steps, however, or risers, by which the font is surrounded, are richly panelled; of this treatment there is no better example, unless it be that of Little Walsingham, Norfolk.

A note of warning should be given as to small almeries or recesses, originally fitted with doors, which are now and again found in church walls at the west end of the nave, near to the font. These are usually pointed out, with confidence, as intended for the safe keeping of the chrism or holy oil used in mediæval days at baptism; they may quite probably have been used for the salt, or for a bowl used by the sponsors for washing the hands, or for small napkins, which formed part of the conventional adjuncts to the baptismal rite in the unreformed Church, but most certainly not for the chrism. The chrismatory, a small case, containing the three usual kinds of holy oil for (1) anointing the sick, (2) for confirmation, and (3) for baptism, was kept under lock and key in the chancel. The chrismatory was treated with much reverence; it was carried in a cloth of silk or some other costly material, at the time of baptism, from the chancel to the font.*

The writer on a parish church should also be warned against giving further currency to that nonsensical name, of comparatively recent invention, of "Death's Door" to the north entrance to the nave or north aisle. This silly talk took its rise from a wholly imaginary tale, as to this door being left open in old days at the time of baptism to allow for the exit of the Devil!

It may be as well to add the curious fact that in late post-Reformation days one or two old churches in England have been supplied with tanks, wherein the total immersion of adults can be accomplished if desired. A rectangular baptistry was erected in 1721 on the north side of Cranbrook Church, Kent, with a descent of steps into a deep bath. The church of St. Mary, Lambeth, chiefly rebuilt on the old foundations in 1851, is provided with " a deep pool or bath for baptism by immersion."

Font Covers.

According to a provincial English Synod of 1236, the font was always to have a locked cover, the key of which was to be kept by the parish priest or curate, for the twofold reasons of cleanliness, and for the prevention of any superstitious use of consecrated water. The water at that date was to be changed every seven days.

But the use of a locked cover prevailed long before the date of that Synod, for we do not recollect ever having seen a Norman font which did not, if untouched, bear the marks on the rim of the staples of a cover.

The earliest font covers were mere flat wooden lids; gradually they assumed a domed shape, later narrowing to an ogee-shaped canopy, with the finials and ribs more or less elaborately carved. During the 15th century they became higher and higher, and were carved with crockets and niched figures, sometimes painted and gilded. The finest remaining example of these lofty spire-like canopies is that of Ufford, Suffolk. This cover (Figs. 76-77) rises up like a spire, level with the top of the clerestory windows, and the whole is surmounted by a pelican. The elaborately crocketed work is of singular delicacy (Fig. 77), and this cover retains much of the original painting and gilding, though somewhat restored. There are three other towering covers of this kind in the same county, four in Norfolk, two in

---

* See Dr. Cox's *Early Churchwardens' Accounts*, pp. 151-2.

Lincolnshire, one in Oxfordshire, at Ewelme, and two in Yorkshire, at Almondbury and Thirsk, the last of which attains a height of 21 feet. We also illustrate two tabernacled font covers of the more usual type (Figs. 79 and 80), both late Perpendicular in date. At Methley, near Leeds, there is an Elizabethan cover of much grace, a bequest of 1584-5, but examples of this reign are infrequent.

There was a considerable renewal of feeling in favour of the decent use of font covers during the revival of church ritual in the days of Laud. Especially was this the case in Middlesex and elsewhere in the neighbourhood of London. There are ornate examples at Kemsing, Kent, and at Poynings, Sussex, whilst there is a nearly plain one at Northolt, Middlesex, dated 1624. The font and cover of Great Stanmore, Middlesex, are of much interest, not only because they were both the work of Nicholas Stone in 1634, but because the church itself, now a picturesque brick ruin, was erected under the immediate auspices of Archbishop Laud.

At Burgh-le-Marsh, Lincolnshire, the font has a finely carved lofty cover of the same date with the pulpit (1623); doors on hinges open when the font is required for use. The top of the cover bears a plain cross, which was substituted by Bishop Tozer (vicar of Burgh, 1758-63) for a gilded eagle of strange design, standing on an open book, and carrying in its beak two pendant devices, which are intended to represent an inkhorn for registering a baptism and a sand-box for drying the entry. This nondescript bird now stands at a considerable elevation on the top of the tower screen (*see* Fig. 78).

Renaissance font covers still surviving exceed in number those of mediæval date, and would be still more numerous if certain restorers had not, during recent years, regardless of the historical continuity of our churches, seen fit to regard them as out of harmony with Gothic surroundings!

Fonts and font covers were treated with avowed contempt by the Puritans during the few years of the Commonwealth period, but, with the Restoration of Episcopacy and the Monarchy, old fonts were replaced and many new ones were supplied; these latter were as a rule furnished with covers of a more or less ornamental Renaissance design. After the Great Fire those in the old London churches often followed beautiful Classic conceptions. As a good instance of the former an illustration is supplied of the enriched font cover at Arksey, W.R., Yorks, over a plain octagonal font; it is dated 1662 (Fig. 81). Of the latter, one of the most stately covers is that which covers the classical font of St. James', Garlickhythe (Fig. 83).

In the church of St. Botolph, Cambridge (Fig. 82), is a remarkable style of font cover, which is well worth mentioning, as it is typical of several others where the old font has been enclosed in wooden panelling. Here the old octagonal font bowl has been encased in painted Renaissance panelling, whilst the actual cover has a canopy above it, supported on classical piers. The whole is raised on a wide stone platform of two steps.

Those who desire to follow up the story and date of any particular font and font cover should be sure to consult the Churchwardens' accounts of that period, and if they are extant they will often be rewarded for their trouble. In the rare instances of mediæval survivals of parish accounts, such an entry may be found as that at Yatton, 1449, where the exact payments to the carpenter *pro cooperatione baptystorii* is recorded, as well as payments for the key of the cover and for the line and pulley wherewith to raise it. Simpler entries of a like character in 17th century accounts are frequent.*

---

* For further information as to font covers, see Dr. Cox's long article on the Middlesex Churches in *Memorials of Old Middlesex* (1909), pp. 14-84; and Mr. Tavernor Perry's *Renaissance Font Covers*, in the "Architect and Contract Reporter" for 30th July, 1915.

Fig. 84. CAMPSALL, YORKSHIRE: Stone Seat.

Fig. 85. SKIRBECK, LINCOLNSHIRE: Stone Seat round Base of Column.

Fig. 86. GT. BUDWORTH, CHESHIRE: Early Stall Work.

Fig. 87. SOUTHWOLD, SUFFOLK: Late 15th Century Stalls.

CHAPTER V

THE SEATING OF CHURCHES

THE original seats of the church were of stone, and formed part of the structure. Seats were not then a necessity, since the posture adopted in worship was chiefly kneeling or standing, as it still is throughout all the communions of the Eastern Church. For the aged or infirm, stone seats or bench-tables were provided against the walls. An early example of this can be seen in the small church of oratory of St. Perran Zabuloe, on the Cornish coast. This little church is of 6th or 7th century date, and has a stone seat, 16 inches high and 14 inches wide, running round the building, interrupted only by the doorways and the altar. Quite a long list of surviving stone bench-tables, chiefly against the walls of naves, but occasionally against the chancel walls, could be readily compiled.

During the 13th and 14th centuries the bases of the piers of the nave arcades were often encircled with stone bench-tables at a convenient height and width for serving as occasional seats. These are wholly unknown in some shires, but they are not infrequent in Nottinghamshire, where they can be seen at Coddington, Kirton, Kneesall, Lowdham, North Muskham, South Searle, South Bonington, St. Michael, Warsop and Walkeringham. There is a good instance of this kind of structural seating round the base of the early English piers at Skipwith, E.R., Yorks, and Fig. 85 shows an instance from Skirbeck, Lincs. Fig. 84 shows the early stone seating of the chancel of the Transitional church of Campsall, W.R., Yorks; at this church there is a stone bench-table on each side of the chancel, but it does not extend to the sanctuary.

From an early period stalls or seats were provided within the chancel for the ministers and singing clerks. These stalls are almost always of wood, although there are some few examples in stole. The early stalls were plain and massive, as for instance the example from Great Budworth, Cheshire (Fig. 86), but during the latter part of the 14th century, and more especially during the 15th century, these stalls were carved with the utmost richness, and were further elaborated by handsome canopies of tabernacle work. The finest examples of these stalls are to be found, naturally, in the Minster or Cathedral churches, but many a parish church, both large and comparatively small, retains sets of stalls of remarkable beauty and richness. East Anglia can show many extremely fine examples, as can be seen by the illustration (Fig. 87) of the stalls at Southwold, Suffolk. Wingfield, Blythburgh, Dennington and Fressingfield rank among the more noteworthy remains in that county. A singularly complete and rich set of stalls for a parish church is that possessed by Nantwich, Cheshire (Fig. 88). It will be seen that these handsome stalls, with their richly traceried backs and splendid canopies compare not unfavourably with the examples in the larger foundations.

Misericords are the hinged seats of the chancel stalls. These could be conveniently turned up to facilitate passing, but their chief use was to serve as supports for the priests and other clerks when reciting the psalms during the Canonical hours. Few subjects are of greater fascination than the misericord carvings, which illustrate for us so vividly almost every aspect of mediæval life, religious and secular. There are happily hundreds of misericords remaining in England, including a considerable number in the parish churches.* A few are carved with sacred symbols and religious subjects, but by far the greater number show incidents from every-day life. There are hawking and hunting scenes, weapons, agricultural and other implements, subjects from the bestiaries so popular in the later Middle Ages, grotesque figure carvings, and a host of other similar subjects that to modern thought may seem rather incongruous in a church. But it must be borne in mind that the Mediæval Christian was no Puritan in the invidious sense; his religion embraced every activity of life.

It would be possible to illustrate a multiplicity of these misericord carvings, but we must content ourselves with two examples: (Fig. 89) a cleverly treated owl from Edlesborough, Bucks, and (Fig. 90) a quaint lion from Higham Ferrers, Northants, where are twenty fine stalls with misericords dating from 1415.

Fixed Seats in the Nave.

Fixed seats in the body of the church were introduced about the end of the 14th century. It is sometimes said that the earliest fixed

* Numerous instances are set forth under each county in *English Church Furniture*, pp. 255, 261, with details; but the reader is specially directed to the finely illustrated volumes on this subject, the one on *Stalls and Tabernacle Work*, and the other on *Misericords*, together with the recently issued volume by Dr. Cox, entitled *Bench Ends*, and Messrs. Crossley and Howard's magnificent new book on *English Church Woodwork* (Batsford).

FIG. 88. NANTWICH, CHESHIRE: 15TH CENTURY STALLS (LOOKING WEST).

Fig. 89. EDLESBOROUGH, BUCKINGHAMSHIRE: Misericord.

Fig. 90. HIGHAM FERRERS, NORTHAMPTONSHIRE: Misericord, 15th Century.

Fig. 91. CLAPTON-IN-GORDANO, SOMERSETSHIRE: Early Seating. Early 14th Century.

107

FIG. 92. WIGGENHALL ST. MARY.   FIG. 93. UFFORD, SUFFOLK.

FIG. 94. RATTLESDEN, SUFFOLK.   FIG. 95. WESTHALL, SUFFOLK.

EAST ANGLIAN 15TH CENTURY POUPEE HEADS.

Fig. 96.
WINTHORPE, LINCOLNSHIRE.

Fig. 97.
WALSOKEN, NORFOLK.

Fig. 98.
GRUNDISBURGH, SUFFOLK.

EAST ANGLIAN TYPE OF 15TH CENTURY BENCH END.

seating in a parish church is that of Clapton-in-Gordano, in northwest Somerset (see Fig. 91). But it may be doubted whether that of the north side of the church of Dunsfold, Surrey, is not somewhat earlier; indeed, they are considered by so good an authority as Mr. P. M. Johnstone to date from c. 1290. They are plain massive benches with good mouldings and ends cut out of the solid. Plain benches of this description are also met with at Fen Ditton, Cambridgeshire; at Willington, Bedfordshire; and at Eckington and Suckley, Worcestershire.

During the 15th century seating in the body of the church became practically universal, and the benches were carved and traceried. The bench ends received particularly elaborate treatment, being carved with naturalistic, symbolic, or grotesque ornament in infinite variety. As is the case of almost every kind of church woodwork during the Mediæval period, certain well-defined local types can be distinguished; in the case of bench ends the chief divisions are (1), the East Anglian Counties, where the finials or standards of the bench ends terminate in tall " poppy heads," and (2), the western counties Somerset, Devon, and Cornwall, where they are generally square headed.

The name " poppy head " was in use as early as the 14th century. It has no connection with the flowering plant of that name, but is derived from the French " poupee "—a puppet or figurehead. The " poppy head " developed into various forms, saintly and grotesque human heads and figures, beasts, monsters, etc., but the best and purest type is the carved fleur-de-lys. Fig. 92 is a fine fleur-de-lys head flanked by a cock and a dog carved with much spirit. This is from Wiggenhall St. Mary, Norfolk, a church which is remarkable in possessing almost all its fine original seating, dating from about 1400. A similar fleur-de-lys head, with charming little attendant figures, is shown in Fig. 93, from Ufford, Suffolk. Other East Anglian churches which retain much of their original seating with noticeably fine bench ends are Dennington, Fressingfield, Rattlesden and Westhall, in Suffolk; and Irstead, Horsey and South Walsham, in Norfolk. Poppy heads from Rattlesden and Westhall are illustrated in Figs. 94 and 95; they are very beautiful examples of graceful forms with delicate carving.

Backless benches, with good poppy-headed ends, used to be by no means uncommon in the larger churches of Norfolk and Suffolk; but in most cases they have been supplied with backs during recent years. The best instance is at Cawston, Norfolk, where they have been suffered to remain in the north aisle.

Lincolnshire is also noted for its bench ends, though in a less degree than Norfolk and Suffolk. The old benches mostly terminate in poppy-headed standards, but at Walcott there are some good square-headed ends. Holton Holgate is famed for the number and great variety of its poppy heads. The special feature of Winthorpe, on the coast near Skegness, is its old woodwork. In addition to the superiority of its screen work, the body of the church is fitted throughout with old late 15th century seating; the bench ends have poppy-headed terminals and elbow rests. In the chancel are four singularly beautiful and elaborately carved stall ends of considerable size, having a height, exclusive of the platform, of $58\frac{1}{2}$ inches. The best of these (Fig. 96) is the most exquisite piece of carving of its kind in all England. In the centre is wrought the legend of St. Hubert found in the forest by a stag, that bore a sword or crucifix between its horns. The poppy head of this stall end is thick with delicately carved acorns and oak-leaves, and up, as it were, the branches of this tree climb three little manikins, one of whom has caught a bird. A fine stall end from Walsoken, Norfolk, is also illustrated (Fig. 97). This has a finely carved figure within a niche, and the poppy head is flanked by two seated figures now headless. The stall end from Grundisburgh, Suffolk (Fig. 98), has elaborate tracery and a well-carved griffin on the shoulder.

In Somersetshire, the number of the well-wrought square-headed bench ends, mostly of late 15th or early 16th century date, is very large. In the large church of Bishop's Lydeard, the bench ends are most varied and interesting. We illustrate (Fig. 100) one of the most striking, carved with a windmill, in naïve and homely fashion. Note the miller and the horse at the base, and more especially the three birds between the sails, possibly intended to signify the animating breath of the Holy Spirit, of which a dove was the emblem.

The church at Curry Rivell is rich in original designs; note the suggestions of the Resurrection and Ascension in the selected illustration (Fig. 99). Monksilver is another Somersetshire church with beautifully carved bench ends (Fig. 101), while Milverton (Fig. 102) shows interesting traces of Renaissance influence.

Cornwall has an abundance of square-headed bench ends, mostly of late 15th century date, not a few of them with pairs of double initials, pointing to the appropriation of seats in pre-Reformation dates. They are so numerous and boldly carved that it is almost invidious to particularize, but to our mind, the church of St. Winnow, near Lostwithiel, has the finest series of bench ends, including a striking one of a ship. Launcells is another church remarkable for good carving of the standards and the backs of the end benches, and for the curious symbols of the Ascension, Resurrection and Washing of the Feet, in

Fig. 99.
CURRY RIVELL, SOMERSETSHIRE.

Fig. 100.
BISHOP'S LYDEARD, SOMERSETSHIRE.

WEST COUNTRY TYPE OF EARLY 16TH CENTURY BENCH END.

Fig. 101. MONKSILVER, SOMERSETSHIRE: 15th Century Bench Ends.

Fig. 102. MILVERTON, SOMERSETSHIRE:
Early Renaissance Bench Ends.

Fig. 103. KEDINGTON, SUFFOLK: 15th Century Pew.

Fig. 104. HOLCOMBE ROGUS, DEVONSHIRE:
Early 17th Century Pew.

Fig. 105. Rycote Chapel, Oxfordshire: Early Renaissance Pews.

addition to the emblem of the Passion, so common throughout the county.*

Devon also abounds in a multiplicity of good bench ends, chiefly of the Perpendicular type. In those parts of the county which adjoin Cornwall the bench ends are mostly square, but in the parts bordering on Somerset they are not infrequently ornamented with the poppyhead finial. At least fifty of the Devonshire churches are still exceptionally rich in carven benches, and among the most remarkable are those of Abbotsham, Atherington, East Budleigh, Colebrook, Ottery St. Mary, Plympton, Sutcombe, Tavistock and Weare Gifford.

The *Manor Pews*, which multiplied soon after Reformation days, had their origin in the parcloses which surrounded the endowed chantries of the local lords. The parcloses were usually placed at the east end of the aisles, and were constructed not only to hold an altar for special celebrations, but also a seat or two for members of the family. After obituary masses were forbidden, the lords of the manor often retained the site of the chantry, which in course of time became the family pew. This has clearly been the case with the old manorial pew of the Barnardiston family on the north aisle of Kedington church, Suffolk (Fig. 103).

Rycote, Oxon, is peculiarly interesting from its historical associations. The fine old manor house has long been ruined, but the chapel, which was founded in the middle of the 15th century, is still standing. Here the Princess Elizabeth spent some time partly as prisoner and partly as guest, and when she came to the throne she visited it on two separate occasions. Charles I was also twice a resident here; firstly when Parliament met at Oxford, in 1625, in consequence of the Plague, and also during the Civil War, in 1643-4. The rood screen has been replaced by two elaborate Renaissance pews (Fig. 105); the canopied one of the south side is Elizabethan; the north pew, of two storeys, was occupied by Charles I, the upper part being then used as an organ loft.

At Holcombe Rogus, Devonshire, there is a very curious great pew, which pertained to the Bluett family, who held the manor for several centuries. It is of early 17th century and the design is of an Italian fashion; the screen-work displays a series of medallions carved with Biblical and other subjects in relief (Fig. 104).

The offensive and irreverent custom of the squire claiming a large family seat within the chancel, had its origin in the right granted in mediæval days to the patron of a church to a seat in

* See Dr. Cox's *Churches of Cornwall* (1912), in the County Church Series, pp. 37-44 and *passim*.

the chancel. This was the custom in Durham diocese as early as the 13th century.

However offensive the large and ostentatious canopied pews, fitted occasionally with fire-places and every contemporary convenience, may seem to the reverential mind, there is no gainsaying that a number of them are of much artistic merit. The patron's pew at Stokesay, Salop, is a fine example dating from the late 17th century (Fig. 106), while many of the Renaissance churches of London can show pews of stately design and well-executed ornament, as instanced in the illustration from St. Margaret Pattens (Fig. 107).

Fig. 107. ST. MARGARET PATTENS, LONDON: PEW.

Fig. 106. STOKESAY, SHROPSHIRE: LATE 17TH CENTURY PEW.

Fig. 109. WITHERIDGE, DEVONSHIRE: Stone Pulpit, late 15th Century.

Fig. 108. LONG COOMBE, OXFORDSHIRE: Stone Pulpit, late 14th Century.

Fig. 111. KENTON, DEVONSHIRE : Oak Pulpit, 15th Century.

Fig. 110. MELLOR, DERBYSHIRE : Oak Pulpit, 14th Century.

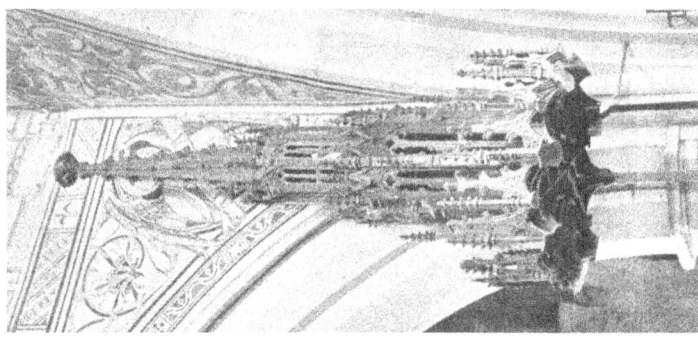

Figs. 112, 113, 114. Edlesborough, Buckinghamshire: Showing Canopied Tester, 15th Century.

CHAPTER VI

PULPITS AND LECTERNS

THE pulpit* was specially honoured in the Mediæval Church of England. There may have been preaching from the altar or chancel steps in quite small churches or chapels, but in nearly all parish churches the pulpit was almost as much an adjunct of the interior as the altar or font. The evidence is conclusive, from a variety of early manuals, that it was considered as much a Christian man's duty to hear sermons as to hear Mass. There is a popular notion that much preaching, and consequently the multiplication of pulpits, came in with the Reformation; but this notion is completely false. There are a large number of pre-Reformation parish accounts extant and in every one of them the repairs or reconstruction of the pulpit is mentioned. The reports of Edward VI Spoliation Commissioners bear witness to their universality; for instance, those for Surrey state that " the formes and pulpits were necessarily left in every parish churche within the countie."

The craftsmen of mediæval England, recognizing that the pulpit was a centre of attraction second only to the altar itself, frequently gave the best of their art, whether in stone or wood, to its construction.

The stone pulpits of pre-Reformation date yet extant in our churches number upwards of sixty. They naturally occur most frequently in districts where there is fine grained and easily worked white stone, such as Somerset, Gloucestershire or Devon. They almost invariably date from the 15th century, but are of different periods of the Perpendicular style. Long Coombe, Oxon, has a fine stone pulpit of the close of the 14th century (Fig. 108), for the church of that parish was begun to be rebuilt on a higher site in 1395; the traceried panels are divided by slender crocketed buttresses, and the cornice is embattled. There is a delightful group of stone pulpits round Banwell, in north-east Somerset, all about 1480, of which Banwell and Worle are perhaps the richest. They are all octagonal in plan, and are for the most part divided into two-light blind windows

---

* See F. T. Dollman's *Examples of Ancient Pulpits* (1849), and Dr. Cox's *Pulpits and Lecterns in English Churches* (1915); also Crossley and Howard's *English Church Woodwork*, for the finest mediæval timber examples.

with quatrefoil heads, with cornices of two orders and a vine trail below. Kewstoke is another good example, differing in the tracery of the panels. In the same county, Stratton-on-the-Fosse, near Shepton Mallet, has a much earlier and simpler Perpendicular pulpit, *circa* 1400. A plainer character of advanced Perpendicular may be noticed at Rowington, Warwickshire. Devonshire, on the contrary, has ten examples of stone pulpits of extraordinary richness; they are all octagonal. South Molton appears to be the oldest, about 1450. It is beautifully carved throughout, stands on a slender panelled stem, and has statuettes of the Apostles under canopied niches. Witheridge pulpit (Fig. 109) is somewhat plainer and later in the same century; the squared panels have crocketed canopies over some figures; one of these is the rood with Saints Mary and John.

It may be well here to note that there was no " correct " position for the old pulpits. They generally stood on one side or the other of the chancel screen. The north or gospel side was the commonest, but the south side, on which the men sat, was sometimes used. Occasionally, too, in the larger churches they were attached to a western pier of the nave, as in the grand stone example at St. Peter's, Wolverhampton.

The early pulpits were far more commonly made of oak than of stone. There are still upwards of one hundred pre-Reformation wooden pulpits remaining in our churches; but it must be remembered that this total includes a few that have been reconstructed out of old panels or bench ends; and others, as at Henley-in-Arden and Southam, Warwickshire, and at Crawley, Sussex, which have been made up out of fragments of screenwork. These extant oak pulpits are almost exclusively of 15th century date, but a 14th century date has been assigned to the pulpits of Mellor, Derbyshire; Dummer, Hants; Fulbourn, Cambs; Hannington, Northants; Stanton, Gloucestershire; and Upper Winchendon, Bucks. It should be recorded of the hexagonal pulpit of Mellor (Fig. 110), that it is the only known example of one carved out of a solid block of oak.

Norfolk and Devon are the two counties which have the largest number of old oak pulpits. Devonshire pulpits have all the richness characteristic of West Country woodwork in general. Usually they are carved with vine trails and other naturalistic foliage in flamboyant profusion; Kenton (Fig. 111) being a fine example of the type. Some Devon pulpits, for instance, those of Harberton and East Allington, are overloaded with extravagant ornament, but where the decoration is kept within reasonable bounds, the effect is one of extreme beauty. The craftsmanship is always excellent. The octagonal pulpit of Coleridge, dating from the early 15th century, is an exceptional type for

Fig. 116. BURNHAM NORTON, NORFOLK: Pulpit with Painted Decoration, 15th Century.

Fig. 115. ROSSINGTON, WEST RIDING, YORKSHIRE: 15th Century Pulpit.

Fig. 118.
ST. MICHAEL'S CHURCH, ST. ALBANS:
Carolean Pulpit, with Hour-Glass Stand.

Fig. 117. ABBEY DORE, HEREFORDSHIRE: Jacobean Pulpit.

Fig. 119. NEWPORT, ISLE OF WIGHT: Carolean Pulpit.

Fig. 120. ST. JAMES, GARLICKHYTHE, LONDON: Pulpit, c. 1680.

this part of the country. The pierced tracery at the head of the canopies in each panel is delightful.

Nor must it be forgotten that our forefathers still further emphasized the pulpit as an object of attraction by a free use of vivid colouring, and occasionally by striking figure painting. Considerable traces of original colouring still remain in not a few cases, but it has usually been removed or somewhat renewed. Cheddar and Dartmouth are bright with colouring among stone pulpits. Painted decoration reached its zenith in East Anglia, so that it is not surprising to find that Norfolk bears the palm in painted oak pulpits. The best of these is at Burlingham St. Edmund; it is of early 15th century date, and most delicately coloured in alternate panels of red and green. Burnham Norton, *c.* 1475, bears the four Latin Doctors, and has kneeling figures of the donor and his wife (Fig. 116). In this connection the coloured pulpits of Southwold, Suffolk, and Burford, Oxfordshire, may also be named.

At Edlesborough, Bucks, there is a considerably restored 15th century pulpit, of small but good design, which used to have figures on the panels standing on brackets; the remarkable feature of this pulpit is the elaborate tabernacled canopy over it, which attains to a height of 14 feet. The underside of this canopy is elaborately groined, as shown in Figs. 112-114.

Yorkshire, notwithstanding its vast extent, has, so far as we know, only one wooden pulpit of pre-Reformation date, namely at Rossington, in the West Riding. This pulpit is one of the best 15th century examples; it has much more dignity than the over-enriched and more famous ones of Devonshire. The good photograph (Fig. 115) speaks for itself; round the top is the carved inscription: *Orate pro aia Picardi Stansall et uxoris ejus.* This pulpit is supposed to have come from the destroyed church of St. Mary Magdalene, Doncaster.

As to post-Reformation pulpits, there are only a few belonging to the many years of Elizabeth's reign, when preaching, save the reading of authorized homilies, was almost in abeyance. Dated examples occur at Bungay (1558), Knebworth (1567), Lenham (1574), and Rothersthorpe (1579). With the accession of James I came a great change; pulpits began to multiply and there are many of this reign extant; particularly in Bucks, Somerset, Nottinghamshire, Suffolk and Surrey. They are executed in the best taste of those days, and well worthy of careful preservation. The pulpit of All Saints, Hereford, dated 1621, is a striking example of late Jacobean work. The panels, divided by classical pillars, are arcaded below. Beneath the cornice is a strip of strap work, and in the centre of each panel is a short piece of vine trail, a faint reminiscence of Gothic work. There is another good example at Abbey Dore, in the same county (Fig. 117), which is strikingly like the one at All Saints. It stands close to the bold Jacobean screen, with which it harmonizes.

The Laudian revival had a general effect on decency of worship, and the numerous instances of finely carved pulpits were part of the result. The Carolean pulpits are, as a rule, better designed and more delicately executed than their Jacobean predecessors. The fine pulpit of Burgh, Lincolnshire, is dated 1623. There are good ones to be noted in most counties, as at Odiham and Winchfield, Hants, 1634, and St. Michael's, St. Albans (Fig. 118). Perhaps the most beautiful of them all is the elaborate canopied pulpit at Newport, Isle of Wight, of the year 1636 (Fig. 119). It is extremely fortunate that when the taste for novelties, encouraged by the late Prince Consort, swept away the old church in favour of a showy successor in 1844, this pulpit, the gift of one Stephen Marsh, was spared.* There is another fine Carolean pulpit, dated 1635, at Sefton, Lancs.

When complete with pulpit, tester and pedestal these Jacobean, and more especially the Carolean compositions, make a dignified presentment of the best woodwork of the 17th century. But, alas, the tastelessness of much of the last half century has succeeded, only too often, in dismembering them, and not infrequently in casting them out as worthless. Within our own recollection this latter course has been adopted in at least a dozen cases—the worshipful art of the first half of the 17th century has been broken up, or has been transhipped abroad.

A whole chapter might easily be written on the migration of pulpits, as one of the results of some of the unhappy restorations of the last century, which were too often based on a vulgar love for newness or uniformity, or else regulated on commercial lines. Thus, out of a score or more of cases, Chediston, Suffolk, possesses a really beautiful and comely Carolean pulpit of 1636, which had been ejected from the neighbouring church of Cooksey, on the avowed ground of being inharmonious with its surroundings. But after a considerable sojourn in a loft, its intrinsic value was recognized by the better taste of Chediston. The love of novelty seems specially to beset chapters. Westminster Abbey has discarded more than one pulpit which has found shelter elsewhere! An exceptional pulpit of distinct value was turned out of Southwell Minster and found shelter at Blidworth in the same county. Quite recently (1915), a well-carved mahogany pulpit was ejected from the nave of Lincoln Minster to give place to a singularly inharmonious successor from Amsterdam. Part of a

* For a full description, see Dr. Cox's account, in the Church Art series, of *Pulpits and Lecterns*, published by the Oxford University Press (1913), p. 114.

Fig. 122. WIGGENHALL ST. MARY, NORFOLK: Brass Lectern, 1518.

Fig. 121. ASTBURY, CHESHIRE: Wooden Lectern, 15th Century.

Fig. 123. BURY, HUNTINGDONSHIRE:
Desk Lectern, 14th Century.

Fig. 124. ROMSEY, HAMPSHIRE:
Desk Lectern, 15th Century.

most deplorable scheme of alteration at All Saints, Derbyshire, in 1873, involving the turning out of a distinctly good pulpit cœval with the rebuilding of the body of the church by Gibbs; the present writer bought it out of a builder's yard, and it found a resting place in the church of Pleasley. At Worth, in Sussex, there is a pulpit, dated 1577, which was brought across the seas from Holland. One other instance out of many may be cited. A distinctly interesting late 15th century pulpit was thrown out of the Northamptonshire church of Brigstock, and has recently taken a long journey to Sturminster Marshall, Dorset. Attached to it is a panel with a defaced figure of the quasi-saint, Henry VI.

The Renaissance churches of London, built and fitted by Wren and his successors, contain much beautiful woodwork. The pulpits are noticeably fine, many examples being carved with the bold and striking trails of foliage and fruit, characteristic of Grinling Gibbons and his school. The pulpit of St. James, Garlickhythe, illustrated herewith (Fig. 120), is a composition of much beauty and dignity. The carving is beautifully executed and is not over profuse, while the massive sounding board is a fine example of restrained classic design and ornament.

LECTERNS

The subject of lecterns has been so fully discussed and pictured elsewhere, that in this place there is no necessity for more than a cursory treatment of the subject, together with some illustrations of a few of the more striking examples.*

The eagle was the favourite choice for Gospel reading purposes right through the Middle Ages, and this emblem was most frequently reproduced in brass or some compound of bronze. A list of brass eagles recently set forth, including a few of 17th century date, amounted to forty-six, a far greater number than had as yet been chronicled. To this must be added those of Newcastle Cathedral, of Walpole St. Peter, and of Wrexham, since noted. Possibly the true total of old instances extends to fifty. The singularly beautiful and bold example of St. Mary, Wiggenhall, Norfolk (Fig. 122), bears the inscription:

Orate p. aia fratis Robti Barnard, gardio ni de Walsyngham a. di. 1518.

There are upwards of a score of wooden eagles; one of the most striking is that in the church of Astbury, Cheshire, of early 15th century date (Fig. 121).

More often the mediæval wooden lectern is desk-shaped; frequently it consists of a double desk. The best example of this form

* See Dr. Cox's *Pulpits, Lecterns and Organs* (1915).

occurs at Ramsey, Hants, *c.* 1450, and was doubtless used in the old Abbey. It now bears on the one side a 16th century chained Bible. The ridge of this beautiful lectern is embattled, but the chief feature is the shaft, supported by three widely projecting buttresses with pierced tracery (Fig. 124).

Huntingdonshire also supplies the oldest extant example of a single desk wooden lectern at the church of Bury (Fig. 123); its exquisite carving dates from early in the Decorated period.

CHAPTER VII

SCREENS AND LOFTS

THE use of a chancel screen is of extreme antiquity, since the sanctity of the chancel is a fundamental principle of almost every form of Christian worship. Low colonnaded screens are met with in the Italian Basilicas, but of all Christendom England was the country where the use of the chancel screen was most general, and where it was brought to the highest degree of artistic excellence. During the later Middle Ages almost every English parish church possessed a screen, and despite fanatical violence and perverted taste considerably more than a thousand remain to us to-day, sometimes grievously mutilated but always bearing witness to the piety and genius of those who raised them.

Of the remaining screens of mediæval date by far the greater number is of wood. Stone screens are found chiefly in Collegiate and Monastic churches and in Cathedrals; nevertheless, sufficient examples survive in parish churches widely distributed throughout the country to prove that they were once numerous. Wiltshire can show more stone chancel screens than any other English county; they remain at Charlton, Compton Bassett, Great Chalfield, Hilmarton and Yatton Keynell. The screen at Compton Bassett (Fig. 126) is the finest example now remaining in a parish church, being richly carved and the piers adorned with niches.

In the West Country stone rood screens can be seen at Brimpton and Dundon Compton in Somerset and at Awliscombe and Totnes in Devon. East Anglian examples include the fine stone screens of Great Bardfield and Stebbing in Essex; and those at Bottisham and Harlton, Cambs. The stone screen at Bramford, Suffolk (Fig. 125) is probably the finest East Anglian example, dating from the early 14th century. Another example of the same period may be seen at Broughton, near Banbury, Oxon, and there are stone rood screens in the parish churches of Chelmorton and Ilkeston, Derbyshire, and at Sandridge, Herts. The foregoing examples comprise only rood screens, although there are in addition a number of stone parcloses in parish churches throughout the country.

The woodwork of English churches is always of remarkable beauty, but it would seem that the utmost resources of the mediæval woodworkers were brought to the adornment of the rood screen, which by its position would naturally have a strong appeal to the imagination of a pious craftsman, in addition to offering the most striking field for the display of his skill. Timber screens have been dealt with so exhaustively elsewhere* that it is here proposed only to indicate the main types, and to call attention to some of the best examples. Wooden screens may be divided into two groups—the square-framed and the arched types. The former is the earlier method of construction; it consists of a rectangular frame with a central doorway and two side bays. The base was at first of plain solid wainscot, but was afterwards traceried and sometimes decorated with painted figures, especially in East Anglia. Above the wainscot the bays were divided by upright shafts known as muntins, framed into a horizontal beam at the head. Various structural modifications were afterwards introduced, and each feature came to receive more ornamental treatment. The muntins were at first turned, but afterwards moulded; instead of being framed straight into the horizontal head-beam, leaving plain rectangular openings, they were carried into a beam carved with a series of arches immediately below it. These arch-shaped openings were decorated with tracery, confined in earliest examples to the head, but afterwards the tracery became more and more elaborate. In some screens, such as that at Walsoken, Norfolk, the openings are completely traceried, as can be seen from the detail illustrated in Fig. 134. The square-framed screen is the most usual English type, and throughout the country, though it occurs less frequently in East Anglia, Somerset, and Devon, where the arched screen is more common.

The latter type is a development from the square-framed screen. It never entirely superseded the original method in any way, and both types may be found side by side in most counties, but the arched screen reached its zenith in the districts aforementioned, where square-framed screens are in a minority. There are no existing arched screens belonging to a period earlier than the end of the 14th century. The arcade

* The reader is particularly referred to the following sources of more definite information: (1) *Screens and Galleries* (1908), by Francis Bond, Oxford University Press; (2) Cox and Harvey's *English Church Furniture* (1907), pp. 82-144, where every county is treated separately; (3) Aymer Vallance's papers on the Screens of Derbyshire, Kent, Middlesex, Lancashire, etc., in the *Old County Memorials* series; (4) a set of six long articles on *Screens and Rood Lofts*, in the "Church Times" of February and March, 1907, by the present writer; (5) the classification and numerous illustrations of various types of screens in Messrs. Crossley and Howard's *English Church Woodwork* (Batsford).

Fig. 125. BRAMFORD, SUFFOLK: Stone Screen, 14th Century.

Fig. 126. COMPTON BASSETT, WILTSHIRE: Stone Screen. 15th Century.

Fig. 127. SWYMBRIDGE, DEVONSHIRE: West Country Vaulted Type, 15th Century.

Fig. 128. DUNCHIDEOCK, DEVONSHIRE: West Country Vaulted Type, 15th Century.

motif first appeared as a purely ornamental feature in the tracery of the square-framed screens, when the muntins had been framed into arches as previously explained. Then the muntins themselves were expanded into vaulted arches, the spandrels of the arched head-beam disappearing altogether. In these arched screens the decoration is naturally concentrated on the vaulting, which became more and more elaborate, culminating in the pendant vaulting of some of the beautiful screens of East Anglia. The elaboration of the vaulting threw the tracery work of the transom openings rather into the shade, so that where the arched screen developed the tendency is for the tracery heads of the openings to be of the lightest description, in some cases a mere edging of cusping to the arch. Figs. 133 and 137 show the detail of the vaulting of the screen at Bramfield, Suffolk, one of the very finest examples.

It has been said that Devon, Somerset and East Anglia are richest in screens of the arched type. These counties retain more instances of old screenwork generally than any others, and may be counted as the premier districts of England for the number, beauty and variety of their examples. In a second class may be placed Bedfordshire, Derbyshire, Cambridgeshire, Essex, Kent, Lincolnshire, Northants and Oxon. Cornwall, Devon and Kent, which though still extremely rich in fine old screens, are the counties that have suffered most heavily by the almost wholesale destruction of many scores of beautiful examples, owing to ignorance or prejudice on the part of the "restorers."

Four miles from Barnstaple is Swymbridge Church, a fabric of many attractions, though its chief glory is undoubtedly the noble screen, dating from about 1420 (Fig. 127). It is remarkable for the bold and massive character of its general design, as well as for the extreme delicacy and beauty of its ornament, a quality in which all Devonshire woodwork excels. The cornice is especially beautiful, as can be seen from the illustration. The two square spaces now empty originally formed reredoses for side altars. The base panels are carved with foliage in relief, instead of the flat painted treatment usual in Devonshire. This screen has been well and carefully restored on conservative lines, and may certainly be reckoned as one of the finest examples in the county.

Another noble Devonshire screen is at Dunchideock, four miles south-west of Exeter; it is finely groined on the west side and has a rich cornice and cresting (Fig. 128); the special feature is the beautifully carved pier-casing. This screen was most carefully restored in 1893.

The central portion of the once very fine screen of Ugborough church, South Devon, was wantonly cut down to the sill level by a former vicar. Mr. Baring Gould, with his usual vigour of statement, says that it was "a pity that he was not decapitated instead." A parclose screen in the south aisle of this church is of later date but of exceptional beauty, with a fine impaled and quartered coat-of-arms with iron helm, mantling and supporters. It is impossible to attempt its heraldic and family significance, but the effect is extremely striking. A detail from this screen is shown in Fig. 130. The screen at Kenton (Fig. 129), with its vine-trail ornament carved with marvellous intricacy and its cresting of almost lace-like texture, may be taken as typical of the carved wood ornament of the West Country.

In East Anglia, which is one of the richest parts of England for ancient screenwork, it will be seen that although the arched type of screen predominates, the effect is very different from that of the Devonshire examples. The East Anglian churches are lofty, with soaring spires and high-pitched roofs; their screens are lofty too, and their structural form is never overladen with ornament, as is perhaps generally the case in the west. They are chiefly notable for the beauty of their painted decoration, both as regards colour and draughtsmanship. Colour decoration was probably in general use all over England during the Middle Ages. But most of the remaining examples of the art, apart from East Anglia, consist of the application of colour and gilding to carved ornament, or the painting of heraldic devices, and the stencilling of conventional patterns. Painted figures are not uncommon in Devonshire, but it must be admitted that these efforts are rather more remarkable for the *naïveté* and vigour which always accompanies primitive work than for any intrinsic artistic accomplishment. The figures of Saints and Angels at Ranworth, Norfolk, and at Bramfield (Fig. 132), and Southwold, Suffolk, are of extraordinary dignity and beauty. If the figure painting at Eye, Suffolk, a detail of which is illustrated in Fig. 131, is of less merit, the general effect as a decorative scheme is harmonious and pleasing.

Among the counties of East Anglia, Norfolk is the richest in screenwork. Many of its screens are of unrivalled beauty, and over eighty can show remarkably fine colour decoration. In addition to those churches already mentioned notable screens can be found at Barton Turf, Cawston, Burnham Norton, Lessingham, Ludham, Trunch, Tunstead, Walsoken (*see* detail, Fig. 134) and Westwick.

Suffolk is not quite so rich in timber screenwork as Norfolk, but there are a few beautiful painted rood-screens, as at Southwold, Westhall, Somerleyton and Sotterley. Suffolk, however, can show a

Fig. 129. KENTON, DEVONSHIRE: Screen Detail. Late 15th Century.

Fig. 130. UGBOROUGH, DEVONSHIRE: Parclose Screen Detail. Early 16th Century.

Fig. 131. EYE, SUFFOLK.
15th Century.

Fig. 132. BRAMFIELD, SUFFOLK.
Late 15th Century.

Fig. 133. BRAMFIELD, SUFFOLK;
Screen Vaulting, late
15th Century.

Fig. 134. WALSOKEN, NORFOLK.
15th Century.

141

FIG. 135. FAIRFORD, GLOUCESTERSHIRE: PARCLOSE SCREEN,
WEST COUNTRY TYPE, 15TH CENTURY.

FIG. 136. DENNINGTON, SUFFOLK: PARCLOSE SCREEN,
EAST ANGLIAN TYPE, 15TH CENTURY.

Fig. 137. BRAMFIELD, SUFFOLK: An East Anglian Screen with Pendant Vaulting. Late 15th Century.

Fig. 138. COTES-BY-STOW, LINCOLNSHIRE: A Simple Arched Screen bearing a Loft. (*Much restored.*)

particularly fine example of timber pendant vaulting at the church of Bramfield, near Halesworth (Figs. 132, 133 and 137). It is fortunate that the greater part of this magnificent screen is in a good state of preservation. The coved canopy works supporting the rood-loft floor projects from the screen on the west side 30 inches and 27 inches on the east side. Remains of the original delicate painting on the screen itself, as well as on the saint-bearing panels of the lower stage, are abundant. The very small figures of angels in the intricate divisions of the vaulting-work on the south side of the front of the screen (there are none on the north side) should be particularly noticed; they probably indicate the presence here of an altar to St. Michael and the Angelic Host.

The parclose screens, c. 1450, at the ends of the aisles of Dennington church, Suffolk, are of exceptionally beautiful design, with cornices and choir rood-lofts of a rich character. It is shown in Fig. 136, together with another parclose from the highly interesting church of Fairford, Glos. (Fig. 135). Parclose screens were very numerous during the Middle Ages; their function was to enclose side chapels, and much beautiful work was expended on them. Fortunately they survive in considerable numbers, occasionally in the form of pews, as stated in the chapter on Church Seating.

To return to the chancel screen, in the remaining counties of England it will be found that the majority of screens are square framed, but they are, with some outstanding exceptions, of less striking beauty. It is natural that they should be affected by the predominant styles of the counties on which they border; thus the woodwork of Chester, Shropshire, Herefordshire and East Somerset shows the tendency to elaborate surface ornament as in the churches of Wales and the West Country; while Yorkshire and the Eastern Midlands tend more to the East Anglian type. The arched screens of Mobberley, Cheshire, and Aymestrey, Herefordshire, may be cited as examples of the former, while Ashby St. Ledgers, Northants, will serve as an instance of the latter. The screens of Yorkshire are generally somewhat austere and sparing of ornament (*see* Fig. 141, from Fishlake), a notable exception being the beautiful screen of Kirk Sandall. The woodwork of Hertfordshire shows traces of East Anglian influence, one of the aisle screens of Hitchin parish church (Fig. 140) affording an excellent example from this county. It is a square-framed screen with heavily traceried openings, the coving of the head beam shows a frieze of angels with intercrossed wings.

One of the main reasons for the strengthening and elaboration of the chancel screen, particularly of the arched type, was that it might serve as a support for the rood. It is not possible to decide when the custom of fixing the great crucifix at the entrance to the chancel was first adopted in England, but there is evidence of its existence at least as early as the beginning of the 13th century. At any rate it was practically universal during the later 14th and 15th centuries. The earlier method of supporting the rood and its attendant figures of the Blessed Virgin and St. John was to rear them on a great beam above the chancel screen. These beams remain in a few cases, as at Tunstead, Norfolk, whilst the corbels of wood or stone which bore the beam can frequently be noted. But throughout the 15th century it was usual for the figures to rise from the rood-loft supported by the screen itself. In the majority of cases the rood-loft has perished, and sometimes the stairway by which it was approached is the only evidence of its existence. But sufficient examples have been preserved for us to determine the chief types and methods of construction.

There were three ways in which this loft was supported. In the first case, a stout beam was placed parallel to the top beam of the screen, about 2 feet in advance of it. On these two beams a floor rested, and the gallery was protected front and back by panelling. A fine example of this mode of rood-loft construction exists at Flamborough, in the East Riding (Fig. 142), and a less known one at the retired village of Hubberholme, in the West Riding. In the second and most usual method, there projected from the top of the screen, both at the front and back, semi-vaults or canopied groinings, and the top thus expanded carried the gallery. It is in these cases that the loft or floor of the rood-loft has been most frequently preserved, because, when the Reformation Order insisted on the removal of the rood figures, it was found that the lofts could not be taken down without the destruction of the whole screen. These lofts or loft-bases are fairly common in Devon, and sometimes occur in East Anglia.

The most celebrated Devonshire example is that of Atherington. It is constructed of horizontal boarding instead of the more usual vertical wainscot, and the bressummer or supporting beam is carved with the utmost intricacy and richness. The eastern side is divided by mullions, the panels thus formed being decorated with tracery heads; the west side, shown in the illustration, Fig. 139, supports gorgeous tabernacled niche-work over a frieze of painted heraldic ornament. The churches of Wales can show many magnificent examples of this type of loft; Fig. 143 shows one of the simpler kind from Llanegryn; but there are many lofts of the most elaborate description as at Patricio (Fig. 5), Llananno, Llanwnog, Llanrwst and elsewhere.

The best remaining East Anglian example is that of Attleborough,

Fig. 139.   ATHERINGTON, DEVONSHIRE:
South-Western Type, with Loft.   Late 15th or early 16th Century.

Fig. 140. HITCHIN S. MARY, HERTFORDSHIRE: Midland Type. 15th Century.

Fig. 141. FISHLAKE, YORKSHIRE: Northern Type. 15th Century.

Norfolk; fragments of the loft-front, more or less complete, remain at Southwold and Eye, Suffolk; Stamford's St. John's and Cotes-by-Stow, Lincs, the latter of which has an unusual loft in a very good state of preservation (Fig. 138).

The third and most uncommon plan was to construct two parallel screens, some 2 or 3 feet apart, the space between being boarded over, serving as a floor to the rood-loft. The best instances of this method are to be found at the monastic churches of Hexham and Edington (Wilts), and the collegiate church of Manchester.

The roods themselves were so completely destroyed that beside the Calvary carved with skull and crossbones at the base of the rood at Collumpton, Devon, only two other fragments remain. At Cartmel Fell chapel, Lancashire, there is a charred fragment of the central figure, which served for a long time to stir up the vestry fire! Recently two interesting portions were brought to light at South Carney, Gloucestershire, namely, a carved and painted head and a foot, supposed to have pertained to a 12th century rood. It should also be mentioned that in the Powysland Museum, Wales, are the mutilated small rood figures of Our Lord and the Virgin from the church of Mochdre, Montgomeryshire, which were found on the top of the wall-plate during a restoration in 1867.

As to the use of the rood-lofts of the parish church, it is hardly necessary to remind readers that it is a complete mistake to suppose that they served for the ceremonial reading of the Gospel at High Mass. This mistake arises from the confusion between the parish rood-loft and the *pulpitum* or substantial choir screen of cathedral and collegiate churches. In the ordinary church the evidence is irrefutable that the chief use of the rood-loft was to serve as a music gallery, in addition to its ordinary use for lighting and decking the figures, as well as for specific ceremonial on Palm Sunday. The wider lofts also occasionally carried small altars of their own, of which there are traces indicated by the presence of piscinas, etc. The villages where the churches certainly show signs of rood-loft altars, which have been noted by the present writer, are at Maxey, Northants; Burghill and Wigmore, Herefordshire; Bilton, Chesterton and Church Lawford, Warwickshire; Horningsea, Cambridgeshire; Great Hallingham, Essex; Lestbourne, South Harting and Petworth, Sussex; Oddington, Oxon; and Winterbourne, Gloucestershire; also in the large churches of Grantham and New Shoreham, and in the town church of St. Nicholas, Nottingham.

The instances of organs on rood-lofts being mentioned in old parish accounts are fairly numerous, but it must suffice to quote two of the

15th century. In an inventory of the city church of St. Stephen, Walbrook, in the days of Edward IV, occurs this entry:

> Also in the same rode lofte is a payre organs and abydeth the keys with lok and keye, of Burton Wyvis gifte, Also a standyng lectorne for to ley on a boke to pleye by. Also a stole to sit on when he pleythe on the organs.

The parish accounts of St. Patrock, Exeter, for 1472-3, contain:

> Item to Walter Abraham for making a seat in the Rode-lofte when playing on the organys, viis.

Various accounts all over the country are full of interest with regard to rood-lofts, both in the 15th and first half of the 16th centuries; and also in the latter half of that century, with regard to their destruction under Edward VI, their restoration under Queen Mary, and the re-destruction under Queen Elizabeth.*

There was a revival of the use of the chancel screen in the reign of James I, which lasted on into the 18th century. The rood-loft, however, has not been introduced in the Anglican Church. The post-Reformation screen bears some resemblance to its mediæval prototype; Jacobean and Carolean examples retain the traditional square-frame construction with the panelled base, the mullioned shafts and the decorated head beam. The ornament, however, has almost entirely changed, although since the local woodworkers were naturally conservative the mediæval decorative motifs often linger on after the old order has officially changed. An interesting Jacobean screen is that of Yarnton, Oxon (Fig. 144). The screen is at the entrance to the Spencer chapel; it is the traditional square-faced type, although the wainscot panels are carved with pilasters, and the muntins have become classic columns framed into the old round arch. Despite the unintelligent use of classic forms it is an effective and admirable example of its kind. It is crowned, as usual, by the bold carved strapwork ornament characteristic of the period. The Carolean screens, like the contemporary pulpits and other woodwork, show a distinct advance in design and ornament. That of Washfield, Devon, dating from 1624 (Fig. 145), is a fine example, surmounted by the Royal Arms and supporters. Other good post-Reformation screens may be found at Sedgefield, Brancepeth, Ryton and Merrington, Durham; Abbey Dore, Herefordshire, a church which has much excellent work of this period; Tilney All Saints, Norfolk; Stow-Nine-Churches, Northants; and Acton, near Nantwich, Cheshire. This latter church has a peculiar low colonnaded screen, possibly derived from the Italian models then in favour. The most celebrated of the Cheshire post-Reformation screens is that of Cholmondeley (Fig. 146). This fine screen is one

---

* See Dr. Cox's *Early Churchwardens' Accounts*, pp. 175-185.

Fig. 142. FLAMBOROUGH, YORKSHIRE:
Rood Screen, 15th Century.

Fig. 143. LLANEGRYN, WALES: Rood Loft, late 15th Century.

Fig. 144. YARNTON, OXFORDSHIRE. Fig. 145. WASHFIELD, DEVONSHIRE.

JACOBEAN SCREENS.

151

FIG. 146. CHOLMONDELEY, CHESHIRE: SCREEN, 1655.

FIG. 147. PRESTBURY, CHESHIRE: SCREEN, 18TH CENTURY.

RENAISSANCE SCREENS.

Fig. 148. St. Margaret, Lothbury, London: Carved Oak Screen from All Hallows, Thames Street.

of the very few examples dating from the period of the Commonwealth, being dated 1655. The cornice is classic in style, although the frieze is composed of strapwork, the pillars have well-designed Corinthian capitals, and the surmounting shield bears the Royal Arms on one side and the Cholmondeley bearings on the other.

Somerset has an interesting group of 17th century screens, many showing the survival of Gothic ornament. The more noteworthy of these are at Croscombe, Elworthy, High Ham, North Newton and Thurloxton.

Those screens which were erected during the 18th century were certainly superior to the earlier Jacobean work from an artistic standpoint. For church woodwork of this period it is to London we must look for the finest examples. The churches built and fitted by Wren and Grinling Gibbons and their craftsmen have usually magnificently carved timber screens. We have selected one formerly in the church of All Hallows, Thames Street, but now in St. Margaret's, Lothbury (Fig. 148). In design and ornament it may rank as a typical example of the best work of this time. Provincial examples are fewer and much less ornate; Fig. 147 shows a pleasing and refined example from Prestbury, Cheshire, in which the "Adam" influence is very noticeable.

CHAPTER VIII

IRON-WORK

THE smith who wrought the necessary iron-work within a church in mediæval times was, like his fellow craftsmen the mason and the wood-carver, an artist who treated his material with a deference for its nature and an understanding of the purpose for which the work was intended. Much of the finest mediæval smith-work was bestowed on the church door and its fittings, locks, keys, etc. This is naturally outside the scope of the present work, but the reader may be referred to the section in the writer's *English Parish Church* (pp. 291-298). Another feature which received some of the most elaborate work of the mediæval iron-worker was the hearse over the tomb. This has been discussed in Chapter II of the present book. The church chest was often fortified and enriched by decorative smith-craft, and examples will be found in the chapter on church chests occurring later in the book. It is here proposed to deal with the remains of mediæval iron-work within our parish churches which fall in none of these categories.

An early and interesting object is the iron bracket shown in Fig. 149. This is thought to date from the 13th century, and is one of a pair remaining at Rowlestone church, Herefordshire. The branch has a cresting of cocks and fleur-de-lys heads, and is furnished with prickets for lights. The fleur-de-lys was the favourite terminal in mediæval iron-work, and it continued to be the most general motif in English iron-work down to the latter part of the 17th century. At the church of Bunbury, Cheshire, the Ridley chapel, endowed by the will of Sir Ralph Egerton, dated 1525, is enclosed on one side by an iron grille facing the south aisle of the church. This grille (Fig. 150) is contemporary with the rest of the chapel fittings; it is 7 feet 6 inches long and 4 feet 2 inches high. The vertical stanchions terminate alternately with spear-heads and fleur-de-lys.

Decorative iron-work remained persistently Gothic in design and decoration long after the other crafts had succumbed to the Renaissance. In fact there is little advance of any kind in English iron-work from the 15th to the 18th century, such work as was executed in the intervening period being simply adaptation of the traditional model, by no

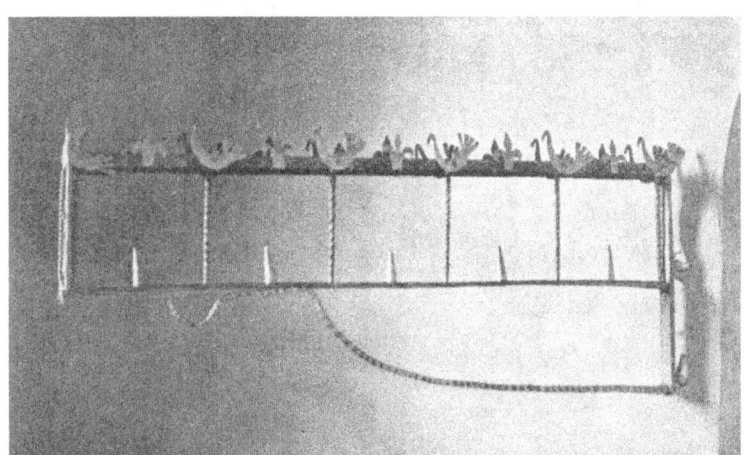

FIG. 149. ROWLESTONE CHURCH, HEREFORDSHIRE:
13TH CENTURY TORCHBEARER.

FIG. 150. BUNBURY, CHESHIRE, RIDLEY CHAPEL:
OLD IRON GRILLE, 15TH CENTURY.

Fig. 152. St. John's, Chester: 17th Century.

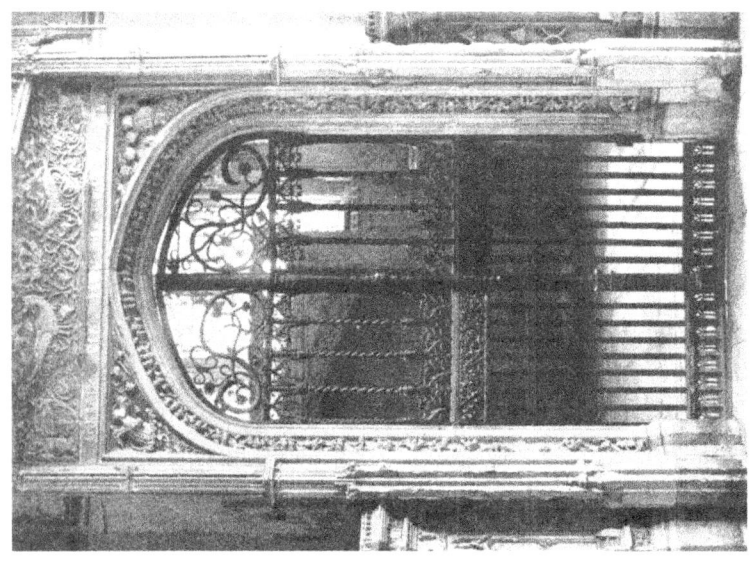

Fig. 151. Ely: Bishop West's Chapel. Early 16th Century.

means improved as time passed. The gates of Bishop West's chapel at Ely (Fig. 151) date from the end of the 15th or beginning of the 16th century, but are thought to emanate from the Low Countries. An example of contemporary English iron-work, perhaps a little later, may be seen in the gates enclosing Bishop Alcock's chapel in the same cathedral. These gates are constructed in vertical bars with a heavy horizontal band across the centre and a panel of quatrefoils enclosed within horizontal bars at the base. Each alternate vertical stanchion terminates in a fleur-de-lys just above the central horizontal bar; the remainder are carried to the top of the gate, where they end in trefoiled arches. These gates are perfectly constructed and are still in acting condition, but there is little or nothing to differentiate them from the work of a century or more earlier. The foreign gate, however, shows unmistakable signs of Renaissance ornament. During the earlier 17th century, iron construction seems to have been largely abandoned in favour of construction in mingled timber and iron, as for example the gates of the screen of the Warbuton chapel at St. John's, Chester (Fig. 152). The principal merit of these gates is their obvious solidity; the iron-work is clumsy and ill-designed. A much more attractive piece of work, dating probably from the end of the 17th century, is shown in Fig. 153, from Farleigh Hungerford, Somerset. The panels are filled with scroll ornament which, if rather feeble compared with later work, is a relief from the shapeless clumsiness of such examples as that from the Warbuton chapel. The central panels contain heraldic shields, which were probably painted, a custom lingering from mediæval times, when most iron-work was coloured and gilt. The cresting is quaint, if rather too heavy for the rest of the composition.

The Renaissance of British iron-work was mainly the work of Jean Tijou. This celebrated smith, probably a French Protestant refugee, came to England in the train of William of Orange. With the exception of the magnificent iron-work at St. Paul's Cathedral, Tijou's work was confined to palaces and great houses, but the publication of his designs gave his style additional publicity, and henceforth the character of English iron-work is entirely changed. The outstanding features of Tijou's work are probably familiar to most people; he employed the minimum of structural divisions, horizontal or vertical, and designed chiefly in bold and intricate acanthus scrolls interspersed with vases, masks, and other classic motifs. The surmounting monogram or cypher was introduced by him. But with all his florid ornament he almost invariably preserves a strong sense of design, so that very few of his compositions can be termed vulgarly ornate. The native smiths proved worthy successors to Tijou; the work of such men as William Edney, Robert Bakewell, the brothers Roberts, etc., being almost if not quite equal to that of the foreign master. Such a gate as that from St. Nicholas's church, Bristol (Fig. 155), is obviously craftsmanship of a very high order. In the same city there is similar beautiful and delicate iron-screenwork at the Temple church. Both were executed by William Edney, a notable Bristol smith, early in the 18th century. The gates at Stanton Harcourt (Fig. 154) are of more modest proportion, and the ornament is quite simple but well designed and wrought. The iron communion rail at Lydiard Tregoze, Wilts (Fig. 156), is a very florid piece of work obviously inspired by Tijou's most ornate compositions. The acanthus scrolls are rather clumsy, and, combined with the large eagles, massive garlands of fruit and cherubs' heads, give a somewhat heavy effect for its size.

The Wren churches of London contain much good iron-work, for the smiths employed by that great architect were in no wise inferior as craftsmen to the wood-carvers under Grinling Gibbons. Wren may be considered fortunate in obtaining such co-operation from the various craftsmen, although probably much of this good fortune was due to his own capacity for recognizing fine work of all kinds. Apart from the compositions of Tijou at St. Paul's, the city churches can show gates, screens, altar rails, grilles, etc., of splendid design and execution. Figs. 157 and 158 show details of the altar rails from St. Mary Woolnoth, and St. Alphege, Greenwich, respectively, and they may be taken as typical of many in London and elsewhere. A noteworthy feature of these city churches is the careful and exquisite craftsmanship bestowed on small details and accessories, such things as brackets and sword-rests. Figs. 159-161 illustrate 17th and 18th century sword-rests. The two plainer examples are both from Bristol churches, Fig. 159 from St. Philip's and Fig. 161 from Christchurch. The fine example shown in Fig. 160 is from the London church of Allhallows, Barking, where there are a number of sword-rests of varying degrees of elaboration. The one illustrated is the finest; it commemorates Slingsby Bethell, who was Lord Mayor in 1755.

The excellent design of much provincial iron-work of the Renaissance period has not, however, saved it from being discarded or destroyed in favour of modern "church furnishers'" cheap patterns. Thus at Warkworth, Northumberland, we have seen handsome iron altar-rails, during 1910 and 1914 visits, lying rejected under the tower, their place being supplied by very common modern successors. At Edlaston, Derbyshire, the singularly fine altar rails, the work of that great Derbyshire craftsman, Robert Bakewell, were thrown out, during a costly but unhappy and drastic recent restoration, and have been cut up to form some churchyard gates leading to the Hall.

Fig. 154. STANTON-HARCOURT, OXON.
18th Century.

Fig. 153. SOMERSET: FARLEIGH-HUNGERFORD.
Late 17th Century.

Fig. 155. St. Nicholas, Bristol. Iron Screen by William Edney, early 18th Century.

Fig. 156. LYDIARD TREGOZE, WILTSHIRE: Style of Tijou.

Fig. 157. S. MARY WOOLNOTH, LONDON.

Fig. 158. ST. ALPHEGE, GREENWICH.

RENAISSANCE COMMUNION RAILS.

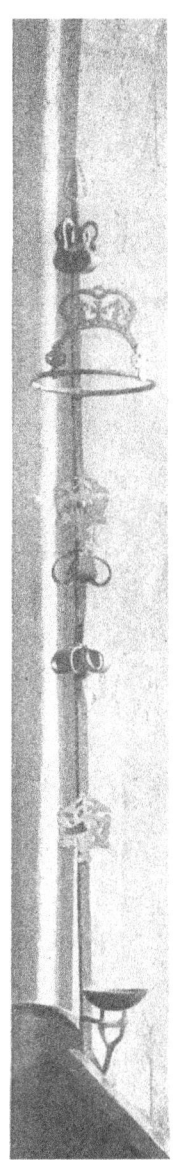

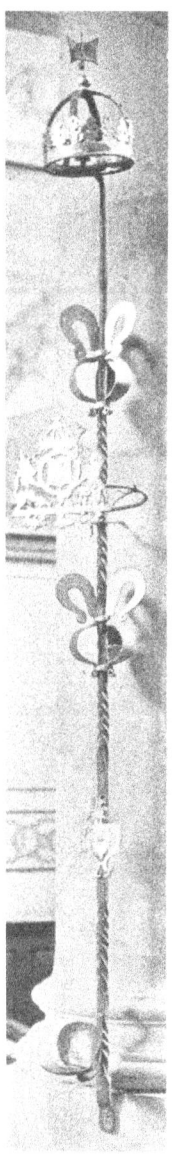

Fig. 159.
ST. PHILIP'S,
BRISTOL.

Fig. 160.
ALL HALLOWS, BARKING.

Fig. 161.
CHRISTCHURCH,
BRISTOL.

SWORD RESTS: 17TH AND 18TH CENTURY.

IRON-WORK

Recent years have also dealt shamefully with other fine wrought iron-work. For instance, by far the best feature of the body of the great church of All Saints, Derby, which was pulled down and rebuilt after the designs of Gibbs, between 1723-5, was the exceptionally fine screens of wrought iron-work by Robert Bakewell, which divided the east end into three divisions. These screens were shamefully maltreated and the chief parts consigned to the crypt, as part of a wretched re-arrangement of the interior in the year 1876; but parts of it have been now replaced. Then, again, the Hampshire church of Wolverton, rebuilt and fitted in 1715 after an excellent classic style, by a pupil of Christopher Wren, fell into the hands of ignorant destructive "restorers" in 1872, when one of a number of blunders was the ejection into the churchyard of handsome wrought-iron chancel gates.

It is now, however, being recognized that English iron-work reached its highest point of excellence during the 18th century, and now that a better understanding of the gradual growth of our church fabrics is becoming more general, it may be reasonably hoped that we have little more to fear from the prejudices of half-educated æsthetes, clerical or lay.

Iron Slabs

Cast iron sepulchral slabs are naturally to be found chiefly in Sussex, where iron foundries existed from an early period. The oldest of these slabs, undated but apparently 14th century, is in Burwash church. It bears a small cross and an inscription asking prayers for the soul of Thomas Coline. Others of pre-Reformation date may be noted at Rotherfield and Playden, whilst later examples occur at Ardingly, Burwash, East Grinstead, All Saints', Hastings, Lamberhurst (just over the Kent border), Mayfield, Mountfield, Penhurst, Salehurst, Sedlescombe, Wadhurst (thirty in number), West Hoathly, and Withyham. A remarkable example is on the church floor of Crowhurst, Surrey: that of Anne Forster, a figure in a shroud with kneeling children, shields, and inscription in raised letters, dated 1591.

At Cowden, in Kent, at the foot of the church steps, is an iron slab to the memory of John Bolting, 1612. In Chiddingstone church, in the same county, are two iron grave slabs, cast in the local ironstone. The oldest, in the centre aisle, with a striking epitaph, is to Richard Streatfeilde, who died in 1601, "greene in yeres but ripe in faith and frutes." The second one, in the south aisle, is dated 1714. There are several cast-iron headstones in the graveyard of the parish church at Leiston, Suffolk, where Messrs. Garrett established their famed iron-works in 1778. There are also several iron slabs, with the lettering in high relief, in the churchyard of Brilley, Herefordshire, on the Welsh border, the oldest of which is dated 1667.

CHAPTER IX

ARMOUR, ROYAL ARMS, HATCHMENTS

Armour

AT least as early as the 14th century it was customary to suspend armour over the tomb of the deceased, especially if he was lord of the manor or of other high estate, or had distinguished himself in battle. These trophies used to assume an elaborate form which was termed an achievement of arms, consisting of the surcoat of arms, surmounted by helmet and crest, with gauntlets and spurs on either side, and in front an oval shield or target. These accoutrements were supported by iron brackets, and above them hung banners and pennons (see *Bloxam Gothic Arche. v, iii*, 204-220).

But we have nothing to do with elaborate examples such as still remain in great churches like St. Mary Redcliffe, Bristol, or St. Mary's, Warwick, or with the historic trophies of the Black Prince at Canterbury, or in the helmet and shield of Henry V at Westminster Abbey. It is of the ordinary parish church we are treating, and though more than half of the genuine old armour, together with the later funeral equivalents, has certainly disappeared or been stolen from the churches within the last sixty or seventy years, a considerable amount of it survives and has to be looked for, not only on the walls, but in chests, vestries, tower chambers and other deposits of "rubbish."

The term "stolen" is used advisedly. At the sale of the famous Brett collection at Christie's, in 1894, of which we have a vivid recollection, an English tilting helmet of the 14th century fetched £210, and several later helmets about £100 each. It was almost openly admitted at the sale that many pieces had been deliberately removed from various churches. The high prices that unscrupulous collectors are prepared to give for remains of old armour are a sore temptation to those who ought to be their jealous custodians. Then again, certain families coolly take upon themselves the assumed right to remove at their pleasure the armour of their ancestors from parish churches; and still more pieces disappear during careless restoration.

A word or two of caution as to church armour is necessary. From the days of Edward II every parish was bound to furnish a soldier or soldiers fully equipped for home and foreign service. The necessary armour seems to have been invariably kept in the church, both in town and country parishes, as we have abundantly shown elsewhere.* In Elizabethan and early Jacobean days, the room over the porch, which was then but little wanted for its original purpose, was often turned into a well-stocked parish armoury, as at Chelmsford, Essex, and Baldock, Hertfordshire, and at Repton, Derbyshire. Hence remains of inferior parish armour have been pointed out at Woodbridge, Suffolk, as armour pertaining to a monument of a person of distinction. We have noticed pieces of corselets, targets and brigandines in the chests of two Essex and one Suffolk churches; whilst in West Somerset we were once just in time to save an incumbent from fixing over the tomb of a manorial lord the morion or open helmet, provided in Elizabethan days for parish soldiers.

In the several volumes of the 5th Series of *Notes and Queries* (1874-9), followed up also in the 6th Series, there are various communications as to church armour then extant in a considerable number of churches. Of the examples then cited so lately as that date, at least eight have, to our knowledge, been looked for in vain.

The custom of placing these armorial trophies in our churches fell into disuse by degrees after the Civil War of the 17th century, but the idea may be said to have survived in the cheap and tasteless form of hatchments.

The following are some of the more important churches where remains of old armour may be found. They are arranged alphabetically, according to counties; but this list must not be regarded as in any way exhaustive or complete:

Bletchley, Chenies and Weston Underwood, BUCKS; Lower Peover, CHESHIRE; St. Michael Caerhayes, St. Mellion, St. Paul and St. Tudy, CORNWALL; Bonsall, DERBYSHIRE; Bickleigh and Crediton, DEVON (Fig. 163); Witham, ESSEX; Iron Acton, GLOUCESTERSHIRE; Godshill, ISLE OF WIGHT; Brabourne, Cobham, Lullingstone, Monks Horton and St. John's, Margate, KENT; Telford, LINCOLNSHIRE; Harefield, MIDDLESEX; Great Brington (Fig. 162, probably pertaining to the Spencer family), and Marholme, NORTHANTS; Shelford, NOTTS; Broughton, Stanton Harcourt and Swalcliffe, OXON; St. Decuman, SOMERSET; Barnwell, SUFFOLK; Addington, Mickleham and Stoke d'Abernon, SURREY; Etchingham, SUSSEX; St. Mary's, Warwick, and Wootton-Wawen, WARWICKSHIRE; Bishop's Canning, WILTSHIRE; Norton, WORCESTERSHIRE; Aldburgh and St. Peter's, Sheffield, YORKS.

* See Dr. Cox's *Churchwardens' Accounts*, 326-330; also *Derbyshire Archæological Society's Journal*, i, 36-40.

Royal Arms

It was at one time generally supposed that royal arms in churches were not to be found in pre-Reformation days, and insufficiently educated High Churchmen were in too great a hurry about the middle of the last century either to get rid of them altogether or to place them in ignominious positions such as the basement or an upper stage of the tower; nay, in certain cases we have met with them in the parsonage coachhouse.

The fact is, that royal arms in a church were not regarded in old days as any sign of hostility to the Pope, for they were not infrequently met with in painted glass, bench ends, stalls, and even on vestments, altar frontals and altar plate, long before our rupture with Rome. To this day in such a Catholic country as Spain, the royal arms are often to be seen in various parts of the churches.

The arms of Henry VI are on the chancel screen of St. Ewe, Cornwall.

It is true, however, that their general use on tablets or frames sprang up in the latter days of Henry VIII, and was probably taken to be symbolical of the royal supremacy. The warden's accounts of Yatton, for 1541-2, record a payment *To a gylter of Bristow for gyltyng ye Kyngs armys*. Immediately on the death of Henry VIII, the Protector and Council of his boy successor took steps for the removal of the Crucifix from the rood-screen, substituting the arms of Edward VI. The only instance that we know of the survival of the arms of Queen Mary is in the church of Waltham Abbey.

The custom of placing the royal arms in some conspicuous place seems to have become general in the time of Queen Elizabeth. They were usually placed on the rood-screen; but, when the screens were removed, another favourite idea was to combine the arms with the Ten Commandments, the " Our Father," and the Creed in a quasi-reredos. Thus the wardens' accounts of St. Thomas, Salisbury, for 1573-4, enter a payment of £2 13s. 4d. to one

Adam Marbell peynting and gilting of ye queens arms a making ye X Commandments and other scriptures at the upper end of ye quire.

The arms of Elizabeth remain *inter alia*, at Basingstoke (1576) and Porchester (1577), Hants; at Stanstead Abbots (1572), Herts; at Greens Norton (1592), Northants; and at Beckington (1574), Wilts.

The tympanum of the arch over the chancel screen at Ludham, Norfolk, is filled up in the boarding, and has painted on it the rood, with St. Mary and John. On the reverse, facing east, are the arms of Elizabeth and the words *Non me pudet Evangelium Christi. Vivet*

Regina Elizabethe. It seems that in Elizabethan days this tympanum was reversed to get a smooth surface for the royal arms, but that a second reversion, effected in 1867, brought back the rood to its original position.

The arms of James I are to be found here and there, as at Blisland (1604), Lanhydrock and South Petherwin, Cornwall, and at Winsford (1609), Somerset.

The arms of Charles I are but seldom met with, as they were for the most part defaced, and usually the "Statas Armys," a plain cross, painted over them, as is stated in a large number of parish accounts. They are, however, to be seen at four Cornish churches, viz., St. Feack, St. Newlyn, St. Mylor, and Poughill; also at Mellis (1634) and Ashbocking (1640), Suffolk.

Under the tower of Burstwick, E.R., Yorks, are the royal arms of Charles II, whilst on the back has been painted the King's execution on the scaffold at Whitehall, after a realistic fashion. This picture was the work or gift of John Catlyn, who was the vicar of Burstwick from 1670 to 1678. On the Restoration of the monarchy, the erection in the churches of the royal arms became for the first time compulsory. Consequently, there are a considerable number of survivals of royal arms of Charles II's reign, especially in the West of England. Figs. 164 and 149 show two excellent examples of late 17th century royal arms. They are both extremely well designed and effective, and are marshalled thus : 1 and 4, England and France quarterly ; 2, Scotland ; 3, Ireland.

The arms of the short-reigned and deposed James II are naturally rare; they occur at St. Sampson, Cornwall. The arms of William III are to be noted at St. Breward in the same county.

There are a fair number of examples of the reign of Queen Anne; the arms of the Cornish churches of St. Breock are dated 1710, and those of St. Dennis, 1711.

With the advent of George I from across the seas, in 1714, there came about considerable changes in the royal arms. The royal seal shows that the arms of the beginning of this reign were, quarterly, 1, England impaling Scotland ; 2, France ; 3, Ireland ; 4, Brunswick impaling Luneburg; on a point in point Saxony ; on centre of fourth quarter an escutcheon charged with the crown of Charlemagne, for the arch-treasuryship of the Holy Roman Empire.

The arms of Brunswick were two passant lions ; of Luneburg a lion in a field sprinkled with roses, and in point a horse courant for Westphalia.

But this elaborate and complicated heraldry, which George I brought with him from Germany, was too much to expect from painters and designers of the arms in churches. Moreover, such a muddle of colours and designs could not possibly produce any effect when seen from a distance. Consequently for the most part the far simpler expedient was resorted to of retaining the old quarters of the United Kingdom, with a small escutcheon of pretence in the centre on which was ensigned the white horse of Hanover. So far as we have noticed, this simple way of reminding folk that the new king, who could only talk German, came from Hanover, is usually followed in the few instances in which early Georgian church arms have survived without subsequent alteration.

This is the case with the large panel of royal arms in the west porch of the church of Lymington, Hants. It was originally painted with the arms of Charles II, as the wardens' accounts testify:

1676.—Gave to men, to help set up the Kings Armes 00.02.00
1716.—To workmen in beere about helping doing the Kings Armes .. 1. 0
        To John Cleves for peinting the Kings Armes 1.10.07

The initial C was altered into G, as we see in the plate, the escutcheon of the House of Hanover was inserted into the midst of the arms; the original date of MDCLXXVI was altered into MDCCXVI; and the names of the later churchwardens, William Chappell and William Scorell, substituted for the original names of Robert Edwards and John Huxton.* This can be seen clearly in the illustration (Fig. 166), reproduced by courtesy of the Rev. G. Bostock, of Lymington.

Lymington is by no means unique in the possession of palimpsest royal arms. At North Walsham, Norfolk, the arms of Charles II, dated 1661, bear on the back the simple arms of the Commonwealth. The very interesting church of Giggleswick, N.R., Yorks, has another palimpsest example, now hanging against the north wall of the nave. At Furneaux Pelham, Herts, there is a panel of royal arms which shows the three successive dates of 1634, 1660, and 1683. In fact, so often is it the case that a new reign occasioned the re-painting or re-lettering of the old panel or canvas, that it is always worth while to examine carefully the extant arms. At St. Michael's Church, St. Albans, are the arms of Charles II, " C.R.1660," painted on wood; they were found in 1901, concealed beneath canvas which bore the arms of George III.

Cranbrook, Kent, is one of the few examples of Georgian arms wherein an effort has been made in the fourth quarter to reproduce the German amalgam of arms, already detailed in the account of that king's seal. The other quarters are: 1, England and Scotland impaled; 2, the *fleur-de-lys* of France; and 3, the harp of Ireland. Fig. 165 illustrates this coat of arms, which was granted to the church in 1750.

* See the Rev. G. Bostock's *Notes on the Parish Church of Lymington* (1913), p. 20.

A similar effort was made in the painted royal arms of Combe-Martin, Devon. The later Georgian arms in churches for the most part abandoned all reference to their German extraction, and, as is well known, the *fleur-de-lys* of France disappeared after 1800.

The setting up of the Ten Commandments in churches for edification was not unknown in mediæval days, as is testified both by inventories and bequests; but the custom became general early in the reign of Elizabeth. On 22nd January, 1560-1, the Queen wrote a letter to the commissioners in matters ecclesiastical complaining of the desolate and unclean state of many churches, and they were ordered to see that tables of the Commandments were set up, not only for edification, but also " to give some comely ornament and demonstration that the same was a place of religion and prayer."

They were usually accompanied by tables or tablets bearing the " Our Father " and the Creed.

Churchwardens' accounts abundantly prove that a number of parishes possessed all these before Elizabeth's letter. The earliest instance we have met with is at St. Michael's, Worcester, under date 1547.

In the following year the Ten Commandments were painted on the rood-loft of St. Mary's, Dover. Five shillings was paid at St. Martin-in-the-Fields, in 1559, for the painting of the same.

1561.—Ludlow. For settinge of the commandments in a frame, iijs.
1561-2.—St. Martins, Leicester. For ye paint to ye ten commandments, xiijd. ob.
    To Wyllam Bargand for wrytyng ye ten commandments, ijs.
1565.—Wimborne. For the x Commandments in collers (colours), xxd.
1576.—St. Mary's, Devizes. To the painters for writing the x Commandments on the church wall, xvs.

The usual place for the Commandments in Elizabethan days was immediately at the east end of the chancel, but they were sometimes painted over or on each side of the chancel arch.

In the few cases where Elizabethan tablets remain, much pains have evidently been taken to render the lettering artistic. In the Lady chapel of Ludlow there is a board of " The X commandemens of almighty god " dated 1561, painted after a much abbreviated fashion in black letter, and surrounded with ornamental borders. At Ellingham, Hants, at the back of the rood-loft over a 15th century screen, are the Commandments, Creed and " Our Father " in Elizabethan black letter, within Renaissance borders (Fig. 168). Lanteglos-by-Fowey has the Commandments in black letter with red initials within a painted border; the spelling is quaint, e.g., " Doe no murther." Other Elizabethan examples are to be found at Aylmerton and Gateley, Norfolk; at Haltham, Lincolnshire; at Wistanton, Salop; and at

Abbot's Langley, Herts. In the chancel of Bengeworth, Gloucestershire, is a table of the Commandments cut in boxwood, dated 1591.

The tympanum of the church of Baddeley, Cheshire, was painted in 1663 with the royal arms; the arms of the Mainwarings, lords of Baddeley from the time of Richard II to 1797; the Commandments and a text. This is well illustrated in Fig. 169. The tympanum has survived intact from mediæval time, and it is thought that it may originally have carried a painting of the "Doom."

There are survivals of carefully executed tables of 17th century dates at Combpyne, Devon, *temp*. Charles II, and at Ruyton, Salop, 1668. There are also named as being executed in various churchwardens' accounts of that century, e.g., Minchinhampton (1606), Gloucestershire; Pittington (1607), Durham; St. Mary's, Cambridge, 1634; and at Shipdham, Norfolk, 1630.

At Terrington St. Clement's, Norfolk, the "Our Father" in the north transept (Fig. 170) and the Creed in the south transept, dated 1635, are quite works of art.

During the 18th century tablets of Benefactions and similar notices were often set up in churches. The lettering is generally good and the frames well carved. We illustrate an example from the London church of St. Alphege, Greenwich (Fig. 171).

HATCHMENTS

The word "hatchment" is considered to be a shortened and corrupted form of "atchievement." It is applied to a painted escutcheon or armorial ensign, exhibiting on a large lozenge-shaped framework the arms of a deceased person. The hatchment was exhibited on the second floor of the front of the dwelling house for six months, or more often for a year, after the funeral, and was then moved to the interior of the parish church, or of the church where the deceased's chief landed property lay.

The hatchment consisted of a large wooden framework, usually from 4 to 5 feet square, on which canvas was stretched, and in the centre was painted the shield of the deceased person, with full armorial bearings, crest and motto. The arms were usually rudely figured so as to withstand exposure to the weather, and were frequently false to true heraldry; the "or" and "argent," the metals of gold and silver, being represented by yellow and white. The canvas behind the shield was painted black, in whole or in part, according to the rules of heraldry, which define the distinctions between married persons, widowers and widows, and bachelors and spinsters. The motto below the shield was sometimes that of the family, but more usually some appropriate sentiment, such as *Mors janua vitæ*, or *Memento mori*.

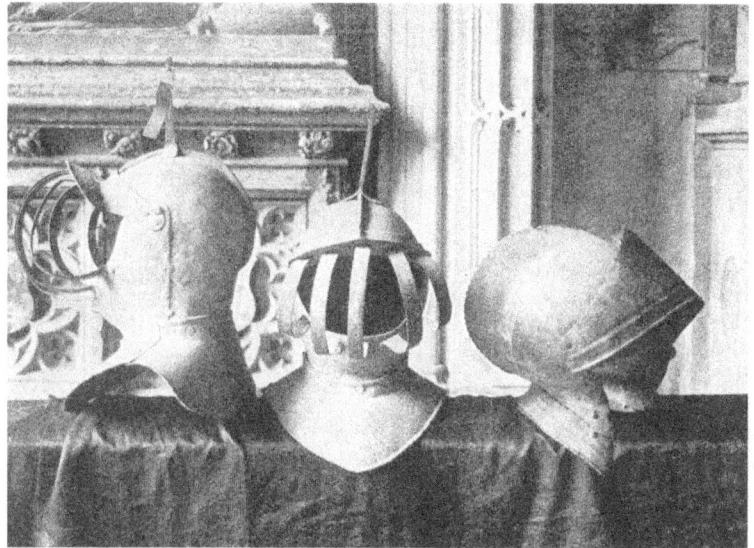

Fig. 162. GT. BRINGTON, NORTHAMPTONSHIRE: Armour.

Fig. 163. CREDITON, DEVONSHIRE: Old Armour.

172

Fig. 165. Cranbrook, Kent: Arms of George I.

Fig. 164. Keynsham, Somersetshire: Royal Arms, late 17th Century.

Fig. 167. Temple Church, Bristol: Royal Arms, late 17th Century.

Fig. 166. Lymington, Hampshire: Palimpsest Royal Arms.

Fig. 168. Ellingham, Hampshire: Commandments and Creed, temp. Elizabeth. Royal Arms, temp. Charles II, 1671.

Fig. 169. BADDELEY, CHESHIRE: Tympanum, Royal Arms, Commandments, etc., 1663.

Fig. 170. TERRINGTON ST. CLEMENTS, NORFOLK: Tablet of the Lord's Prayer, 17th Century.

Fig. 171. ST. ALPHEGE, GREENWICH: Tablet of Benefactions, 18th Century.

There is no doubt that a certain amount of interest pertains to hatchments in the minds of students of heraldry and genealogists. These vainglorious and unseemly disfigurements of the walls of our churches would never have been permitted in mediæval days, and were only introduced in the very worst period of the life of the Church of England, in the days immediately preceding the Commonwealth. In Mr. Christopher Markham's admirable essay on hatchments which appeared in the *Proceedings of the Archæological Society for the Archdeaconries of Northampton and Oakham*, 1910, the oldest known hatchment mentioned is one in Stoke Bruern church, Northants, dated 1655-6 (Fig. 172); but the present writer has noted remains of discarded hatchments of the previous decade in the tower chamber of Holdenby, Northants, and in the stable loft on the rectory of Luccombe, Somerset.

Moreover, the materials of which hatchments were made are so mean and ephemeral, that the opinion of some good archæologists is confirmed, namely, that they were not originally intended to hang on church walls for more than a twelvemonth. Happily the recent revival of the proper use to which a church should be put has put to flight hatchments within a church, and probably no incumbent could nowadays be found to admit such a thing. Moreover, the exhibition of a hatchment outside a house is now almost entirely unknown; the present writer can well remember that they were of quite common occurrence during his boyhood in such towns as Bath and Cheltenham, as well as in the West End of London.

One very wholesome effect of often mischievous " restoration " has been the disappearance of these cheap vulgarities in many scores of cases, whilst in other instances they have been relegated to the basements of the towers. Yet they still remain in sufficient numbers to fully justify, nay, to necessitate, their discussion in these pages.

In Derbyshire we are not aware of any hatchments remaining, save seven of the interesting family of Coke on the south wall of the church of Trusley, and two at Wingerworth. Northamptonshire, on the contrary, has hatchments remaining in thirty old churches, as Mr. Markham has shown. In that county various old families still retain their ancestral estates and reside in houses adjacent to the churches. At Stanford there are sixteen hatchments of the Cave family, dating from 1703 to 1888; at Canons Ashby, eleven of the Dryden family, dating from 1708 to 1850; whilst in the north chapel of Brington there are eight Spencer hatchments, now affixed to the roof.

The single case throughout all England in which the appearance of a church can be said to be improved by hatchments is the small debased Gothic church of Compton Wynyates, Warwickshire, rebuilt in 1663. Here are twelve hatchments of the great family of Compton, varying in date from 1740 to 1860; they have been grouped together after a quasi-artistic fashion.

For the most part hatchments, as the keenest heraldic student must admit, are totally destitute of the slightest claim to artistic merit. We only know of one exception to this rule, which occurs at Upton, Northants, in the hatchment of Sir Thomas Samwell, Bart., 1757 (Fig. 173). On a baronet's helm the *Crest*. On a coronet or, a squirrel sejant gules, cracking a nut proper. *Arms*.—Per pale dexter, ermine, two squirrels sejant addorsed cracking nuts gules, Ulster hand on canton in chief for Samwell. Sinister, azure, three escallops or, between two flaunches ermine, for Clarke. *Mantling*.—Gules doubled, argent. Ornamental borders of foliage, with two palm branches crossed beneath shield. *Background*.—Dexter, black; sinister, white.

A good deal of interest pertains to one of the hatchments in the church of Merton, Surrey: it bears the arms of Lord Nelson.

179

Fig. 173. UPTON CHURCH, NORTHAMPTONSHIRE: Sir Thomas Samwell, 1757.

Fig. 172. STOKE BRUERN, NORTHAMPTONSHIRE: Hatchment for Mrs. Hallow, 1655.

FIG. 174. S. LEONARD'S, SHOREDITCH.

CHAPTER X

CLOCKS AND SAND GLASSES

AS to the origin of clocks, with a wheel and an escapement, we have here no concern, further than to note that their invention is usually assigned to Pope Silvester II, who died in 1002. Mechanical clocks were known in England and used in churches as early as the 12th century, for the purpose of sounding the passage of time at the hours and their sub-divisions, but dials do not seem to have been introduced until the 14th century. As late as the 17th century, the simple clocks of village churches had no dials; for instance, the clock in the tower of Luccombe, West Somerset, with which the present writer was well acquainted in his youth, dated from 1672, and was a very good timekeeper, but it had no dial.

The great majority of clocks, even in large town churches such as St. Edmund's, Salisbury, in the earlier days were not supplied with dials, within or without, until the 15th or 16th centuries, as can be proved from a careful examination of their churchwarden accounts; at all events, they had certainly no outside faces and their works were contained in clock-houses within the churches.*

The hour and its divisions were frequently struck on the bell or bells by ingeniously devised automatic figures, termed "jacks." There are interesting old "jacks," but now disused and not in their original position, at Southwold (Fig. 175), and Blythburgh (Fig. 177), Suffolk; and at Minehead, Somerset. There are striking "jacks" still in use at Rye, Sussex, and at St. Mary Steps, Exeter (Fig. 176), and in one or two of our cathedral churches, such as Wells. The great clock of Rye, the pendulum of which swings free in the church, is erroneously reported to have been the gift of Queen Elizabeth, but the extant parish accounts show that it was ordered and paid for by the churchwardens in 1560-2; it is said to be the oldest English clock still doing its work. The 16th century Exeter clock, projecting into West Street, from the tower of St. Mary Steps,

---

* It is worth remembering that M. Viollet-le-Duc was of opinion, from an architectural point of view, that no provision was made in any church tower for outer dials until the 14th century.

has, in an alcove about the dial, a combination of three jacks, the central seated figure is that of Henry VIII, who nods his head at each stroke of the hour; the two side figures are soldiers with javelins in one hand and long hammers in the other, with which they strike the hours (see Fig. 176).

There are records of former jacks for striking the hours in some thirty other churches, but it must suffice to quote one definite example relative to this part of time-noting mechanism, occurring at St. Laurence's, Reading, under the year 1495; the clock itself is named thirty-two years earlier:

Payed for the settyng of Jak, with the hanging of his bell and mendyng his hand, iiii*d*.

There is no greater mistake with regard to church clocks than to imagine that they were great rarities in the later mediæval days. Even a scholar like Dean Burgon makes the mistake of writing of the church of St. Helen's, Bishopsgate, in bygone days, that it had a clock, "that rare luxury"; whereas it does not appear that there was a single clockless church throughout the City of London in the 15th century. There are upwards of sixty sets of churchwarden accounts of the close of the 14th century, and of the 15th century, and about a like number of the first half of the 16th, all of which have been consulted, either in manuscript or in printed transcript, by the present writer. There is hardly a single parish, in either town or country, which lacks entries as to the repair or purchase or guardianship of clocks. Thus there are entries relative to the clock of St. Laurence, Reading, in 1433; of St. Petrock, Exeter, 1435; Tintinhull, Somerset, 1436; Thame, 1443; All Saints, Derby, 1445; St. John, Peterborough, 1473; and of Wigtoft, Lincolnshire, 1484.*

In Marston Magna church is a clock made by William Monk, a blacksmith, in 1710. He received £15 for his labours. It has no face and is composed of seven cog-wheels placed one above the other. It is driven by the weight of two blocks of free-stone having rings leaded into them. These hang on a thin rope, which is wound on a roller like an ordinary windlass at the head of a well. The clock has no face and makes so much noise in ticking that it is generally stopped during public service. There appear to be several similar clocks by the same maker in various churches.

Several particulars could be given of early clocks pertaining to cathedral churches, but these pages are primarily concerned with parish churches. But one fact can be mentioned relative to old St. Paul's,

* See Dr. Cox's *Early Churchwardens' Accounts* (1913), 228-231, etc. To the lists there given several additions can now be made.

whilst the wondrous clock of Wells calls for more definite mention, In 1334 the dean and chapter of St. Paul's entered into a contract with Walter, the "organer" of Southwark, to supply and fix a dial; from which it may be inferred that the previous clock, certainly extant in 1256, had no face or dial, but simply struck the hour and its divisions on jacks.

The current tradition as to the ancient clock now in the north transept of the cathedral church of Wells having been removed here from Glastonbury when that abbey was pillaged in 1539, though repeated in Mr. Britten's work on *Old Clocks and Watches*, has been shown to be unsupported by evidence and distinctly improbable.* The rolls of Wells show that the cathedral possessed a clock long before the dissolution of the monasteries; in fact there is an entry as early as the year 1394-5, recording the payment of ten shillings to the clock-keeper, and a like entry is repeated in every succeeding roll extant, down to the end of the 15th century. The chapter evidently considered their wonderful clock of greater importance than the great organs, for the organist during a like period only received 6s. 8d. a year.

It is difficult to give any intelligible account of the elaborate functions discharged by this wonderful piece of mechanism with any brevity, and we must refer the anxious to Canon Church's detailed account. It must here suffice to quote the few words concerning this clock to be found in *A Concise History of Wells Cathedral*, written more than a century ago, by John Davis, the verger :

In an old chapel of the northern transept is a curious old specimen of the art of clockmaking; it is a dial constructed by Peter Lightfoot, a monk of Glastonbury, about the year 1325, of complicated design and ingenious execution. On the face the changes of the Moon and other astronomical particulars are represented, an horizontal framework, on the summit (?) of the dial exhibits, by the aid of machinery, a pair of knights armed for the Tournament pursuing each other with a rapid rotatory motion.†

A photograph of the dial is reproduced in Fig 178.

Peter Lightfoot, a Glastonbury monk of the 14th century, the designer of this wonderful clock, is also supposed to be the maker of another clock placed in Wimborne Minster. The twenty-four-hour dial, as it at present exists, has a distinct resemblance to that of Wells, but it is on an inferior scale. The clock of Exeter Cathedral has also been attributed to Lightfoot. The cathedral rolls mention the existence

* See the admirable paper by the late Canon Church, " The Clock and Quarter Jacks in the cathedral church of Wells," vol. 55, *Som. Arch. Soc.*

† The copy of this guide, remarkably good for the days in which it was printed, from which these words are taken, was purchased by the writer's father when passing through Wells in 1820, on the way to his tutor in Cornwall.

of a clock as early as 1317, but the existing timekeeper is generally supposed to have been given by Bishop Courtenay in 1480. If this be correct the clock cannot be by Peter Lightfoot, since he died some years before this date. The old iron works of this clock are shown in the photograph (Fig. 179). They have now been superseded, but the elaborate dial still discharges its function.

It remains to be noted that twenty-four-hour clocks were formerly in use in several other churches, both with exterior and interior dials. On the singularly fine tower of St. Austell, Cornwall, erected during the episcopacy of Bishop Courtenay (1478-1487), there is an ancient clock face with twenty-four small bosses for the hours, below the west window of the tower. Each boss has a small hole in the centre, showing that they once bore metallic discs. This clock face is somewhat later than the tower, for the window-sill has been cut away to give room. In the interior of Raunds church, Northants, at the west end, is another old clock face for the twenty-four hours of night and day.

The interior clocks of several of the city churches of Wren are made conspicuous by the beauty of the wood-carving by which they are surrounded. Probably the best of such carving in any London church is that in which the dial is placed at St. Leonard's, Shoreditch (Fig. 174), where the plain clock dial at the west end stands out amid elaborate wooden carving of fruit, flowers and foliage, surmounted by a well-designed eagle. This church was rebuilt between 1735 and 1740 by George Dance the elder, an architect of some renown in the first half of the 18th century.

Sand Glasses

The subject of church sand glasses is by no means to be lightly dismissed. Since the last list of hour glass stands was issued early in 1915, the number now identified (1917) has grown considerably, and old stands are now known to number over 120, more than a score of which still carry glasses. It is usual to call them all hour glasses, but the term sand glasses is preferable, for some of those in churches, and usually attached to pulpits, record a far less space of time than an hour. Sand glasses were continually used for all kinds of purposes prior to the Reformation; they were probably then used by private individuals within church to time their meditations or spiritual readings, in the same way as they in like manner timed their household duties, such as cooking or egg-boiling. It is doubtful, however, if the sand glass was ever used in an official or public manner in churches till the later days of the 16th century. The earliest known instance of a time-glass attached to a pulpit is one named in 1523, when a new pulpit was placed in Lambeth parish church.

185

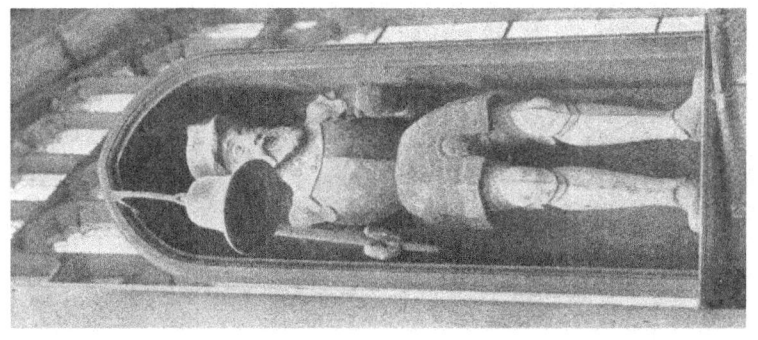

FIG. 175.
SOUTHWOLD, SUFFOLK.

FIG. 176.
ST. MARY STEPS, EXETER.
16TH CENTURY.

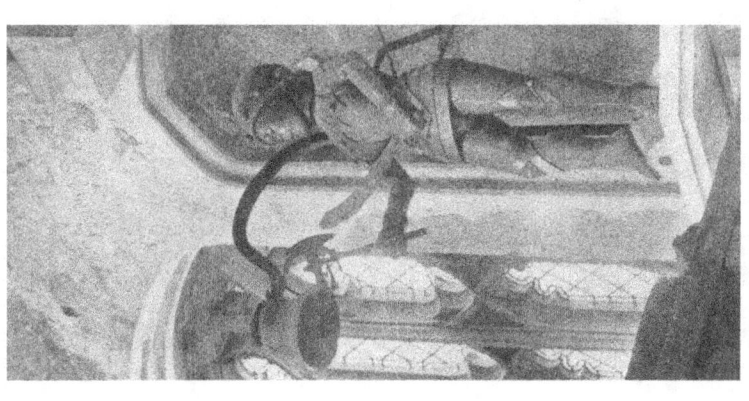

FIG. 177.
BLYTHBURGH, SUFFOLK.

CLOCK JACKS.

186

Fig. 178. WELLS CATHEDRAL: Clock, 14th Century.

Fig. 179. EXETER: Movement of Mediæval Clock, 15th Century.

The frontispiece of the " Bishop's Bible " of 1569 shows Archbishop Parker with an hour-glass in his right hand. Old wardens' accounts show how frequent were their use in the days of Elizabeth. All Hallows, Staines, purchased an hour glass for a shilling in 1561, and St. Peter's church followed suit at a like price in the next year. The parish accounts of St. Katharine, Aldgate, for 1564, show that the sand glass to guide the preacher was then a novelty, otherwise the scribe would scarcely have wasted his time in explaining its purport :

> Payde for an houre glass that hangeth by the pulpitt where the preacher dothe make a sermon, that he may knowe how the houre passeth awaye, xii*d*.

The wardens' returns throughout the 17th century supply many hundreds of entries relative to the purchase or repair of these time measurers. It will suffice to give three extracts as samples :

1613.—(*St. Edmund, Sarum*). An Hourglasse & the ledge to sett him on, 14*d*.

1629.—(*St. Mary, Devizes*). Pd. to John Bennett, Cutler, for a . . . . to carry the hour glass in the church, ii*s*. vi*d*.

1672.—(*Prestbury, Cheshire*). Pd. for the Houre Glasse, Houre Glasse Case, and the guildinge and the setting up the same, 1–7–0.

The iron stand attached to the pulpit, within convenient distance of the preacher's hand, and also projecting from the wall close by, was often a severely plain construction of iron, as at Wiggenhall St. Mary, Norfolk, Dittisham, Devon, or Chelvey, Somerset. But occasionally the smith lavished the best of his craft on the elaborate embellishment of the hour glass. This is most notably the case in the elaborate and intricate work connected with the hour glass bracket at Binfield, Berks, dated 1614 ; the arms of the Smiths and Farriers emerge from oak leaves and acorns, whilst there is the legend, " Watch and pray, that ye enter not into temptation." At Hurst, in the same county, there is another instance of ornate hour glass ironwork, with the date 1636. But in this latter instance the stand, though close to the pulpit, is attached to the adjacent pillar, on which there is also a scroll inscribed :

> As this glasse runneth,
> So man's life passeth.

The humbler but efficient work of the stand attached to the pulpit of St. John Baptist, Bristol, which is here illustrated (Fig. 180), is a fine piece of smith's craftsmanship, as is also the stand from the church at Compton Bassett, Wilts (Fig. 181), here reproduced from the drawing by C. J. Richardson.

The church sand glass was not always confined to the orthodox hour. In 1632 the wardens of All Saints, Newcastle-on-Tyne, bought " one whole hour glasse and one halfe hour glasse." About the same time the parishes of St. John's, Southampton, and of Pleasley, Derbyshire, also purchased half-hour glasses. In the church chest of Earl Stonham, Suffolk, there is a case of three sand glasses arranged to run for sixty, thirty, and fifteen minutes (Fig. 182). A fine Renaissance stand at St. Alphege's, Greenwich (Fig. 183) (never previously illustrated), is arranged to contain four sand glasses. The old church of St. Alphege, said to have been built on the site where the Danes stoned to death the Archbishop of that name in 1012, was entirely rebuilt between 1711 and 1718 in the Classic style.

In recent years it has been stated that the late Queen Victoria provided an eighteen-minute sand glass for the Chapel Royal in the Savoy, as a testimony to her rooted objection to long sermons.

189

Fig. 181. COMPTON BASSET, WILTSHIRE: Sand Glass Frame.

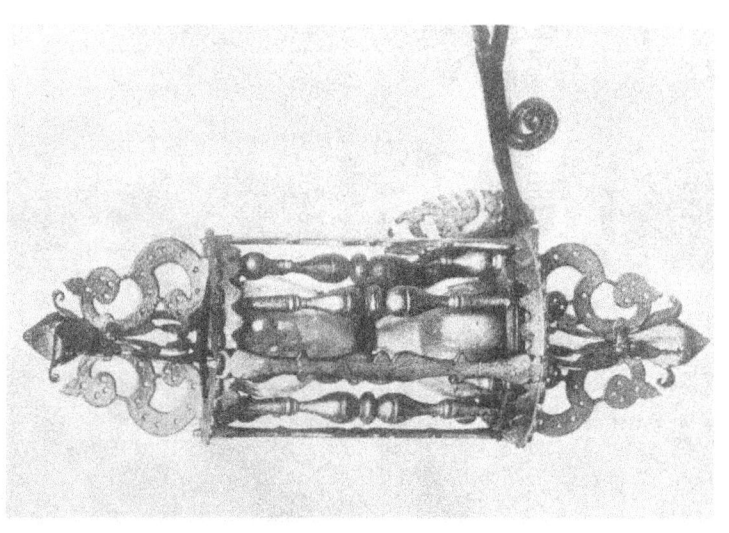

Fig. 180. S. JOHN'S, BRISTOL: Sand Glass Frame.

190

FIG. 183. S. ALPHEGE, GREENWICH: FOUR-FOLD SAND GLASS.

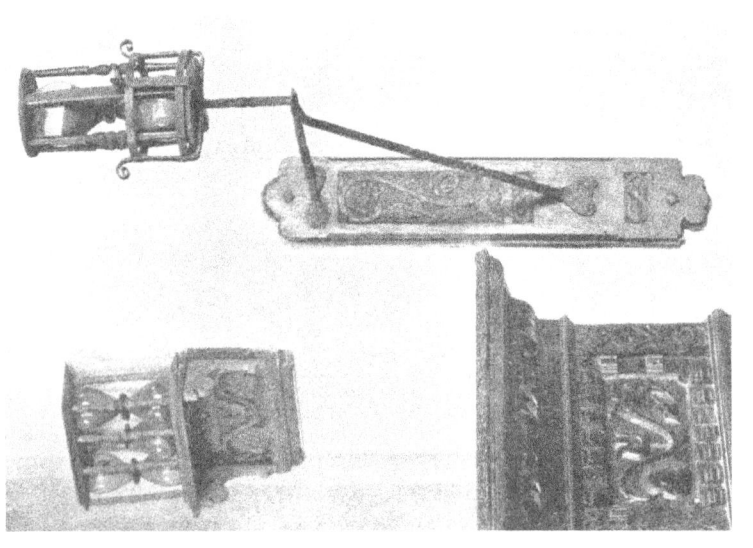

FIG. 182. EARL STONHAM, SUFFOLK: CASE OF SAND GLASSES, RECORDING 60, 30 AND 15 MINUTES.

Fig. 184. GRANTHAM CHURCH: Chained Library.
Founded in 1598.

Fig. 185. WIMBORNE MINSTER: Chained Library.
Bequeathed in 1686.

FIG. 186. HEREFORD, ALL SAINTS: PART OF CHAINED LIBRARY OF 200 VOLUMES.

CHAPTER XI

CHAINED BOOKS AND CHURCH LIBRARIES

THE ordinary man's notion as to a chained book in an English church is that it was a happy invention of the early days of the Reformation, when printed books were so valuable, that it was necessary to secure the safe custody of the printed Word of God. This is, however, a big blunder. Chained books in our churches were no novelty when the Reformation dawned, nor was the Bible excluded before that period.*

Monasteries were the chief homes of English books in mediæval days and their destruction was a grievous blow to literary culture. But the custom of storing manuscripts other than service books, in our cathedral and more important parish churches, was well established long before the dispersion of monastic libraries. For instance, Belinus, a wealthy and learned merchant of Bristol, bequeathed, in 1416, to the church of St. Mary Redcliffe the *Sixth Book of the Decretals* and the *Constitutions of Pope Clement V*, there to be retained so that the vicar and chaplains might study them at their leisure. There can be little or no doubt that these works were chained.

Another instance, definitely showing that chaining was the practice long before the invention of printing had been discovered, occurs in connection with the annals of Salisbury Cathedral. One of the canons, dying in 1452, left some books to the library of that church ; in two of these volumes there are notes in a 15th century hand on the inside of the covers that they were to be chained in the library.

William Lyndwood, Bishop of St. David's, author of the *Provinciale*, by will of 1443, directed that a chained copy of this book should be kept in the chapel of St. Stephen, Westminster Abbey.

---

* Considerable portions of the Scriptures had been translated into Anglo-Saxon and mediæval English at an early date, but it was to Wycliffe that England owed the first translation of the whole Bible. That translation was unhappily so marred by prologues and glosses of an extreme levelling character that the Church of those days naturally did its best to suppress it. This was also more or less true of Tyndale's and Coverdale's translations of the 16th century. See *Early Churchwardens' Accounts*, p. 116. The whole question as to the different versions of the Bible of that century is dealt with carefully and at some length in that volume.

The wardens' accounts of St. Edmund's, Salisbury, for the year 1477, include, in an inventory of the church books: "Huguson chayned in our Lady Chapell." This volume was the *Vocabularium* of Hugutin of Pisa, a book which was never printed but had a fairly wide circulation in manuscript, for it was an admirable book of reference. It also occurred amongst the ten books chained in the Lady Chapel of All Saints, Derby.

The accounts of St. Michael, Cornhill, for 1475, include this entry:

For lengyng of an yron cheyne and makyng to serve to the glossd sawter in our lady chappell, iid.

Sir Thomas Lyttelton, in his will of 1481, bequeathed:

To the Abbot and Convent of Hales of Hales-Oweyn a book of myne called *Catholicon* to thyr own use for ever and another boke of mine wherein is contaiyned the *Constitution Provincial* and *De Gestis Romanorum* and other treaties therein, which I will be laid and bounded with an yron cheyne at my costes, so that all priests and others may se and rede when it pleseth theym.

Thomas, Earl of Ormonde, in 1515, made the following bequest:

I will my suater boks, covered with whyte leather, shall be fixed with a cheyne of iron at my tombe, there to remain for the service of God.

He was buried in the City church of St. Thomas Acon, on the north side of the altar. There cannot be but little doubt that this was a psalter in the vulgar tongue.

A highly interesting record of the chaining of ten theological books in the Lady Chapel of All Saints, Derby, occurs in the wardens' accounts of that church under the year 1535.*

These be the bokes in our lady chapell tyed with chanes yt were gyffen to Allhaloes Church in Derby—

    Imprimis one boke called summa summarum.
    Item. A boke called Summa Raumundi.
    Item. Anoyer called pupilla occuli.
    Item. Anoyer called the Sexte.
    Item. A boke called Hugucyon.
    Item. A boke called Vitas patrum.
    Item. Anoyer boke called pauls pistols (doubtless a translation).
    Item. A greete portuose.
    Item. Anoyer boke called legenda Aurea (probably in print).

* The two earliest volumes of the wardens' accounts of these account-books, which are exceptionally full and complete, beginning as early as 1465, were discovered by the present writer, in 1877, in an attic at Meynell Langley, whereupon Mr. Godfrey Meynell promptly restored them to their proper custody. In 1881 the oldest parts were transcribed in the *Chronicles of All Saints* (Bemrose & Sons).

Full notes on each of these books appear in the *Chronicles of All Saints* (pp. 175-7) from the pen of that eminent bibliographist, the late Mr. Henry Bradshaw, the Cambridge University librarian.

Cromwell, as the King's vicar-general, issued a set of injunctions in August, 1536, one of which required the clergy, before August, 1537, to provide " a whole Bible in Latin, and also in English," and to lay them in the choir for anyone to read. This first injunction as to the Bible appears to have met with very limited obedience ; it was repeated in different phraseology in 1537, and still more explicitly, under Edward VI, in 1547, when each parish was ordered to provide " one Boke of the whole Bible of largest volume in English," an injunction which was yet again repeated by Elizabeth in 1559. These 16th and 17th century Church Bibles seem to have been invariably chained. Those that are yet extant in our parish churches barely number two score.

At Shorwell, Isle of Wight, is a Bible of 1541 ; at All Saints, Worcester, one of 1603 ; and at Windermere, of 1608. The authorized version was issued in 1611, and chained Bibles of that date are still to be seen at York Minster, at Stratford-on-Avon, at Abingdon, at Cumnor, at East Winch, Norfolk, and at Geddington and Walgrave, Northants. Chained Bibles, dated 1617, remain at Backford, Cheshire ; at Kingston and Wrington, Somerset ; and at Dacre and Mungrisdale, Cumberland. Later examples are 1634, East Budleigh, Devon ; and 1637, Lyme Regis.

The injunction of 1547, as to Bibles in every church, gave a considerable impetus to chaining of books in churches, for it also provided that " within one twelvemonth the *Paraphrases of Erasmus* be sette upp in some convenient place." This translation, pronounced by scholars to be very poorly done, is still to be seen in the churches of Barchester, Warwickshire ; Egginton, Derbyshire ; Great Doddington and Kingsthorpe, Northants ; All Hallows, Lombard Street ; St. Andrew, Undershaft ; Mancetter, Warwickshire ; Tavistock, Devon ; Ubley, Somerset ; and Windermere, Westmorland.

Archbishop Parker ordered that Bishop Jewel's *Defence of the Apology* be placed in the churches, and Archbishop Bancroft ordered that Jewel's collected works (editions 1603, 1611) should be similarly placed. Copies of Jewel, in all instances chained or showing traces of a chain, remain in the churches of Bridlington, Bromsgrove, East Budleigh, Cavendish, Chedworth, Chew Magna, Dronfield, Frampton Cotterell, Geddington, Hatfield, Kidderminster, Kingsthorpe, Kinver, Leyland, St. Andrew Undershaft, Mancetter, Newport Pagnell, Shirland, Tavistock, Upton Magna, Wiggenhall St. Mary, Windermere, Wootton-Wawen, Wolverley, Wrington, and All Saints', York.

Another chained work is the *Book of Martyrs*, originally published by John Fox when in exile. An English edition, purged of many gross inaccuracies, but still most inaccurate—as the present writer has frequently had occasion to show—appeared in 1563. " The Government ordered it to be placed in each parish church; more than any other influence, it fanned the flame of that fierce hatred of Spain and the Inquisition which was the master passion of the age. Nor was its influence transient. For generations the popular conception of Popery has been derived from its melancholy and bitter pages."*

This ghastly Sunday picture-book remains chained in the churches of Appleby, Arreton, Borden, East Budleigh, Chalson, Great Chart, Impington, Kingsthorpe, Lewisham, Leyland, Little Petherick, St. Andrew Undershaft, Luton, Mancetter, Newport Pagnell, Quatt, Sittingbourne, St. Michael's (Southampton), St. Teath, Towcester, Tilstock, Whitchurch, Wiggenhall St. Mary and Wrington.

Various other books, chiefly theological, are found in several churches, but at St. Andrew Undershaft, in the City, there is a chained copy of Sir Walter Raleigh's *History of the World*, 1621.

The *Books of Homilies*, referred to in the 35th Article of the Church of England, had their origin in a decision of Convocation in 1542, when it was agreed " to make certain homilies for stay of such errors as were then by ignorant preachers sprinkled among the people." This resolve eventually resulted in a volume issued in 1547, entitled *Certain Sermons or Homilies appointed by the King's Majesty to be declared and read by all parsons, vicars and curates every Sunday in their churches where they have care*. In 1563 a second book of homilies, together with the Thirty-nine Articles, was issued under the title *The second Tome of Homilies*, etc. As the Homily was usually read from the pulpit in the place of a sermon, these volumes were naturally only seldom chained; but in five or six cases they remain chained to a desk, as at Cavendish, Suffolk, from which they were doubtless read.

In a few cases churches possess a number of volumes chained to a large desk; there are fifteen at Sleaford, Lincolnshire, and twelve at Wootton-Wawen, Warwickshire. In the chancel of the church of Breadsall, Derbyshire, there were eight volumes chained to a unique double reading-desk, on the two folding lids fastened at the top by a padlock; but this was wickedly and wantonly destroyed by the militant suffragists when they set fire to the church in July, 1914.

* *Encyclopædia Britannica*, 9th ed.

In old church warden accounts there are many entries as to the cost of chains for chained volumes. Two must suffice :—

1542.—(*Wimborne*). For a desk and chain for the Bybyll, xiiii*d*.
For Three Chaynes of Iron with plates and for the fastenyngs of the Bible, Paraphras of Erasmus, and Mr. Juells booke in the Churche, iiis. iiii*d*.

1636.—(*St. Mary, Devizes*). Pd. for the Chaynes wherewith the Bookes of Martyrs are tyed, 1s. viii*d*.
Pd. for a Chayne and Staple to tye the booke of the phrase of Erasmus, viii*d*.

In the following short account of old church libraries only those that are or were chained are named. There are upwards of fifty of such libraries all told, set forth in the last edition of *English Church Furniture*.

Bolton-le-Moors, Lancashire. The chained books left to this church by Humphrey Chetham, in 1651, are now in the Grammar School Library.

Cartmel, Lancashire. There were a number of books chained to desks prior to 1629. Most of the present library, of about 300 volumes, dates from 1692; it includes various literary rarities.

Chirbury, Salop, has a chained library of 217 volumes, dating from 1530 to 1684. All were originally chained, now chains are 110.

Grantham, Lincolnshire, has a library of 368 books in a room over the south porch, founded in 1598, of which seventy-four books retain their chains. (Fig. 184).

At North Denchurch, Berks, there used to be a valuable chained library of about 100 books over the porch. In 1852 the library was removed to the Vicarage, and the chains taken off, save in a few cases.

Hereford Cathedral library of about 2,000 volumes, with 1,500 of them chained, stands at the head of the list of England's chained libraries, and has probably the largest chained collection in existence.

Hereford All Saints has about 200 volumes of early divinity in the vestry, all of them on chains after an unusual and cunning fashion, which can be best understood by studying the excellent photographic reproduction (Fig. 186).

Blades, in his *Books in Chains*, tells a curious story of the vicissitudes of this ancient library. An Oxford Street bookseller bought these books, chains and all, from the then churchwardens about 1850, and the transfer was agreed to by the vestry. After the books had been carried off to London, catalogued, and the arrangements made for their being transhipped to a foreign dealer, some local feeling was fortunately aroused, and after much trouble the books were brought back to Hereford and restored to the church.

To Salford Church, Lancashire, was left the theological library of

Humphrey Oldfield, in 1684, to be kept in the chancel, together with three yards of chain for the same to prevent them from being stolen. But after many had been lost the remnant of seventy-four volumes were transferred to the Salford Free Library.

Turton, Lancashire, has an oak case with shelves and folding doors, fitted with two iron bars, to which are chained the books presented by Humphrey Chetham in 1651.

Wells Cathedral used to have a chained library. Many of the chains still hang from the shelves, although there are now no chained books.

Wimborne Minster, Dorset, has a famous library of about 240 chained books in a room over the vestry (*see* Fig. 185). They were given to the church in 1686 for the free use of the townsfolk, and include a Bible of 1573, Watts's Polyglot Bible (in seven vols.), of 1657, and Raleigh's *History of the World*, 1614.

CHAPTER XII

PAINTED GLASS*

WHEN Bede brought glass to England in 674, when Benedict Biscop fetched " glasens " from France in 680, and when St. Wilfrid glazed York Minster in 709, each of these events almost certainly refers to the employment of plain glass.

Mr. Westlake has conclusively proved that there was an important school of glass painting in France, near Chartres, in the 12th century, and that there is a very close relationship between the glass of that period preserved in France and in England, pointing to a common origin. There was at that time much friendliness, both in Church and State, between the two countries. In July, 1176, the Dean and Chapter of Chartres visited Canterbury, on the death of their bishop, begging that Becket's friend and counsellor, John, Archdeacon of Salisbury, might be nominated to the vacant See. A still more interesting fact is that a treaty between Henry II and Louis VII made express provision for the emigration to this country of one of the French king's leading artificers in painted glass. Twelfth century medallion windows, probably French, are to be found in the choir of Canterbury Cathedral, in the Minsters of York and Lincoln, in Dorchester Abbey, and in the churches of Lanchester, co. Durham, St. Denys, York, Wilton, Wilts, and Rivenhall, Essex.

All early mediæval glass windows were composed in mosaic ; that is to say that each colour was represented by a separate piece of glass. This early glass was really *stained* glass in a strict sense of the term ; there was little surface painting. Brushwork was at first used only for shading and to add detail to the features, etc. Gradually the glass artists came to rely more and more upon paint and less upon staining. Late Renaissance glass is almost purely *painted* glass. The

---

* As to Painted Glass, the late Mr. Winston's book, for so long the one authoritative work, has been quite surpassed in certain periods by the four volumes of Mr. Westlake's *History of Design in Painted Glass*, 1891-4. The 3rd edition of Mr. Lewis F. Day's *Windows* is most useful and admirably illustrated. But the book of all others invaluable to the student of the old churches of England is Dr. Nelson's *Ancient Painted Glass in England*, 1170-1500 (1913), one of the " Antiquary's Books " series.

mosaic glass necessitated the use of numerous leads, but these were always extremely narrow. They certainly made for rigidity and convention in design, but on the other hand they contributed much of the character and strength of the effect. Their restraining influence compelled the craftsman to respect his material, and they prevented the window from attaining an excessively pictorial appearance.

Early coloured glass was pot-metal glass, that is, coloured in its entire substance by the addition of metallic oxide to the plain glass. This method gives a depth and richness which surface coating and painting can never give. The only colour in early glass not produced by this process was the crimson. This was produced by imposing a thin layer of ruby glass on a sheet of plain glass. The reason for this is that solid ruby glass of any considerable thickness appears almost black, even in a strong light. The most frequent colours in early glass are the ruby, a deep and very beautiful sapphire blue, several shades of green, purple, some brown and yellow. These early windows have a wonderful brilliancy and translucency which more than compensates for the stiffness of draughtsmanship.

Dr. Nelson happily gives the title of Byzantine to 12th century glass, since it is characterized by the stiffness and angularity of the figures general in Byzantine enamels, paintings and mosaics, and by the marked conventionality of the foliage. All this gave way in the second or early Gothic period, which prevailed throughout the reign of Henry III, to a more natural treatment of both figures and foliage, but it shared with the first period in the medallion treatment of the small scenes depicted and was still dependent to a large extent on the geometrical arrangement of the iron framework. During this Early English period *grisaille* glass was largely employed. This was " a clear glass painted with foliate work upon a cross-patched background, a method of painting which not only insured increased light, but in addition economy in production."* Fragments of this second period occasionally occur in parish churches, as well as whole lancet lights, but Early English glass only occurs on a large scale in such cathedral churches as Canterbury or Lincoln. Glass of this second period survives in the two lowest windows on the north side of the chancel of Aldermaston, Berks, and at Lee, Bucks, where in the east window are 13th century figures of saints. We have also personally noted some glass of this date in the churches of Harbledown and Edenbridge, Kent, and of Twycross, Leicestershire. This, of course, is quite exclusive of the considerable remains in abbey and cathedral churches.

As an illustration of early Gothic glass we give a reproduction of a 13th century medallion in the church of West Horsley, Surrey

* Dr. Nelson's *Ancient Painted Glass in England.*

Fig. 188. Aldwinckle S. Peter, Northamptonshire: Figure of S. George, with Canopy.

Fig. 187. West Horsley, Surrey: 13th Century Medallion.

202

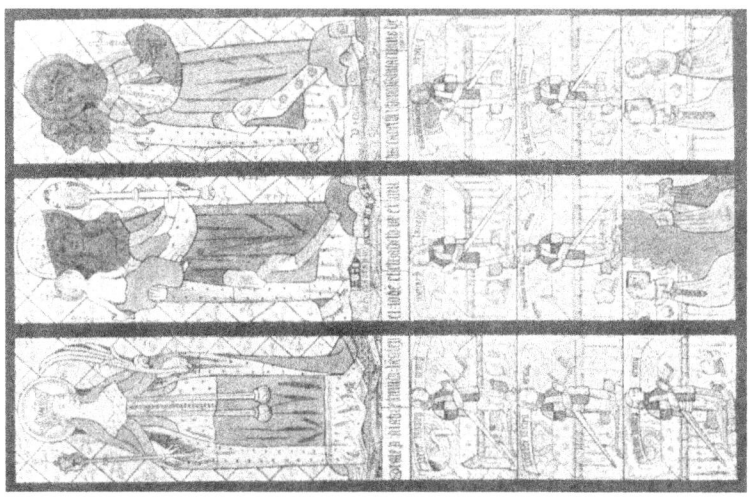

Fig. 190. Siddington, Gloucestershire. 15th Century Heraldic Glass.

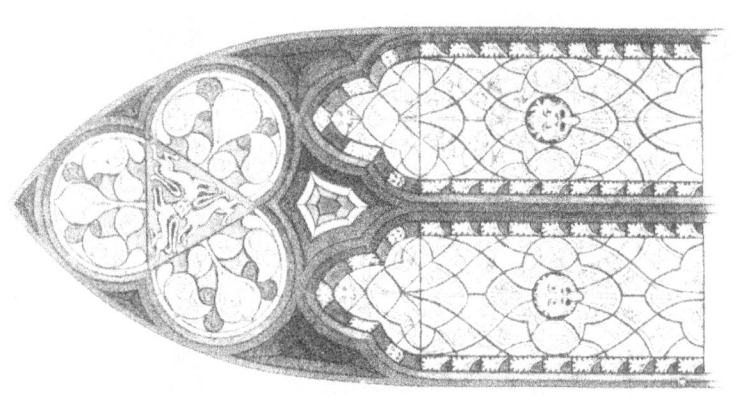

Fig. 189. Trumpington, Cambridgeshire: 14th Century.

(Fig. 187). The subject, which is rather naïvely treated, is the anointing of Christ's feet by St. Mary Magdalene. There is a charming diaper background and scroll work borders. This medallion is from the east window of the church, where is also another medallion of the same period illustrating the deliverance of St. Catherine from the executioners.

A fine example of late 13th century glass is shown in Fig. 188, a figure of St. George from a window in the south side of the church of Aldwinkle St. Peter, Northants. The saint is habited in mail with a white surcoat, his sword is slung across his body, and he bears a spear and a shield. There is a simple and effective canopy on a blue background, and a curious border of running hounds. In the same church is also a figure of St. Christopher of late 13th century date.

The 14th century, mid-Gothic or Decorated glass, forms the third period. The glass painter found in the wider windows of the new style a greater scope for the display of his art, and worthily availed himself of the opportunity. The natural delineation of leaves, so noticeable in the wood carving and stone sculpture of this period, found its reflection in the glass, where leaves of oak, ash, sycamore, maple, hawthorn, ivy, vine and other trees and plants can be readily recognized. Few counties are destitute of more or less distinctive fragments or considerable remains of the delightful glasswork of this century. Mentioning parish churches first as they occur to us, where examples remain extant, they are to be seen at East Bridgeford and Fledborough, Notts; at Bawburgh, Elsing, and Mitcham, Norfolk; at Great Gonerby, Heydour, and Kingerby, Lincolnshire; and at Blithfield, Staffordshire. Norbury, Derbyshire, is, *par excellence*, the parish church where this abounds, and where its history and date can be definitely settled. There is, too, some remarkable painted glass of this style preserved in the windows of Merevale, Warwickshire. What, for instance, on a small scale can be more striking than either the scroll-work background or the personality of the organist of the 14th century (Fig. 191), who sings as he walks in the Sunday procession ? He is playing with his left hand on his portative instrument, whilst he is working the bellows underneath with his right.

If the remains of Decorated glass in our parish churches are far more considerable than is usually supposed, what is to be said of the glass of the 15th century ? The sheer quantity of it is almost amazing, leaving out of consideration great displays, such as are in the windows of Fairford, St. Neots, Cornwall, and at some half a dozen other places. In Dr. Nelson's book may be found the various churches containing considerable remains of the glass of the Perpendicular period preserved from the ignorant fury of Reformers or subsequent Puritans, and the student of old glass can scarcely fail to be greatly surprised.

Such things only reveal themselves to the ardent and systematic ecclesiologist.

Take, for instance, Cornwall—leaving out the fairly well-known work in St. Neots and in St. Kew Church, known to have been moved here from Bodmin in 1469, or in St. Winnow, where there is a fascinating window in the south aisle of early 15th century date—the student will find 15th century glass that will well repay observation at Laneast, Lanteglos-by-Camelford, St. Keyne, Lanteglos-by-Fowey, St. Mellion, Quethiock, South Petherwin, St. Sampson and St. Teath. If you wish to extend the survey of painted glass of 15th century date to the churches of Devon, upwards of fifty churches will have to be visited.

Going to the extreme north of England, although so continuously subjected to border raids, the painted glass enthusiast will find that even in Cumberland five parish churches should be visited in addition to the cathedral church of Carlisle. Or take a representative midland county of limited area, such as Warwickshire—the parish churches with distinctly good portions of Perpendicular glass exceed thirty.

We may here add a word as to the subjects of mediæval painted glass windows. Many elaborate classifications have been made, but for the sake of simplicity we will here divide them into (a) windows introducing figures, either singly or in composition; (b) windows containing floral, heraldic or other ornament. With regard to the figure windows, these illustrate almost every imaginable incident from the Scriptures and from the lives of the Saints. The single-figure windows are sometimes isolated representations of a Saint or other figure; sometimes they have their place in an elaborate allegorical scheme in which all the windows of the church play their part. The single figures often show admirable draughtsmanship; they are generally placed upon diapered or other figured backgrounds, with borders of various patterns, sometimes the arms of the donor or other patron are introduced. The figures are generally depicted beneath canopies of contemporary architectural ornament, increasing in elaboration from century to century. For a good example of a canopy of late 13th or early 14th century tabernacle work the reader may refer to Fig. 188—the figure of St. George, from Aldwinckle St. Peter's, Northants.

It is quite impossible here to attempt to detail the various themes of the subject windows, but there is one type which merits a little special consideration, both from its popularity and from its value as an artistic and symbolic composition. The Tree of Jesse was one of the favourite subjects for stained glass windows throughout the Middle Ages. The general arrangement was to place the recumbent figure of Jesse at the base of the window; from this sprung a vine among whose branches were seated the Kings of Israel, accompanied by Prophets, thus representing the maternal ancestry of Christ. The Blessed Virgin with Our Lord terminated the Tree. The earlier examples of these windows are composed in the most glowing of colours: sapphire and ruby, purple, green and gold. The earliest of all Jesse windows are to be found at Chartres and St. Denys; the earliest remains in England, *c.* 1170, are at York. The finest of these windows are naturally to be found in the great cathedrals, since they are elaborate compositions, requiring no little time and skill. But there are numerous examples, in varying stages of completeness, remaining in many parish churches, and it is here proposed to mention a few of the more remarkable. At Westwell, in Kent, is the upper portion of a Jesse window, dating from the 13th century. This represents the Holy Mother and Son, on a background of very beautiful deep blue glass, enclosed within a vine on a crimson ground. There are 14th century Jesse windows at Ludlow and St. Mary's, Shrewsbury; one also in the church of Mancetter, Warwick, whence it is said to have been brought from Merevale Abbey. The latter is still famous for its beautiful Decorated glass. Parish churches, containing remains of 15th century Jesse windows include: Dyserth, Flintshire, a fine and complete example; Leverington, Cambridgeshire, complete with sixty-one figures, but restored; Margaretting, Essex, a very beautiful example with twenty-four figures, of which four are restored; Morpeth, Northumberland; Petsey, Salop; Rushden, Northamptonshire; Thornhill, W.R., Yorks, much restored; and St. Michael's, York, fragments of two windows.

Jesse windows continued on into the 16th century. Possibly the two best examples of this date are at Llanrhaidr, Denbighshire, and St. James's, Bury St. Edmunds. The striking example in the church of St. George's, Hanover Square, London, is, like most of the glass in that church, of 16th century Flemish workmanship.

Although strictly not within the scope of this book, since the fabric is not a parish church, we cannot refrain from reproducing the unique Jesse window at Dorchester Abbey, Oxon (Fig. 195). Here the figure of Jesse is carven in the stone base of the window, and the mullions also are carved with figures and foliage, which combine with the figures in the glass to form a most striking representation of the subject. This window is on the north side of the chancel.

Turning to non-subject windows, mention has already been made of "grisaille" or trails of foliage painted on a cross-hatched background of clear glass. These grisaille windows were usually further elaborated by shields within tracery, roundels bearing masks, etc., as in Fig. 189, from Trumpington, Cambs. In the 15th century Grisaille was more or less superseded by "quarry" windows. A quarry is a small pane of glass, usually square or diamond shaped bearing floral and conventional patterning, an heraldic device or cypher, etc. (*see* Fig. 190). These quarries were used in the less significant windows of the church, the subject compositions appearing in the larger and more important ones.

Heraldic glass occasionally combines figure work with the armorial patterns and inscriptions, especially in memorial windows. A most elaborate specimen of Perpendicular heraldic glass is shown in Fig. 190. This window commemorates various members of the Langley family, arranged beneath the Holy Mother and Child and two saints. This glass was originally in the church of Siddington, Glos., but has now been removed to Cirencester.

It remains now to draw attention to a few illustrations of some of the less known examples of the Perpendicular period. In the six-light south transept window of Cheddar, Somerset, is some striking 15th century glass, including figures of SS. Barbara and Katherine, whilst several pieces about the windows of this church of the like period are executed with effective boldness. Especially is this the case with the half-length figure of a priest in albe, amice and crossed stole, bearing a processional cross (Fig. 192).

At Almondbury, W.R., Yorks, there is good Perpendicular glass in the windows of the north or Kaye Chapel. The east window contains SS. Elizabeth, John Baptist and Helena, with the kneeling donors of the Kaye family at the foot. The north window contains St. Anne teaching the Blessed Virgin to read, flanked by SS. Barbara and Margaret (Figs. 193 and 194). Above St. Anne is a scroll bearing *Parvulus enim natus est nobis, et filius datus est nobis;* below is the Kaye motto "Kynne Kynde Knawne Kepe."

The special glory of Thornhill church, W.R., Yorks, lies in its wealth of Perpendicular glass. The east window of the chancel contains a vestured Jesse Tree of six lights, dating from 1499, and the east window of the Saville Chapel has a remarkable Doom of 1493. The west window on the north side is a three-light rood window, with the Crucifixion in the centre, and the Blessed Virgin and the Beloved Disciple in the side lights, whilst beneath are the three shields of (1) Bradbourne, (2) of Saville quartering Thornhill, and (3) of Leeds, by North Milford.

The church of Melton-on-the-Hill, also in the West Riding, contains a quantity of fine old glass, but it is impossible to assign any precise date or origin, for, as the Yorkshire historian, Hunter, says (i. 369): "the late Dean Fountague introduced into this church much painted

FIG. 191. MEREVALE, WORCESTERSHIRE:
15TH CENTURY STAINED GLASS.

FIG. 192. CHEDDAR, SOMERSETSHIRE:
15TH CENTURY STAINED GLASS.

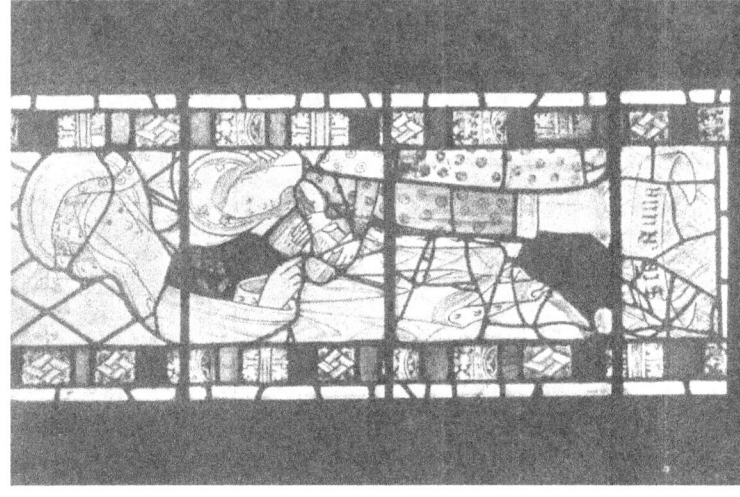

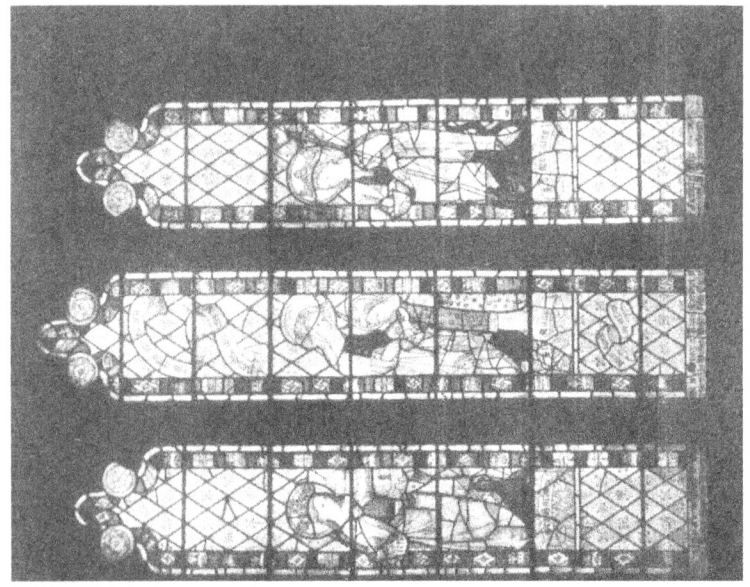

Figs. 193, 194. ALMONDBURY, WEST RIDING, YORKSHIRE: North Window of Kaye Chapel, with Detail. 15th Century Glass.

209

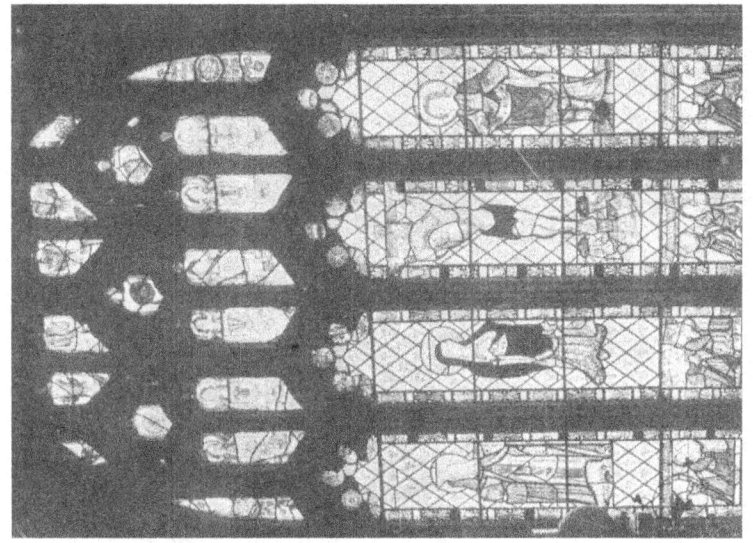

Fig. 196. Winscombe, Somersetshire.

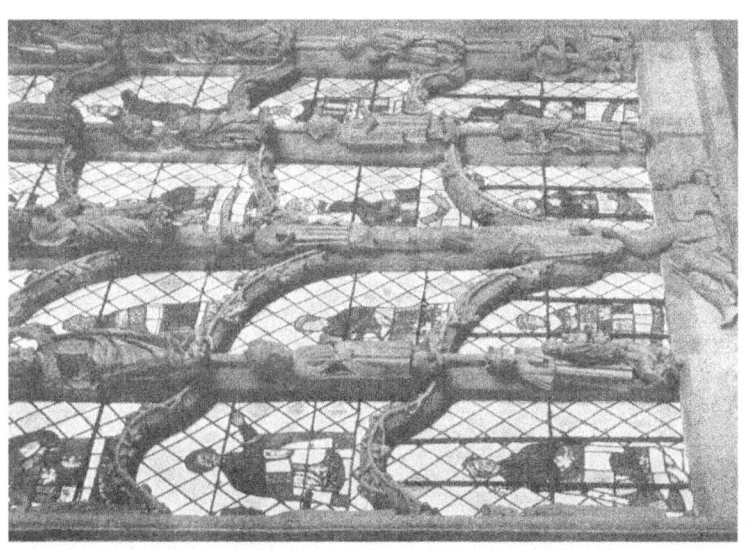

Fig. 195. Dorchester, Oxfordshire: Tree of Jesse. 14th Century.

FIG. 197. MELTON-ON-THE-HILL, YORKSHIRE.

FIG. 198. YARNTON, OXFORDSHIRE.

glass, partly by Becket of York, and partly collected by him from old ecclesiastical edifices in that city. Fig. 197 illustrates a very spirited heraldic motif from this church, a shield bearing a golden lion rampant on a crimson ground.

At Winscombe, Somerset, is good 15th century glass. The large east window of the north aisle, illustrated in Fig. 196, contains figures of St. Anthony, the Blessed Virgin, the Crucifixion, and St. John, while in the tracery above are angels bearing emblems of the Passion. The lower panels of this window are restored.

Our last illustration of 15th century painted glass is from Yarnton, Oxon. In this church there is a large amount of ancient painted glass, collected from various buildings, the gift of Alderman William Fletcher, of Oxford, who died in 1827. A north aisle window contains figures of the Virgin and Child and of St. Christopher; the portion of it here shown gives quarries of enamel Tudor badges surmounted by quarries in which is displayed two bright-looking little birds, with scrolls bearing respectively the enigmatical words *Greete richyinge greete* and *Who blameth thys ale* (Fig. 198). This glass is sometimes thought to be of secular origin.

The Renaissance in English glass need not detain us long, for it was not a renaissance at all, but a distinct decadence. Much 16th century work is very beautiful—the celebrated Fairford windows date from this century—but it retained its high standard only so long as it followed the earlier Gothic models. Late 16th and 17th century glass is marked by feeble colour, due to thin coating, much surface painting, excessive naturalism in modelling, and few leads which are of most aggressive thickness in order to endeavour to add some structural weight. Windows of this period are almost invariably found to be more dilapidated than the early mediæval ones, where the latter have been spared violence or accident, for the construction in narrow leads is obviously more lasting than the wide panels held by a few leads, and the " pot-metal " colour has an ineradicable brilliancy that weather or dirt cannot fade. These facts are now realized by stained glass workers, so that present-day glass is mostly designed and carried out with true understanding of the principles of the best mediæval work.

CHAPTER XIII
MURAL PAINTINGS

THERE can be no doubt that the habit of decking the walls of our churches with brightly coloured pictures of sacred subjects to arrest the attention of worshippers was practised in England prior to the Conquest. This has been proved by that expert in the history of church wall-paintings and in their preservation, Mr. P. M. Johnston, F.S.A., in his scholarly illustrated article on Hardham Church, Sussex, and by his general remarks in a catalogue of the remains of this decoration in the ancient churches of that county.* He gives good grounds for believing that the churches of Ford and Lyminster had painted consecration crosses of the 10th century, and Amberley of the 11th century. The wondrous series of paintings which used to cover the interior of the small church of Hardham were first brought to light in 1866, but perished sadly till they were taken in hand by Mr. Johnston in 1900. They date from 1098 to 1100. At Patcham in Surrey, the early Norman church shows a remarkable "Doom" over the small chancel arch, brought to light in 1880.

The roof paintings of the chapel of St. Gabriel in the crypt of Canterbury Cathedral, c. 1100, are of great importance in the history of Art, and so too is the picture of St. Paul shaking off the viper at Miletus in the apex of St. Anselm's chapel of the same cathedral; but as we are only concerned with parish churches in these pages, we must not be beguiled into discussions on the Greek tendency of the art of Canterbury. For the like reason we pass over certain notable wall-paintings at Peterborough, Durham, Romsey Abbey, St. Albans, and Chichester.

The parish church of Chaldon, Surrey, is unique in possessing on the west wall of the nave the sole instance in this country of "The Ladder of Salvation and the Heavenward Way," a most remarkable allegory, and a favourite subject in the adornment of the churches of Eastern Christendom. This complex early design of Norman date, brought to light some forty years ago, is in good condition and has been often described in detail and illustrated.†

* *Sussex Arch. Coll.*, vols. xliii and xliv.

† Perhaps the best account is the initial one by the late Mr. Waller, *Surrey Arch. Coll.*, vol. v.

Claverley church, Salop, is remarkable for having a long frieze of a secular subject extending along the north wall of the nave above the Norman arcade; it is upwards of 50 feet in length and has a breadth of 4 feet 8 inches. The mode of treatment of these armed knights is so strikingly like that of the Bayeux Tapestry that it seems impossible to resist the conclusion that the artist was well acquainted with that piece of needlework, or was possibly the designer of the pattern from which it was wrought. A portion of this frieze is illustrated in Fig. 182.

The highly interesting church of Copford, Essex, a small Norman fabric, was originally rich in paintings, which covered all available wall spaces as well as the roof of the apse. The latter feature was the most remarkable, and obviously of 12th century date, c. 1150. When it was being carefully restored by Mr. Daniel Bell, in 1872, Sir Gilbert Scott considered the painting a surprising and valuable discovery, and, " with the exception of that in the chapel at Canterbury Cathedral, he knew of no similar work to be compared with it in beauty." Round the fine central figure of Our Lord in Majesty are grouped angels in the vaulting (Fig. 199).

The church of Clayton, Sussex, shows a variety of interesting remains of mural painting dating from the 11th to the 17th century. The illustration (Fig. 201) is taken from the remains on the north aisle wall. The original composition is probably of 12th century date, but the various re-paintings and the later ornament have produced a rather confusing effect.

Mural adornment of the 13th century is often to be found, especially in the splays of the windows, and occasionally in imitative masonry patterns on the walls; also now and again in finely painted figure subjects, such as at West Chiltington, Sussex, where there are many scenes of Our Lord's life under trefoiled arches on each side of the nave. Fragments of earlier painting of this age are not infrequently brought to light beneath the paintings of later periods.

In the 14th century the figures in mural painting, as in glass painting, lost much of their angularity and stiffness, whilst the foliage gradually approached to some likeness to nature. In naming just a few of the better examples exposed on the walls of our churches, mention may be made of Avebury, Barnstaple, Battle, Bedfont, Chalgrove, Faversham, Godalming, Houghton Conquest, Islip, Kimble Parva, Melbourne (Cambs.), Newington (Kent), Somerton, Stedham, and Yarmouth. The martyrdom of St. Thomas of Canterbury occurs several times during this period, perhaps the most vivid and notable instance is on the south wall of the chancel of Burlingham St. Edmund, Norfolk. Arundel is famous for striking examples of the Seven Acts of Mercy, and the Seven Deadly Sins, c. 1370.

The mural paintings of the 15th and early 16th centuries far outweigh in number and merit, as is only natural, the whole of those of earlier dates. In every county the number and the variety of the subjects of the Perpendicular style, still to be traced on the walls, distinctly predominates, though in many cases ignorant Philistinism has caused once exposed pictures to be again obscured by whitewash.

The most favourite subject with the English church wall painters of the 15th century, when they produced a group, was the " Doom " or day of judgment; the main features of which were, Our Lord in Majesty pronouncing the final doom on the quick and the dead, the redeemed being conducted by angels on the right hand to the New Jerusalem, whilst the wicked on the left are being pronged by demons, with more or less realistic horrors, into the open jaws of hell. A recent manual on the mural paintings of our old churches much understated the matter by saying that over a hundred examples of this composition had been exposed to view. It is nearer the truth to say well over one hundred and fifty, though several, as we have seen, were far older than the 15th century.

The most effective position for the " Doom " is doubtless at the east end of the nave, facing the congregation, where the apex of the chancel arch afforded a triumphant position for the Great Judge, often represented seated on a rainbow, whilst the spaces on either side of the archway readily lent themselves to the imagination of the artist. About nine-tenths of the " Dooms " occupy this position; but a variety of readily imagined objections in divers instances prevented this space being thus used, and " Dooms " are occasionally found in less suitable places. For instance, the Last Judgment is depicted at Oddington, Gloucestershire, and at Bedfont, Middlesex, on the north wall of the nave; at Axbridge, Devon, over the archway of the south transept; at Pickering, N.R., Yorks, in the north transept; at Newington, Kent, on the east wall of the north aisle; and at Winchfield, Hants, in the last place where we should expect to see it, namely, on the west wall of the nave. No two examples of the normal position are precisely alike, but usually a broad similarity is maintained. At Long Coombe, Oxon, is the upper part of the " Doom," showing the Court of Heaven, in a fair state of preservation; it is here given as a fair example of a village " Doom " (Fig. 202). The restored Doom of St. Thomas's, Salisbury, is one of the most effective; here the skill of the artist has been chiefly spent on the cleverly grouped many mansions of the City of God. Below, on the north side of the chancel arch, the dead rising from their graves are conducted to their bliss by an angel. The conductor, in the case of the Doom of St. John's, Winchester, assumes the shape of a Franciscan friar. In this last case, the resurrection of the élite of the righteous is represented after a curiously realistic fashion; two of the ten figures wear crowns and two others mitres. The resurrection scene is generally somewhat comic; it is, for instance, impossible to give any dignity to a bishop nude to his waist and wearing, as in several cases, a bright red mitre.

One of the covenants made for the decoration of the celebrated Beauchamp Chapel of St. Mary's, Warwick, in the year 1449, runs as follows:

> John Brentwood, citizen and steyner of London, 12 Feby. 20 Henry VI, doth covenant to paint fine and curiously to make at Warwick, on the west wall of the New Chappell there, the dome of our Lord God Jesus, and all manner of devices and imagery thereto belonging of fair and sightly proportion, as the place shall serve for, with the finest colours and the finest gold: and the said Brentwood shall find all manner of stuffe thereto at his charge; the said executors paying therefore xiiili. vi$s$. viii$d$.

Of single subjects, the one repeated with most astonishing frequency is that of St. Christopher, a gigantic figure bearing the Holy Child Jesus on his shoulder and wading through a river. It almost invariably occurs on the north wall of the nave, so that it was at once seen by worshippers entering by the principal or south doorway. The popular belief, strangely prevalent in the 15th century, was that whoever beheld the figure of St. Christopher would for that day be exempt from evil, or at all events from fatal sickness.

> *Xpoferi sancti speciem quicumque tuetur*
> *Illo nempe die nullo langore gravetur.*

No fewer than 125 instances of the occurrence of St. Christopher on the walls of our churches were chronicled by Mr. Keyser, in 1887, and there can be no doubt that those by now discovered are well in advance of 200, though many have faded away or have been obliterated. The beautiful story of St. Christopher is found in the Golden Legend and is too well known to cite at length. Far the best representation of the whole legend is to be found in the church of Shorwell, Isle of Wight (Fig. 204). This composition, over the north doorway, measures 11 feet by 6 feet 6 inches, and is of *c.* 1470 date. All the events are set forth—the ride of Reprobus with the Evil One; the abjuration of bad companions at the foot of the cross; the fording of the dangerous river with the Child Jesus, from whose lips proceed the words *Ego sum Alpha et Omego*; the hermit holding a lantern outside his oratory to guide the afterwards named St. Christopher; the martyrdom of the saint; and the king of Lycia receiving an arrow in his eye. The artists of this oft repeated picture rivalled each other in the quaintness of the details; in at least three cases mermaids are introduced on the river-banks, and a great variety of fish disport themselves in the water, whilst in one painting a crab grasps the great toe of St. Christopher.

One of the next in frequency is the portrayal of St. George slaying the Dragon, which often accompanies St. Christopher on the north wall of the nave. The legendary tales of St. Catherine and St. Margaret were also favourite subjects with the church artists who could secure large spaces for their treatment above the nave arcades of the Perpendicular period.

A Christian mediæval conceit, imported here from France, which became popular in the 15th century, was the morality picture as to the vanity of life, generally known as The Three Living and the Three Dead, or with the French title of *Les Trois Rois Vifs et Les Trois Rois Morte*. About thirty copies of this allegory, in whole or in part, still adorn the walls of our old churches. There are many variants; it mostly takes the form of three crowned kings on horseback enjoying sport in a forest, and three other grisly skeleton kings forcibly reminding the living monarchs of their eventual end. Perhaps the most remarkable representation of this morality is the one on the north side of the nave of Raunds, Northants. The figures of the living kings are remarkably well proportioned and admirably draped.

But all allegorical or legendary pictures were completely thrown into the shade, so far as frequency is concerned, by the far greater number that are representations of Bible incidents, particularly from the New Testament.

Those ignorant persons who still persist in speaking and thinking of the two or three centuries preceding the Reformation as the " Dark Ages," would be at once convicted of the folly of their statement if they made an intelligent study of the wall paintings of England's mediæval churches. A prominent writer among the more bitter of the Protestant school has recently stated that " the very walls of our churches bear witness to the sad way in which the simple teaching of the Gospel story was obscured by the foul legends of imaginary saints, until the cleansing wave of the Reformation relegated them to obscurity, putting in their place more helpful passages from Holy Writ." A more hopeless travesty of the truth it is hardly possible to conceive. Surely the life and sufferings of Our Saviour are the very essence of the Faith ? That being the case, it will perhaps surprise this ignorant traducer of times that have passed, to learn that the artists who decked our churches with pictures from the Conquest to the days of Henry VIII and those who controlled them were obviously saturated with a full knowledge of the Scriptures, and more especially of the New Testament.

217

FIG. 200. CLAVERLEY, SHROPSHIRE: PART OF FRIEZE OF NORMAN KNIGHTS.

FIG. 201. CLAYTON, SUSSEX: PART OF PAINTINGS ON NORTH AISLE WALL.

FIG. 199. COPFORD, ESSEX: PORTION OF THE APSE, SHOWING 12TH CENTURY PAINTINGS.

Fig. 202. LONG COOMBE, OXFORD: Painting of the "Doom." 15th Century.

Fig. 203. PICKERING CHURCH, YORKSHIRE: Part of Series of Mural Paintings, showing S. George, S. Christopher, Herod's Feast. etc. 15th Century.

FIG. 204. SHORWELL, ISLE OF WIGHT: THE LEGEND OF ST. CHRISTOPHER. 15TH CENTURY.

Fig. 205. TEMPLE CHURCH BRISTOL: Mediæval Candelabra.

The fact is, as the work of Mr. Keyser on *Mural Paintings* (1883) conclusively proves, and it has been further substantiated by a great number of subsequent discoveries, that the mural paintings depicting every incident in the evangelistic life of Our Lord infinitely surpass, both in number and worth, the whole of the saintly biographical incidents. In short, if we could imagine a wholesale destruction of the copies of the New Testament, it would conceivably be possible to reconstruct it in almost every detail from the Bible Picture Book, with which our forefathers covered the walls of our churches, at a time when reading was altogether unknown save to the lettered few.

On these walls were blazoned, in church after church, representations of the Annunciation, the Nativity, the Adoration of the Magi and the Shepherds, the Presentation in the Temple, the Flight into Egypt, Our Lord amongst the Doctors, the Baptism, the Temptation in the Wilderness, the Call of the Apostles, the Preaching to the Multitude, the Woman of Samaria, the Performing of divers Miracles, the Transfiguration, the Triumphal Entry, the Last Supper, the Washing of the Disciples' Feet, the Betrayal, and every incident of the Passion, more especially the actual Crucifixion, the Descent from the Cross, the Pieta, the Entombment, the Descent into Hell, the Resurrection, the Appearing to St. Mary Magdalene, the Incredulity of St. Thomas, the Ascension, and Christ in Majesty or in Judgment.

The writer will never forget the eloquent words that fell from the lips of the Dean of York, Dr. Arthur Purey-Cust, some thirty years ago, when preaching on the occasion of the completion of the restoration of the grand series of wall paintings in the church of Pickering, N.R., Yorks. He said that the walls around were simply studded with figures of holy men and the representations of holy scenes. The great truths of the Gospel were literally blazing forth before them, and the " voices " (his text was from Psalm xix, 3) which " are heard amongst them " are preaching nothing short of the whole Gospel of God.

Purists declare that this magnificent series of mural paintings in Pickering church are over-restored, but for our own part we rejoice that we can point to at least one church in England where an honest and most careful attempt has been made to conscientiously reinstate, in something like their original brightness, the pictures with which our forefathers loved to adorn their sacred walls some four centuries ago. This great range of pictures were first uncovered in 1853, when Puritan folly caused them to be again speedily white-washed over as " heathenish." Under a more intelligent rector (Rev. G. H. Lightfoot) they were, however, cleaned and restored in 1889. On the north side of the nave are pictures of (1) St. Christopher ; (2) St. George ; (3) Herod's Feast, in three acts ; (4) Coronation of the Virgin ; (5) The Martyrdom of

St. Edmund; and (6) The Martyrdom of St. Thomas of Canterbury. On the south side of the nave are (1) the Passion of St. Catherine of Alexandria, in eight acts; (2) the Seven Corporal Works of Mercy, each separately illustrated; (3) the Passion of Our Lord, in three scenes; (4) the Descent from the Cross; (5) the Entombment; (6) the Descent into Hades; and (7) the Resurrection. Between the clerestory windows are also mutilated scenes from the life of the Blessed Virgin. The date of the whole of these is *c.* 1450. Part of these paintings, showing St. George, St. Christopher and scenes from Herod's Feast, is illustrated in Fig. 203.

It should also be remembered that, next to the four Gospels, the Acts of the Apostles was the most important book to suggest subjects to English wall-painters of mediæval days. Groups of the Apostles are of very frequent occurrence, as well as individual portraits of each one of them, besides St. Mark, St. Luke, St. John Baptist, and St. Paul. As to the Virgin Mary, she can be traced in incidents, Scriptural or of an early legendary character, in at least 250 churches.

It is at first sight surprising to find that the references to church paintings are so very few amidst the full records of churchwardens' accounts both in town and country during the 15th century. In fact, almost the only one that we can recollect is from Cowfold, Surrey, where there is a receipt of a comparatively small sum, in 1470, toward "payntyng of the Churche of devocione de parische." These paintings were frequently the gifts of special parishioners or other donors, with which the common accounts of the parish had no concern. There are various references to such gifts in pre-Reformation wills; a single instance will suffice. William Porte, of Mayfield, Kent, by will of 1471, bequeathed £10 " towards a new picture of St. Mary of Maghfeild if the parishioners are willing to repaint the same."

It is not a little remarkable how many able and well-read men will persist in styling our old church wall or mural paintings " Frescoes." Such a term is an absolute falsity, and not a mere blunder. A fresco is a design carried out in wet plaster; there is not a single design in all our old parish churches carried out on such lines, the whole of them are executed in *tempera* or distemper, that is to say, painting on dry walls in various pigments prepared with gum.

During some repairs in 1909 to the church of Boughton, Lincolnshire, an interesting discovery was made beneath the pulpit of several small pieces of late mediæval pottery, usually termed "tygs," and with them, in diminutive cases, pigments of divers colours, black, white, red, and blue. They were doubtless intended for use in beautifying the church with wall paintings; these remains are now placed in a small glass case on the south side of the west entrance within the church.

Notwithstanding the injunctions of the 16th century calling for the obliteration of mural paintings from church walls and the substitution of sentences from Holy Writ, post-Reformation pictures ere long crept in again. The two subjects generally favoured were life-sized figures of Moses and Aaron in conjunction with the Ten Commandments, and more or less gruesome figures of Time and Death.

In the course of the 17th and 18th centuries the fashion came in of decking the church with large figures of Moses and Aaron, usually painted on canvas, but sometimes on panel. The following receipt is taken from the church records of All Saints, Hastings, for 1755:

Recd. of Mr. John Sergeant and Mr. Thatcher the sum of seven pounds seven shillings in full for painting the 10 Commandments, the Creed, the Lord's Prayer, Moses and Aaron, and the King's Arms.   B. MORTIMER.

All these were heedlessly destroyed, including the life-size oil paintings of Moses and Aaron on oak panels, during a restoration of 1870.

At the west end of the timber-framed church of Marton, Cheshire, there are two 18th century pictures of Moses and Aaron, painted on panels in conjunction with the Ten Commandments. We can well remember similar full-sized pictures in the chancel of Porlock, West Somerset, in the fifties of last century, and at a yet earlier date in the church of Parwich, Derbyshire, as well as other examples, during the sixties and seventies, in several churches of Dorsetshire, Devonshire, and Cornwall. Mr. Bloxam, in his *Companion to Gothic Architecture*, named Badley, Leicestershire; Halston, Salop; Brightlingsea, Essex; and Helpringham, Lincolnshire, as all possessed of this pair of patriarchs, but we believe that in each of these cases they have now disappeared.

In the case of Time and Death, the former is usually represented as an old man, with wings displayed, and having a scythe in his right hand, and an hour glass in his left, whilst Death was represented as a skeleton with a dart. Bloxam cites Chipping Norton, Oxon and East Leake, Notts, as churches possessing this pair of paintings.

CHAPTER XIV

CANDELABRA AND CRESSET STONES

IN these brief pages, it is only proposed to deal briefly with the two subjects of cresset stones and old candelabra.

The most beautiful and most ancient candelabra now extant in any English church is that in the Temple church, Bristol. It is of latten or an amalgam of brass, and is about 3 feet high, with twelve branches arrayed in two tiers, the lower of eight, the upper of four. The branches, which are gracefully curved and richly foliated, terminate in sconces for candles; they spring from two globes which are held together by slender uprights, forming a sort of cage, within which is a beautifully executed statuette of St. George and the Dragon. On the pedestal at the upper end is another statuette of the Holy Mother crowned, with the Holy Child in her arms. The lower globe terminates in a grotesque head with a large ring in its mouth, for convenience in drawing down the chandelier for lighting or cleaning. The date of this chandelier, a fine example of craftsmanship, is about the end of the 14th century. We give two illustrations from a recent photograph, and another from the drawing by Henry Shaw (Figs. 205 and 206).

The Welsh county of Denbigh has the honour of possessing two somewhat similar brass candelabra of pre-Reformation date, though much later than that at Bristol. They are both of the first quarter of the 16th century, and show a slight approach to Renaissance design. The brass candelabra in the church of Llanarmon-yn-Ial has a statuette of the Virgin between the two tiers of branches. This chandelier is said to have been brought here from the Abbey of Valle Crucis at the time of its demolition. There is another brass candelabra, nearly as good, but rather smaller in the village church of Llandegla; in this case the figure of the Virgin rests upon the upper tier of branches and is easier to see.*

In the Kent church of St. Nicholas-at-Wade there is a chandelier, said to be *c.* 1500. There are perhaps some half-dozen other churches

---

* Both of these fine candelabra are well illustrated in the 4th vol., p. 84, of the Inventories issued by the Royal Commission on the *Ancient Monuments of Wales* (1914).

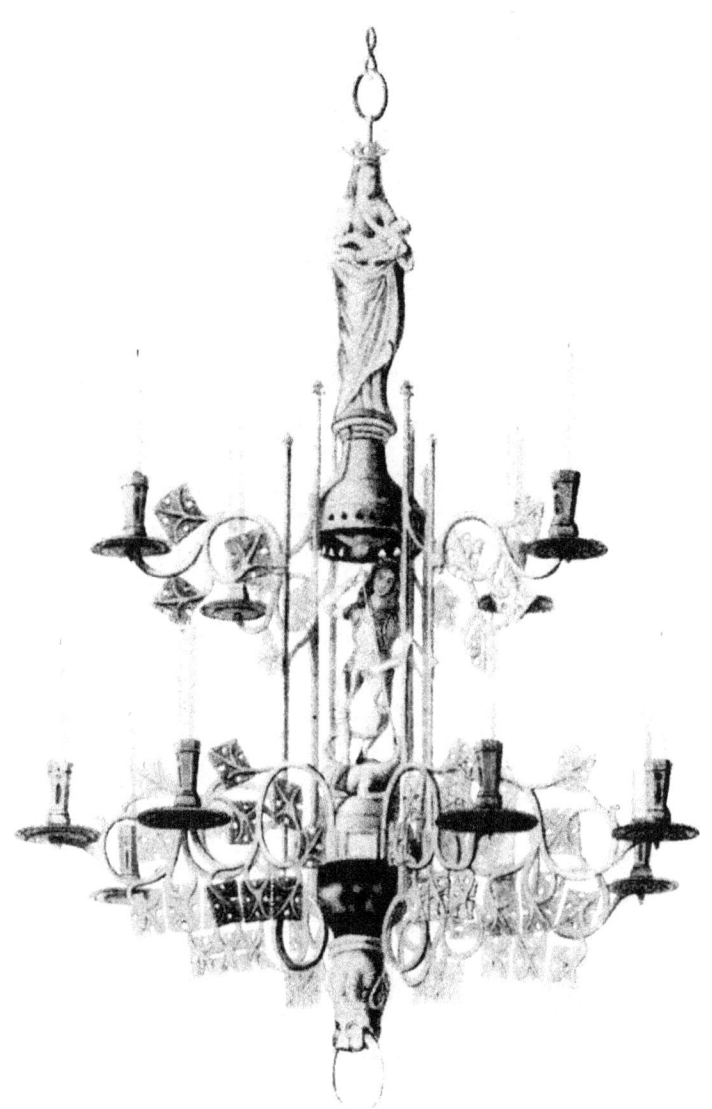

FIG. 206. TEMPLE CHURCH, BRISTOL: MEDIÆVAL CANDELABRA.
From the Drawing by Henry Shaw.

Fig. 207. WEDMORE, SOMERSET: Renaissance Candelabra.

Fig. 208. HORSMONDEN, KENT: 18th Century Candelabra.

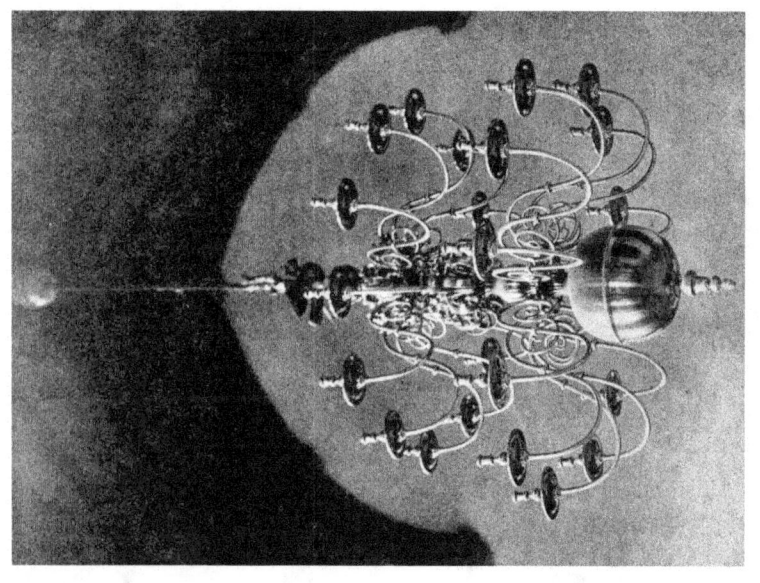

Fig. 210. WYMONDHAM, NORFOLK.

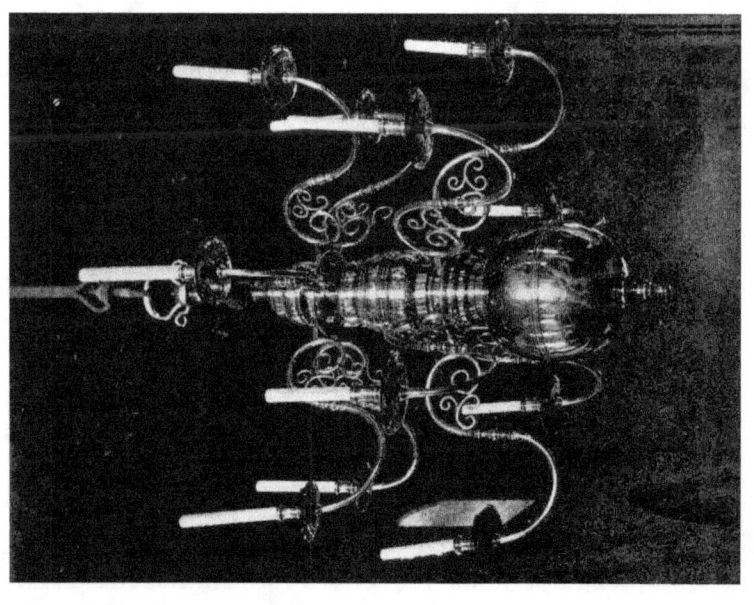

Fig. 209. NORTHIAM CHURCH, SUSSEX: FREWEN CANDELABRA.

FIG. 212. KENSEY, NR. LAUNCESTON.

FIG. 211. LEWANNICK, CORNWALL: CIRCULAR CRESSET STONE ON PLINTH.

FIGS. 213, 214. WESTON, EAST RIDING, YORKSHIRE: CRESSET WITH 12 CUPS. REVERSE CARVED WITH SAXON ROOD.

CRESSET STONES.

which contain candelabra or portions, of late mediæval date, as at Lew Trenchard, Devon, and Rowlston, Herefordshire. An ancient bracket with prickets for lights from the latter church is illustrated in the Chapter on Iron Work (Fig. 149).

The use of branched candelabra by no means died out with the Reformation. Those of the 17th and early 18th centuries are generally of brass, and are of distinctly Flemish design, if not in some instances of actual foreign workmanship, although many of the finest can be identified as the work of local craftsmen. These candelabra usually have two tiers of branched candlesticks on rounded stems springing from a central globe. From their resemblance to the radiating legs of a common household insect they were commonly, if somewhat irreverently, known a century ago as "spiders." We usually look in vain for any reference to their date or price in old churchwardens' accounts, for they were costly, and were therefore generally the gift of private benefactors. The central globe of the chandeliers usually bears the name of the donor and the date.

One of the best of the smaller examples of a brass candelabra of this kind in a parish church is that which is dependent from the roof of Horsmonden church, Kent (Fig. 208); the orb bears this inscription:

To this parish of Horsmondean The gift of Stephen Bate Rector. Anno 1703.

Among the good early examples worth noting are those of St. Helen, Abingdon, 1710; Kingsclere, Hants, under the central tower; and Whitchurch, Salop, both of 1713. There are also excellent specimens at Ightham, Kent; Wymondham, Norfolk (Fig. 210); Lingfield, Surrey; Mayfield and Northiam, Sussex, the candelabra in the latter church being the gift of the Frewen family (Fig. 209); Tilstock, Salop; and Over Stowey, Somerset. There are two gilt brass chandeliers of historic interest hanging in the Cumberland church of Penrith. They were purchased by the parishioners with the fifty guineas, as a long inscription records, bestowed on the town as a reward for the active part they took in helping to suppress the invasion of England by Prince Charles Edward in December, 1745.

Not a few of these dignified candelabra have, alas, fallen victims, within comparatively recent years, to Philistine church restorers, who in their ignorance eject everything not "purely Gothic." In a midland town we have seen an almost majestic 18th century chandelier hanging in an hotel hall, with the name of the church whence it was taken imperfectly erased. It will be scarcely credited that the would-be restorers of the interesting church of Gedling, Notts, in 1890, actually mutilated three old 17th century chandeliers, twisting them up to make therefrom a singularly tasteless lectern!

Several of our larger or cathedral churches have been stripped in like manner. Thus the great quire of York Minster was sometime ago bereft of the seven "large branches," formerly dependent from the roof. The great collegiate church of Manchester formerly possessed five fine Renaissance candelabra; two only of these remain in the restored quire, which were originally given to the church in 1690. The noble church of St. Mary Redcliffe, Bristol, used to be formerly lighted throughout in this fashion, but only one of the original candelabra now remains, dated 1650; it has happily served as a model for the reproduction of a new series now placed throughout the aisles.

The fine old Somersetshire church of Wedmore, near Wells, used to be adorned with an exceptionally handsome brass candelabrum hanging from the centre of the nave (Fig. 207), bearing the inscription: "The generous gift of Mr. John Tucker, of Blackford, in this parish, in 1779." It hung there in solitary grandeur till 1854, when a good maiden lady was moved to add two more modelled on the same plan. The first of these is inscribed : "The generous gift of Miss Ann Redman, of Wedmore, 1854. Thomas Hall & Co., fecit, Bristol." The second additional one repeats the donor's name and date.

In the parish church of Bermondsey there are two fine brass candelabra, the gift of the Elwood family, respectively dated 1699 and 1703.

It is worth noting that the City of Bristol and the adjacent districts supply various instances of these later forms of effective English-made candelabra, owing no doubt to the establishment of the manufacture of brass in that town at as early a date as 1705.

A pleasant instance of the improved taste of modern days, in this respect, is afforded by the interesting Kent church of Otford. When formerly inspected there used to be a solitary old candelabra of rather unusual Flemish design, but in 1912 we found that the church was provided throughout with new chandeliers of like pattern.

Cresset Stones.

The word cresset was originally a term applied to a cup of earthenware or metal fastened on the top of a pole, and used in mediæval days as a kind of portable lantern. This cup or receptacle contained oil and a floating wick, and was eventually transformed to a stationary light formed out of hollow cups carved in the surface of a stone, and hence termed cresset stones. The *Rites of Durham* mentions three of these, one in the church and two in the dormitory, to light the monks at the night offices. They are of fairly frequent occurrence in the ruins of abbeys, as at Brecon, Calder, Furness, Waverley, Romsey, Llanthonne, Priory and St. Mary's Abbey, York; whilst two were found in 1837 at Ramsey. The number of depressions in the various examples vary from sixteen to four. The cresset now at the Priory of St. John the Evangelist, at Brecon, has thirty depressions—the largest number met with as yet.

The late Mr. Romilly Allen devoted much research to the subject of cresset stones and contributed a good deal of fresh information on the subject. The student is also referred, for further information, to an interesting paper in *The Reliquary*, by Mr. A. G. Langdon, F.S.A., and another in the *Proceedings of the Clifton Antiquarian Club*, by Dr. Alfred C. Fryer, F.S.A. The present writer is indebted to all these sources.

It has been stated that cresset stones are not infrequently found in monastic ruins, but examples also are seen occasionally in parish churches, and doubtless many more have been cast away by careless restorers. Cornwall can show two interesting examples, including the rare cresset stone at Lewannick (Fig. 211). This cresset is shaped like a low truncated cone, it is of the local granite, and has seven depressions, six being arranged symmetrically round the central one. The upper surface of the stone measures 1 foot $6\frac{1}{2}$ inches; the lower, 1 foot $3\frac{3}{8}$ inches, while it is 8 inches thick. The outer cups are 3 inches in diameter and from 3 to $3\frac{1}{2}$ inches deep; the central one is slightly larger. The most interesting feature of this cresset stone, apart from its circular shape, is the octagonal stand, constructed of the same stone as the cresset itself, and probably contemporary with it. This stand is $13\frac{1}{2}$ inches high and 14 inches wide, and it has chamfered stops on alternate faces. Mr. Langdon, from whose paper this description is taken, suggests that the plinth has been at some time inverted, for it would certainly add to the appearance and stability of the whole if the chamfered stops formed the base. This stone, being of an exceptionally hard substance, is extremely well preserved.

Another cresset stone was found in Cornwall, in 1901, in the wall of a house near Launceston. No satisfactory explanation of its presence there can be given. It is of yellow sandstone, in fairly good condition, with five cups, four arranged round the central one (*see* Fig. 212). The cups are 4 inches deep and $2\frac{1}{4}$ inches in diameter across the top. This cresset stone is now at the church of Kensey, near Launceston.

Dorsetshire churches containing cresset stones number two, viz., Wool and Wareham, the former with four depressions. Nothing is known of their history or association, but as the churches are both within a short distance of each other, it is not improbable that the cressets came from some local monastic foundation, such as Bindon Abbey.

At the church of Dearham, Cumberland, is a curious corbel, with a cup hollowed in the stone. Mr. Fryer considers that this also was used as a cresset stone.

In Derbyshire there is a cresset stone at Parwich; and the present writer has twice had the good fortune of discovering a cresset, once at North Wingfield, Derbyshire, during the reconstruction of a wall, in 1872; and again during the excavations at Watton Priory, E.R., Yorks, in 1894.

But by far the most interesting discovery in this direction is the finding, as recently as 1915, of a cresset stone in Weston Church, E.R. Yorks. The stone measures $22\frac{1}{2}$ inches by 14 inches, and is 7 inches thick, and the twelve cups are $4\frac{1}{2}$ inches in diameter. The stone is of coarse limestone, and now rests on the sill of a window between the chancel and the north aisle. It probably was brought here from the neighbouring abbey of Kirkham. The reverse of the stone is carved with a late Saxon rood, which much adds to its interest. There are other instances of the utter disregard shown by Norman monks to the sacred carving of their predecessors.* Both sides of this interesting stone are shown in the illustration (Figs 213-214).

* The account of this stone, together with the two prints, were kindly sent to me by Mr. Reginald H. Barker, of Grosvenor Bank, Scarborough.

CHAPTER XV

ORGANS AND OTHER MUSICAL INSTRUMENTS

ORGANS were used in this country within churches at a very early date. There is record of one at Malmesbury at the dawn of the 8th century, and at Abingdon, Glastonbury, and Winchester in the 10th century.* By the 13th century the larger parish churches were well equipped with these instruments. During the 14th and 15th centuries organs multiplied to such an extent in England, that it would have been difficult to find any decent-sized church fabric destitute of such an instrument.

Out of the great number of pre-Reformation churchwarden accounts still extant, there is not a single one in which repairs of old organs or the purchase of new ones do not occur. Among those of the 15th century, there are full parish records as to the organs of St. Petrock, Exeter; St. Margaret, Southwark; and of St. Peter Cheap and St. Mary-at-Hill among the City churches. These accounts tend to show that the general position of the organ was on the rood-loft, and that in certain churches there was also a smaller " pair " in the quire. " A pair of organs " is the usual mediæval nomenclature for this instrument; it is equivalent to a " pair of beads," or a " pair of stairs," and refers to more pipes than one.

The reason why the remains of old organs or organ cases are so trifling in number, and to be looked for rather in museums than in churches, is the unhappy set that was made against them by the more puritanical and gloomy of the Reformers. It is not generally known that on a division in the Lower House of Convocation, on the 15th of February, 1562, a motion to the effect that " the use of Organs be removed," the continuance of these instruments was only saved by a majority of one, out of a vote of 117! Bishops Grindal and Horn were among their active opponents. In 1644, ordinances by the Lords and Commons enacted that " all organs and the frames and cases in which they stand, in all churches and chapels, shall be taken away and utterly defaced, and none other hereafter set up in their places." Just a few escaped in cathedrals and colleges.

---

* For fuller information, see Dr. Cox's *Pulpits, Lecterns, and Organs* (1915).

The only organ case now remaining throughout England and Wales that has any claim to be considered pre-Reformation is that of Old Radnor, on the Welsh border (Fig. 215). It has been carefully restored and fitted to a new instrument. This handsome case shows a blending of Renaissance with late Gothic ornament, and probably dates about the end of Henry VIII's reign; it is certainly not Jacobean as has often been asserted.

After the Restoration, the general re-use of church organs set in apace, especially in the more important towns. At Framlingham, Suffolk, there is a beautiful organ case (Fig. 216), which was originally set up in Pembroke College Chapel, Cambridge, in 1674 (the living of Framlingham is in the gift of that College). The organist is screened off by scroll-work of exquisite Renaissance design. The natural notes of the keyboard are black, whilst the short keys or semi-tones are white.

Organs were occasionally, during the 17th and 18th centuries, placed in a gallery across the west end of the nave. An example of this occurs at Alderley, Cheshire (Fig. 217). The gallery is painted with coats-of-arms within the panels. It is similar to, but less elaborate than, the eastern gallery, which shows a curious mixture of debased Gothic and classic feeling.

The numerous city churches, rebuilt and refitted after the Great Fire, vied with each other in the merit of their organs, both in the instruments themselves and in the beauty of their cases.

The organ of All Hallows, Lombard Street, is enclosed in a richly gilded case of refined and delicate carving (Fig. 218). The organ is the work of Renatus, or Rene Harris, and was erected in 1694. This distinguished organ builder, the rival of Father Smith, also supplied organs, from 1676 to 1705, to the city churches of All Hallows Barking, St. Andrew Undershaft, St. Giles', Cripplegate, St. Andrew Holborn, and St. Sepulchre.

Another grand instrument, with a noble and beautiful case, is that of St. Magnus the Martyr, London Bridge (Fig. 219). This organ is by Abraham Johnson, of a great organ-building family, and is remarkable for the first introduction of the "swell" or sliding shutter.

The Pitch-Pipe.

The pitch-pipe is a small stopped diapason pipe, with movable graduated stoppers, blown by the mouth, and only to be depended on for giving the pitch for vocal music; it is inferior in accuracy to the tuning-fork, invented in 1713. The pitch-pipe used to be the almost invariable instrument of the conductor of the village choir from the 17th to the first half of the 19th century, especially where it was simply vocal.

Fig. 215. OLD RADNOR, RADNORSHIRE: Pre-Reformation Organ Case

Fig. 217. ALDERLEY, CHESHIRE: ORGAN GALLERY.

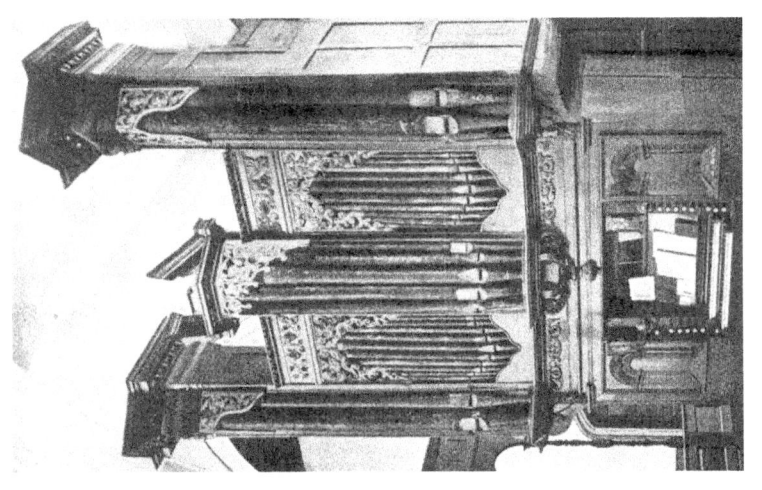

Fig. 216. FRAMLINGHAM, SUFFOLK. 1674.

Fig. 218. LONDON: ALL HALLOWS, LOMBARD STREET. 1694.

Fig. 219. LONDON: ST. MAGNUS-THE-MARTYR

As the country church choir, whether vocal or instrumental, gave way, in cases where they had no organ, to the leadership of the harmonium or afterwards to that of the American organ, the pitch-pipe fell into disuse, and was very rarely used after the middle of last century. When once put on the shelf, together with the tuning-fork, it was soon mislaid, or became the perquisite of the old parish clerk. The pitch-pipe, however, remains as a curiosity in at least a dozen churches; we need only mention three instances. In the parish chest of Morton Morrell, Warwickshire, there is an old wooden pitch-pipe, with a sliding stopper. The old pitch-pipe of the secluded little church of Matterdale, Cumberland, is nailed to the jamb of the west doorway, opening out of the church into the small belfry, presumably to secure its retention as a symbol of extinct sacred music. In a glass case at Aberedw, Radnorshire, are a pitch-pipe and flute formerly used in the church.

Vamping Horn.

A far more curious relic of ancient singing is the vamping horn, a kind of church megaphone, which seems to have come into use in the days of Charles II. To "vamp," in a musical sense, is now an almost obsolete term. In the *Church Times*, of February 25th, 1898, a correspondent wrote that "In music the performer on an instrument 'vamps,' when, while the air is played on another, he improvises harmonies to fill up the body of sound, and help out the other instruments." To put it plainly, vamping is a loud humming through a large kind of speaking trumpet. Five of these horns or trumpets still survive in English churches, namely at East Leake, Notts; at Bradbrook and Harrington, Northants; at Charing, Kent; and at Willoughton, Lincolnshire. The best and largest example of a vamping horn—spoken of in the parish to me by more than one old inhabitant, who had heard it used in church, as a "shawm"—is the one at East Leake. It hangs in the vestry, and is a large tin trumpet, measuring 7 feet 9 inches long when extended, and 4 feet 1 inch when closed; the mouth is 21 inches in diameter. It was in use as part of the gallery orchestra up to 1855, and was vamped through by one of the bass singers. The stories of these horns being used to call parishioners to church, are, we feel sure, modern inventions. There are substantial traditions of their having been used in two churches of the Lake District. The second largest is that at Willoughton, which stands 6 feet high, and has a mouth of $16\frac{1}{2}$ inches. When tested, for curiosity, in the open air as speaking trumpets, it is said that these horns carry the human voice with ease for a mile.*

* There is an interesting article on Vamping Horns by Miss Florence Peacock in the *Reliquary and Illustrated Archæologist*, vol. iv. (1898), 731-746; but the writer was not acquainted with the Notts example.

The "shawm," as the local name for the big tin trumpet at East Leake, is quite incorrect, for the true old English shawm (*see* Pr. Bk. version of Psalm xcviii. 7 : "with trumpets also and shawms,") had a wooden tube and was a form of clarinet. In the Wimborne, Dorset, wardens' accounts for 1531 occurs the entry: "an iron bar for the shawm, viii*d*."

In the museum of the Surrey Archæological Society at Guildford is an example of the curious old instrument not unreasonably called a "serpent." Readers of Hardy's *Under the Greenwood Tree*, will remember the disquisition of one of the ancient village choristers regarding the serpent. "There's worse things than serpents," says he, "old things pass away, 'tis true ; but a serpent was a good old note ; a deep rich note was the serpent." Looking at its massive coils, one can easily believe in that "good old note." But it has passed away utterly, and even its traditions are few. The example from the Guildford Museum, reproduced in Fig. 220, by courtesy of the Surrey Archæological Society, is said to have been used in a local church.

The Bassoon.

The bassoon, a long wooden reed instrument played through a bent metal mouthpiece, was the favourite English church instrument for some two centuries. It served as the bass to hautboy and clarinet in the gallery orchestra, and in the smaller churches was frequently the only instrument to accompany the singers. This was the case in the small church of Kingston, Isle of Wight, where a bassoon hangs in the vestry, with a label attached stating that it was "used by a member of the choir occupying a small west gallery before its restoration in 1872."

The wardens' accounts of the 18th century contain frequent references to the large amount paid for a bassoon. The following entries occur at Hayfield, Derbyshire, in connection with this instrument:

1772.—Spent with singers when the new Bassoon came	.. ..	.. 2s. 6d.
„ Charges when the Bassoon came	.. .. ..	.. 3s. 6d.
1779.—For repairing the Bassoon	.. ..	.. 1s. 6d.
1783.—For reeds for the Bassoon	.. ..	.. 1–1–0

In 1751 the wardens of Youlgreave, Derbyshire, spent 3s. to buy new reeds for the bassoon. The old bassoon is carefully preserved in the church of Church Broughton, Derbyshire (Fig. 221). Visiting that church in 1871, when the bassoon was in the parish chest, I could not find anyone who recollected any other instruments being played in the church. At Bunbury, Cheshire, a bassoon was bought in 1712 for five guineas ; at Farndon, in the same county, the new bassoon cost £6 0s. 8d. At St. Giles', Northampton, the churchwardens paid £4 13s. 6d. to Bland, of Holborn, for a bassoon ; a balance of 5s. 9d. being reserved for " new reeds for the bassoon if wanted." In the same year, and for several years following, 10s. 6d. was the payment to the bassoon player ; in 1799 his salary for the year rose to a guinea.

The Bass-Fiddle.

Next to the bassoon in popularity with church music comes the bass-fiddle, bass-viol, or violoncello. In the voluminous and varied church accounts of Youlgreave, Derbyshire, there is an entry under 1742 of 8d. " For hairing the bowe of the viole." From a loose sheet of paper in the church chest of the same parish, it appears that the parish acquired in 1785 a new " Base Voile," when the wholesome resolution was carried by the vestry that the instrument should be appropriated solely to the use of the church, " and not to be trundled about to Wakes or any other places of profaness and Diviner, except to the club feasts of Youlgreave and of its chapelries of Elton and Winster." Bunbury, Cheshire, expended £6 16s. 7d. on a bass-violin in 1811, and in 1816 the wardens of St. Giles', Northampton, spent 3s. 6d. on " a string for the base." The old " bass-fiddle," of which we give an illustration (Fig. 222), of the highly interesting church of Giggleswick, W.R., Yorks, still stands in the Vicar's vestry and is occasionally used. It is 4 feet 5 inches high.

Hautboy or Oboe, and Clarinet.

These wooden reed instruments were also in favour in village church orchestras. At Hayfield, Derbyshire, a guinea was paid in 1793 for a hautboy, and at Hartshorne, in the same county, the like instrument, in 1789, cost 19s. The more modest price of 14s. was paid for a hautboy in 1801 at Bunbury, Cheshire.

At Farndon, Cheshire, in 1785, two new " clarinets and reeds " cost £5 12s. 9d. ; at the same time a new hautboy was bought for £1 8s.

The village orchestra in the west gallery was a leading feature of the more important country churches up to the middle of last century, the favourite instruments being the bassoon, violin, bass-viol, flute, clarinet, and hautboy, whilst in later days an occasional wind instrument of brass was introduced at festivals. It was the custom, during their performance of the hymns or occasional anthems, for the whole congregation to face westwards. The present writer well recollects the church band of Luccombe, West Somerset, which ceased to exist in 1859. In the neighbouring village of Selworthy, the church orchestra continued to occupy the west gallery until after the death of " Old Sir Thomas Acland " in 1871. In short, throughout West Somerset there were far more village church bands or single instruments than organs down to 1875 or somewhat later. The Rev. F. W. Galpin, in his *Old English Instruments of Music* (1910) carries the recollection of the church band to a much later date, for it did not expire at Winterbourne Abbas, Dorset, till about 1895 ; the instruments were a clarinet, a flute, and a violoncello, which were played respectively by a shepherd, a thatcher, and a farm labourer.

243

Fig. 222. GIGGLESWICK, WEST RIDING, YORKSHIRE
The Bass Fiddle

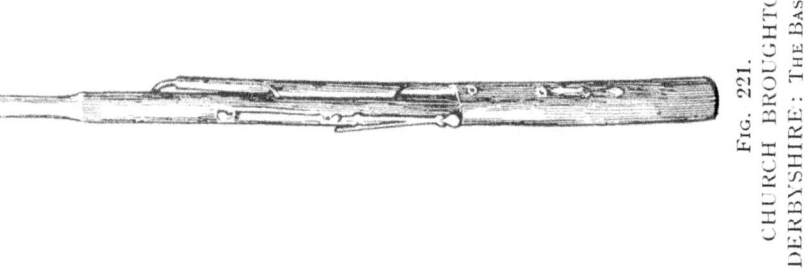

Fig. 221.
CHURCH BROUGHTON, DERBYSHIRE: The Bassoon.
MUSICAL INSTRUMENTS.

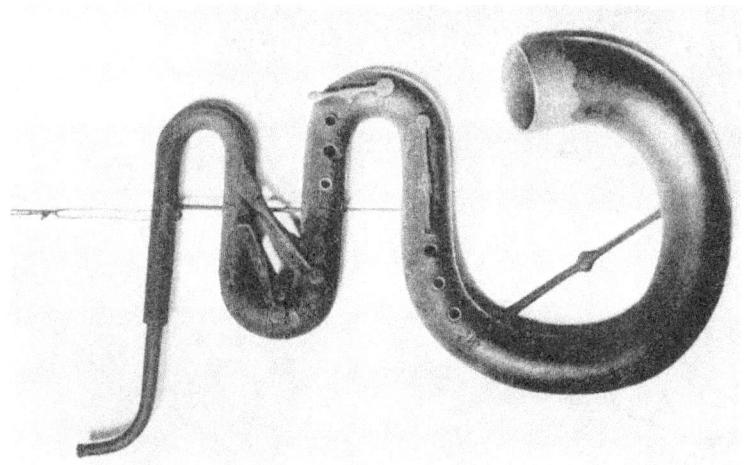

Fig. 220. GUILDFORD MUSEUM:
The Serpent.

FIG. 223. ENSTONE, OXFORDSHIRE: STONE ALTAR, 15TH CENTURY.

FIG. 224. DRAYTON, BERKSHIRE: ALABASTER REREDOS.

FIG. 225. SOMERTON, OXFORDSHIRE: SCULPTURED REREDOS.

CHAPTER XVI

ALTARS, REREDOSES, ALTAR RAILS, PLATE, Etc.

OLD stone altars of the Church of England remaining in their original position are not so rare as is usually supposed; there are well over a score, chiefly in chapels, as at Tintagel, Cornwall; Abbey Dore, Herefordshire; Northleach, Gloucestershire; and Shotteswell, and Weddington, Warwickshire.

The most interesting feature of the parochial chapel of St. John Baptist, Belper, Derbyshire, c. 1250, is the original small altar, resting on brackets below the east window. (Fig. 222a.) The *mensa*, which retains some of the consecration crosses, measures 3 feet 6 inches by 1 feet 1½ inches and stands 2 feet 7 inches in height.

In one of the 15th century south chapels of Enstone, Oxon, the original altar, with reredos over it still remains, though it has lost the *mensa* (Fig. 223).

It is a mistake to imagine that our pre-Reformation altars were invariably of stone, though this was undoubtedly the case with the vast majority. Early examples were usually of wood, and the appellation of " Christ's Board " was in common mediæval use. The Council of Winchester, under Lanfranc and the papal legates of 1076, ordered the altars to be made of stone. But this order was by no means always obeyed. Thus a priest in 1072 bequeaths a vestment to the wooden altar (*altare lignes*) of St. Martin, Aldwark; whilst Erasmus mentions a wooden altar standing in Canterbury Cathedral.

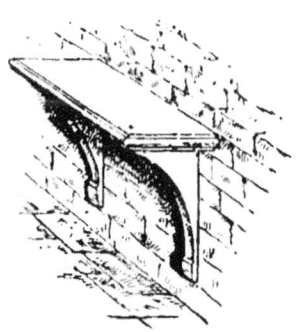

Fig. 222a. Altar. St. John Baptist, Belper, Derbyshire. C. 1250.

Several surviving examples of Elizabethan altars or Holy Tables are beautifully carved and supported by bulbous legs. Probably the best instance of such work is at Blyford, Suffolk (Fig. 226).

In Jacobean days the altar usually assumed a plainer and more severe form, as in the historic chapel of Rycote, Oxon (Fig. 227). This altar is of peculiar interest, as it is the one before which, in 1625, Charles I knelt when the Parliament was held at Oxford on account of the plague, and again in 1643-4 during the Parliamentary strife.

An illustration is also given of the highly ornate mahogany altar in the chapel of St. Clare, in the church of Rye (Fig. 228). It has all the characteristics of Kent's work and dates *c.* 1730. It was probably the gift of one of the Lamb family, who have for several years had no representative living in Rye, but " Lamb House " still exists. A brass chandelier of many lights is inscribed *Ex dome Thom. Lamb armigeri* 1754.

The Sanctuary Table from St. Catherine Cree, London (Fig. 229), is of later 18th century date. It is very elegant in shape and is carved with typical " Adam " acanthus and medallion ornament.

Reredos or Altar Screen.

The whole subject of retables and high altar screens, together with the attached reredos of aisle or chapel altars, has been thoroughly treated in *English Church Furniture* (pp. 20-27), where a list of upwards of 125 mediæval examples are set forth under counties. Suffice it here to draw attention to certain remarkable examples which are not therein mentioned.

The beautiful Marshland churches of Lincolnshire have three good instances in close proximity to each other, namely, at Theddlethorpe All Saints, Theddlethorpe St. Helens, and Saltfleetby All Saints. In the last case there is a most interesting and exceptional reredos of three tiers, *temp.* Edward I, against the east wall of the south aisle. At Theddlethorpe All Saints there is a singularly handsome reredos in the south chapel, consisting of a large crocketed recess elaborately carved, 8 feet high and 5 feet 10 inches wide, evidently designed for a group of sculpture. The one good feature of the much-rebuilt and over-restored church of Theddlethorpe St. Helens is the yet finer reredos than that of its sister church, now at the east end of the north aisle, but formerly in the south aisle. It originally contained a considerable group of imagery. It is elaborately crocketed, and on the centre crocket has stood a crucifix, $14\frac{1}{2}$ inches high ; this ornament is now detached and seems to have been removed at the time of the rebuilding, as it interfered with the low pitch of the aisle roof. The total height is 7 feet, and the outside width 6 feet 2 inches ; the depth of the recess is 15 inches. There are two diminutive figures, $5\frac{1}{4}$ inches long, at the top of the carving on the right hand, which are possibly intended for the man and wife who gave this elaborate and remarkable reredos. It will scarcely be credited that, when we visited the church in 1910, the actual stonework of this noble relic of Christian art was peppered with nails (of some size) and various tacks and pieces of string, the usual traces of modern " decoration."

Alabaster was a favourite material for reredoses, as for effigies, in the Middle Ages. The finest of existing alabaster reredoses is that of Drayton, Berks, which was found buried in the churchyard. It

247

Fig. 226. BLYFORD, SUFFOLK: Elizabethan Communion Table.

Fig. 227. RYCOTE CHAPEL, OXFORDSHIRE: Jacobean Holy Table.

248

Fig. 228. RYE, SUSSEX: 18th Century Altar Table.

Fig. 229. LONDON, S. CATHERINE CREE: Sanctuary Table.

ALTARS, REREDOSES, ALTAR RAILS, PLATE, &c.

has fortunately suffered little damage, and, as can be seen from the illustration (Fig. 224), its beautiful carvings, including representations of the Annunciation, the Nativity, and other scenes from the life of Christ are more or less complete. A reredos, representing the Last Supper, remains at Somerton, Oxon (Fig. 225); it is inferior to the Drayton reredos, but is nevertheless a fine piece of work.

In the church of Northwich, Cheshire, at the east of the south aisle is a stone reredos of unusual design. It consists of a row of twelve crocketed niches of late 14th century design; they were probably filled with little figures of Our Lord and His Apostles.

There are but few altar pieces of the 17th century of any degree of merit outside the metropolis; but there are several fine and dignified examples in the city churches which were rebuilt and fitted after the Great Fire. Undoubtedly the finest of these compositions is contained in the church of St. Mary Abchurch, where Wren, Thornhill, and Gibbons wrought some of their best work. This altar piece, which was not completed until 1686, is of the usual classic design (*see* Fig. 230). It is supported by Corinthian columns, and the central pediment is broken to give place to carven swags and garlands in Gibbons's most naturalistic manner. Another good altar piece, more sombre but very dignified, is that of St. Magnus the Martyr, London Bridge (Fig. 231), where are also notably good iron altar rails.

At the church of Harefield, Middlesex, is a most beautiful and unusual reredos with altar rails to match (Fig. 234). It is carved in a bold continuous scroll design, with cherubs' heads interspersed; the effect is not unlike that of the late 17th century staircase carving in Dunster Castle and elsewhere. Nothing is known of its origin. The church itself is a rather uninteresting fabric, badly restored in the 19th century, but a remarkable feature is the collection of monuments to the Newdigate family. Some of these are of 17th century date, so that it is not inconceivable that this handsome altar piece was a gift from some member of this family, obviously then of considerable local importance. It is curious that so beautiful and unique a fitting should have been passed over by most ecclesiological writers entirely without comment; as far as we are aware it has never previously been illustrated. It may or may not be of foreign workmanship, but it is impossible to conjecture further.

Altar Rails.

When chancel screens with doors were the invariable rule of the Church of England in mediæval days, there was no need for altar rails, so far as keeping dogs and other profanities at a distance were concerned. Kneeling benches for the aged or infirm were occasionally to be found, and thereon would be placed the houseling cloths of white linen, which were otherwise held by clerks at the time of communicating the laity, as is shown in several missal illuminations. In several places this use of the reverential houseling cloths outstayed the Reformation, as is proved by such wardens' entries as these:

1602.—(*St. Botolph, Cambridge*). Two Lyninge Towell for the Chancel at Communion tyme.
1617.—(*St. Margaret, Westminster*). For twenty yards of diaper towelling for the desks, i*li*. iiis. iiii*d*.

The necessity of rails across the chancel, a little way in advance of the altar piece, became obvious in Elizabethan days when the majority of rood-screens were either removed or stripped of their doors. No bigger blunder can be committed in the ecclesiastical history of those days than to assert, as is often done by writers who ought to know better, that we owe the introduction of altar rails to Archbishop Laud. Such a statement as this has been already so flatly contradicted and so completely disproved in two recent works,* that it is unnecessary to re-argue it for a third time. The instances that prove the contrary from the statements of bishops, from various parish accounts, and from examples yet extant therein set forth could be readily doubled.

The true story of altar rails can be put in a nutshell. They were almost universally adopted in early Elizabethan days; but the Puritan clergy, though episcopally ordained, set episcopal rule and church customs at defiance, and before the end of the reign and throughout the reign of her successor these ministers were strong enough in many cases to secure the removal of the rails, and to do much else that was deliberately irreverent. Archbishop Laud was promoted to Canterbury in 1633, and at once began, through his Vicar-General, Sir Nathaniel Brent, his celebrated visitation, wherein he chiefly aimed at the restoration of altar rails, which had been illegally removed by certain of the Puritan and practically non-conforming clergy. In 1641, Parliament ordered the removal of altar rails, an order which was at that time resisted by the royalist half of England. After the Restoration altar rails were again restored. But in out-of-the-way and badly supervised districts, the rails were not readily re-supplied. Thus, in Bishop Nicholson's 1703-4 visitation of neglected Cumberland, he found thirty-five chancels lacking rails.

Our four illustrations of altar rails are (1) St. Marcella, Denbigh (Fig. 232), where the three-sided altar rails, as well as the Holy Table,

---

* See Dr. Cox's *English Church Furniture*, pp. 17-19; and *Early Churchwardens' Accounts*, pp. 124-5.

Fig. 230. LONDON, ST. MARY ABCHURCH: Reredos, 17th Century.

Fig. 231. LONDON, ST. MAGNUS-THE-MARTYR: Reredos and Communion Rail, 17th Century.

253

Fig. 232. DENBIGH, S. MARCELLA: Communion Rail, early 17th Century.

Fig. 233. WORMLEIGHTON, WARWICKSHIRE: Communion Rail, temp. Archbishop Laud.

Fig. 234. HAREFIELD, MIDDLESEX: Communion Rail and Reredos, late 17th Century.

are at the very least twenty years older than the consecration of Laud to his first bishopric of St. David's in 1631; (2) an exceptionally fine example of Laudian altar rails at Wormleighton, Warwickshire (Fig. 233); (3) later 17th century rails of a different design at Acton, Cheshire, which are supposed to be Laudian (Fig. 235); and (4) one of the exceptional instances, of four-sided rails, of post-Restoration date, at Branscombe, Devon (Fig. 236). The spiral rails came in with Charles II, and lasted till about the end of the century.

Altar Slabs.

When the old altars were overthrown at the time of the Reformation, many of the *Mensae* or slabs were often deliberately used in the paving of the churches.

Another fairly frequent use of these altar slabs was to employ them as stones commemorating subsequent interments. Occasionally they had the decency not to remove them far from the site on which they had stood, but simply to lower them to the ground, and several yet remain immediately below the later altar tables. A large number of them, which from their size became useful as pavers in the aisles, were reversed so that the five crosses, with which they are almost invariably marked at the time of their consecration, typical of the Five Wounds of Our Lord, are not readily detected. Since 1840 a considerable number have been replaced and again serve their original function. The number of them to be found, after careful search throughout our ancient churches, is far larger than is usually supposed. In the list the present writer compiled, in the first edition of *English Church Furniture* (1907), these old altar slabs number 158, but by the close of 1916 those that had been detected rose to nearly twice the number. The size of the *Mensae* differed considerably, those that we have ourselves measured vary from 9 feet 6 inches in length and 4 feet broad down to 5 feet by 2 feet 3 inches wide. The larger ones were of course for the high altar, whilst the smaller ones were those of the side altars. We have every confidence that careful and intelligent survey of the flooring of our country churches will reveal a yet larger number which have escaped destruction. In few instances it is on record that the Puritans wilfully broke them up.

Altar Plate.

We have no concern in these pages with many of the details of ecclesiastical plate, such as cruets, pyxes, ciboria, censers and incense vessels, the Pax and Chrismatory, and, at a later period, the

Monstrance; but a few words ought to be said about the chief sacramental vessels, namely the chalice and the paten.*

From the 13th century downwards the English wine-cup was always of one of the precious metals, usually of silver or silver-gilt, and sometimes of gold. These chalices were always stately vessels, about 7 inches in height, and consisting of a spreading base, a stem for holding, and a wide, fairly shallow bowl; they were often richly decorated. The great majority of old plate bears certain hall-marks, by which the precise date can be ascertained; for particular information such a work as Cripps' *Old English Plate* should be consulted.

The mediæval chalices now extant in our old churches, including two of English make in Wales, number forty-seven. A good example of the Tudor or late type is in use at the Carnarvonshire church of Llandudwen, *c.* 1500 (Fig. 237), reproduced from Mr. E. A. Jones' Monograph on the Church Plate of the County, by kind permission. The plain hemispherical bowl is supported by a hexagonal stem, divided by a large ornate knop. The foot is a sexfoil with wavy points; one of the compartments is engraved with a representation of the Crucifixion. The only Welsh example of a pre-Reformation chalice left in Wales is at Llanelian, Denbighshire, and is an almost exact counterpart of the one at Llandudwen.

With the chalice was always found the paten, a small flat shallow dish, of circular form, for the reception and distribution of the consecrated wafer. Each chalice had its own proper paten, of like material and workmanship, designed to form a cover. In old inventories the term "chalice" may be always taken to include its paten. There are now in use in our churches ninety-six mediæval patens, including one in Wales, at Llanmaes, in Glamorganshire. The mediæval paten selected for illustration is that in use at Dronfield, Derbyshire; its date is *c.* 1530, but it was not detected until a visit by the present writer in 1907. An illustration of it appeared in the *Derbyshire Archæological Journal* for the following year, and it is here illustrated (Fig. 238), by courtesy of the Derbyshire Archæological Society. The diameter of this fine example is $6\frac{1}{4}$ inches; in the centre of the six-lobed depression is the Sacred Monogram. The lettering of the inscription round the rim is of exceptionally fine design. It consists of the first five words of the Song of Zacharias, ending after a strangely abrupt fashion—*Benedictus Dominne Deus Israel quia.* It has been suggested that the rest of the verse was on a coeval chalice.

* For details as to all of these and other Church Plate, see cap. ii of *English Church Furniture*, pp. 28-59. As to English examples of pre-Reformation chalices and patens, see *Arch. Journ.*, vols. xliii and lxi.

FIG. 235. ACTON, NR. NANTWICH, CHESHIRE: 17TH CENTURY RAILS.

FIG. 236. BRANSCOMBE, DEVONSHIRE: FOUR-SIDED ALTAR RAILS, END OF 17TH CENTURY.

258

Fig. 238. Dronfield, Derbyshire: Pre-Reformation Paten. c. 1530.

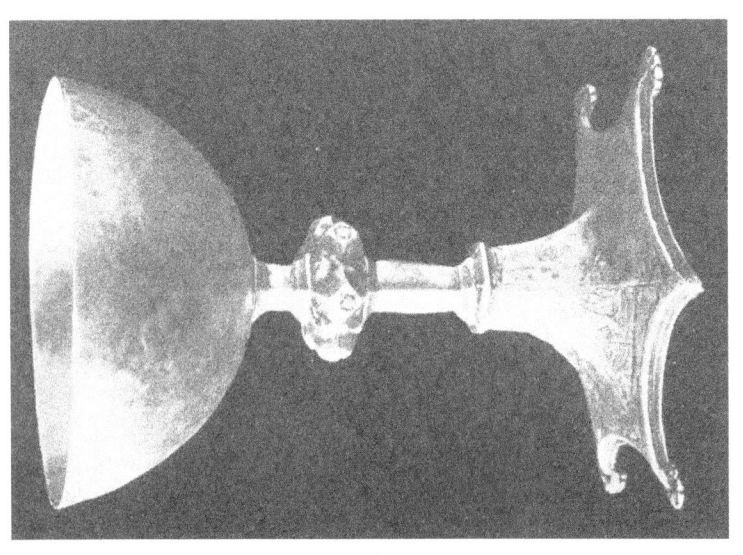

Fig. 237. Llandudwen, Carnarvonshire: Pre-Reformation Chalice, c. 1500.

Nothing suffered more grievously during the Reformation period than the altar plate. After most of the plate had been locally embezzled or seized by the crown in the early days of Edward VI, the covetous Council of the boy-king coolly decreed, in 1551, that "forasmuche as the King's Majestie had neede presently of a Masse of Mooney therefore commissions should be addressed into all shrines of Englande to take into the Kinges handes such church plate as henceforth to be emploied unto His Highness use." This commission swept away all save a single chalice and paten, and a bell or two, and in cases where Puritanism was rampant, the old mediæval chalice with all its beauty was melted down to make a repellently plain and ugly Edwardian cup.

But worse was in store, for soon after Elizabeth came to the throne a cry was raised for the old Mass chalice to give way to a cup and cover of new design. By degrees the abandonment of the old chalice was insisted upon at various visitations, and when Archbishop Parker made his metro-political visitation in 1569, he inquired: "Whether they do minister in any profane cuppes, books, dishes or chalices heretofore used at Masse; or else in a decent Communion cuppe, provided and kept for that purpose." The destruction of the ancient vessels speedily followed, and it appears to be only by accident or by temporary concealment that any exist.

The Elizabethan cup, still so widely prevalent, especially in Somerset and Kent, was avowedly made in direct contrast to the ancient chalice. Instead of a wide shallow bowl the Elizabethan cup is bell-shaped with a baluster or trumpet-shaped stem expanding into a plain foot. The paten is very slightly domed and has a foot or stand. The bowl is generally ornamented with an engraved band or bands, the space between them being filled with arabesque ornament. An example of this type is the communion cup in use at the fine old church of Mobberley, Cheshire (Fig. 239); it has all the characteristic Elizabethan features, but the writer has been unable to ascertain its date or history.

On the whole, Elizabethan cups although perhaps monotonous by repetition, and lacking the individual touch and luxuriant fancy of mediæval work, are not unpleasing vessels; they are at least of silver and not, as happened under the auspices of some of the later Puritans, of base metal unworthy of the sacred usage.

Fig. 240 shows the type of cup most prevalent during the first half of the 17th century, and it will be seen that it is more severely plain than its Elizabethan predecessor. This cup is $9\frac{1}{4}$ inches high, and bears the London hall-mark for 1635-6. The bowl is shaped like a truncated cone, and is connected with the trumpet-shaped stem by a flat calyx with a thin projecting collar. The circular foot is moulded.

The paten cover is very slightly domed, and has a trumpet-shaped foot. There is absolutely no ornament, but the vessel is less clumsy than many of the period. It is inscribed, in contemporary script, "*Poculum Charitas*," and, in later lettering, "the gift of the Rev. Oswald Leycester, Rector of Stoke, December, 1826." Its history is unknown, and it is now in the Victoria and Albert Museum. An exactly similar chalice, although not quite so tall, is in use at Melton Mowbray; this is dated for 1630-1. Communion cups of this type, very little varied, may be met with in almost every county. Similar examples, generally well made and of good proportions, abound in the district of Norwich. The church of St. Peter Mancroft, Norwich, has a notably good example, the work of a local silversmith of considerable merit.

In the latter half of the 17th century, there was a half-hearted attempt at a Gothic revival—at least where ecclesiastical plate was concerned. A ciborium of the period of Charles II has been found, and a good many communion cups of this period show a tendency to return to the mediæval form, although the ornament is pure Renaissance. The well-known chalice at Ashby-de-la-Zouch is a product of this period; it is marked for 1676-7, and has a fairly wide bowl covered with cherubs' heads and shields in repoussé, with an octagonal stem and foot and an ornate knop. The paten is fairly flat, and has a projecting rim; it is surmounted by an upright cross-fleuri. There are a fair number of this type extant, although they are more common in Ireland than in Great Britain.

Occasionally there is found in churches a tall and florid standing cup, with an elaborate steeple cover, as at Ipplepen, Devon; St. John's, Hampstead, and elsewhere. These were made during the 16th century, and were almost certainly originally intended for secular purposes, being adopted for ecclesiastical use at some subsequent period. They are often beautiful examples of the silversmith's art, but they have no bearing on the design of purely ecclesiastical plate.

Eighteenth century plate continues mostly in the plain tradition of the 17th century, with occasional ornate examples of beautiful workmanship, but in no wise differing from contemporary domestic plate in design or ornament. The 19th was a century of continual and conscious revivals, and, of course, the old mass-chalice reappeared with the wholesale and undiscriminating adoption of Gothic accessories.

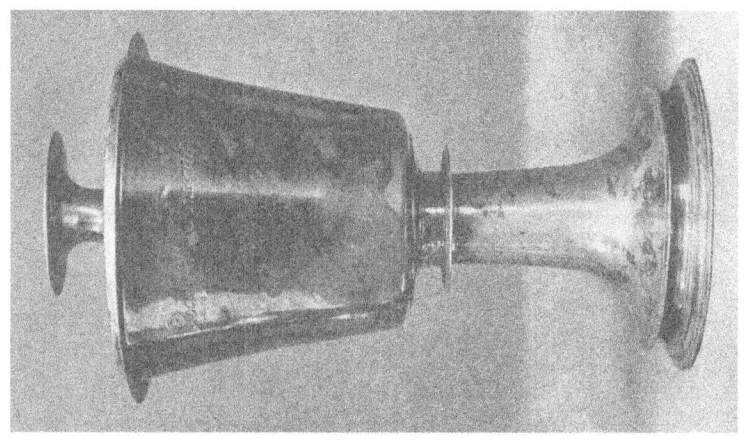

Fig. 240. English Communion Cup with Pattern Ewer. Hall Mark London. Early 17th Century.

Fig. 239. Mobberley, Cheshire: Communion Cup, Elizabethan Type.

Fig. 240a. KING'S NYMPTON, DEVON.

Fig. 240b. CARTMEL, LANCASHIRE. Pewter Communion Plate.

263

Fig. 243.
GREAT GRANSDEN, HUNTINGDONSHIRE: Piscina, 15th Century.

Fig. 242.
MILTON KEYNES, BUCKINGHAMSHIRE: Piscina, 14th Century.

Fig. 241.
CHERRY HINTON, CAMBRIDGESHIRE. Double Piscina, 13th Century.

Fig. 244. MONYASH, DERBYSHIRE: Norman Sedilia.

Fig. 245. UFFINGTON, BERKSHIRE: 13th Century Sedilia.

CHAPTER XVII

PISCINÆ, SEDILIA, EASTER SEPULCHRES

THE PISCINA.

IN the wall to the south side of the altar there is generally to be noted the piscina or water drain, placed as a rule within a more or less ornamental niche. The piscina itself is a shallow stone basin with a hole at the bottom to carry off the water into the ground beneath. The mouldings of the niche usually plainly exhibit to what architectural period it belongs. There are a large number extant of the Norman period, as well as of the three successive Gothic periods.

Pope Leo IV, about 850, directed that a place was to be provided near the altar for the disposal of the water used for the ablutions of vessels and of priests' hands after Mass. Pope Innocent, at the beginning of the 13th century, enjoined the washing of the priests' hands before the canon of the Mass, and deemed it unseemly that these manual washings should be done in the same basin; consequently he ordered that there should be two piscinæ within the same niche. Hence a large number of niches with double basins appear in the Early English period, and occasionally at a later date.

The drain or basin nearest to the east is often more ornamental in its treatment than its fellow; this was the one which was used for the cleansing of the chalice. But a further ritual change in the 14th century brought about the custom of the celebrant drinking the ablutions; hence the reversion to a single drain.

It must be remembered that a piscina was required for every altar, so that we may naturally expect to see them at the east end of the aisles, in transepts, or wherever chapels were established.

A common feature of the piscina niche is to find within it, just below the spring of the arch, a stone credence shelf whereon to place the cruets for wine and water, and also the box for the wafers. Sometimes this shelf was of wood, and grooves remain for its insertion.

Then again it must not be forgotten to look for the presence of a piscina drain in the flooring to the south of the altar. It was at one time, chiefly in the 13th century, the habit to use such floor-drains in conventual churches. They have been noted in the ruins of the

Cistercian abbeys of Fountains, Furness, and Rievaulx, as well as in the ruins of the Austin house of Kirkham and of the Premonstratensian house of Langdon, Kent. They have also been noted in recent years in several parish churches. They remain in the churches of Little Casterton and North Luffenham, Rutland; and at Barton Bendish and Tilney All Saints, Norfolk, the latter in the south-east chapel. There are, we believe, some three or four other cases known, and it is quite possible that further examples will come to light when the level of pavements near altars is changed.

It is supposed that these ground piscinæ were for the purpose of pouring out a small quantity of the contents of the altar cruets before using them, with the intention of removing any possible dust or impurity.

The piscina niches in several dioceses were ordered to be walled up in Reformation days. Many have been opened out, in a more or less mutilated condition, during recent years, but there are probably several others still concealed in the walling awaiting exposition.

Some of the most handsome piscina niches are those that are worked continuously with the sedilia; these are to be noted of all periods, but those of the Decorated period are specially beautiful.

In exact contrast to these are the instances, not infrequent in the Midlands, where the shallow basin and drain are carved in the sill of the window without any kind of niche above it.

Cherry Hinton, Cambs, affords a beautiful example of a double piscina (Fig. 241) of the 13th century, with dog-tooth mouldings. The piscina niche in the north chapel of Milton Keynes, Bucks, with ball-flower mouldings, illustrates early Decorated treatment (Fig. 242); while Great Gransden, Huntingdonshire (Fig. 243), is one of the numerous and varied instances of 15th century workmanship. The arched niche is enclosed in the characteristic Perpendicular rectangular framework, the spandrels being filled with the typical quatrefoil-within-circle ornament.

Sedilia.

The sedilia or three stone seats on the south side of the chancel, near to the altar, are a usual distinctive feature of the old English chancel. These structural seats are of far commoner occurrence in England than on the Continent. Occasionally they were of wood, but very few instances have survived. These triple seats were intended for the use of the priest, the deacon, and the sub-deacon at High Mass. Though sometimes on a level, they are more usually graded, and the highest one nearest the altar was used by the celebrant. It is generally stated, no doubt with a certain degree of truth, that they came to be placed on the same level at the time when the assistants at the Mass were themselves priests. The Council of Trent enjoined that the celebrant should occupy the central seat. Though three sedilia were the general rule, there are about a score of old churches wherein there are only two. On the other hand, there is a divergency of cases, chiefly in the larger churches, such as Ottery St. Mary and Stratford-on-Avon, wherein the sedilia are fourfold. The tabernacle work above the sedilia is often strikingly executed, and in the 14th century sometimes towers to a considerable height.

A second set of sedilia in the south aisle is not altogether uncommon in important churches. At St. Mary's, Leicester, in addition to the fine Norman sedilia of the chancel, there is a beautiful Early English example in the south aisle. They are also to be noted in the south transept of Filey, Yorks.

In some districts, particularly in East Anglia, is found the comparatively mean expedient of lowering the sill of the window on the south side of the chancel nearest the east, so as to form a kind of cheap sedilia bench.

The following illustrations serve as good examples of sedilia pertaining to the four main architectural periods; they are in each case combined with the piscina niche at the east end: (Fig. 244), Monyash, Derbyshire, *Norman;* (Fig. 245), Uffington, Berks, *Early English;* (Fig. 246), Milton Keynes, Bucks, c. 1330; (Fig. 248), Swavesey, Cambs, *Decorated;* (Fig. 247), Tilney All Saints, Norfolk, *Perpendicular.**

In the handsome church of Wymondham St. Mary, Norfolk, there is, within the chancel arch, a fine Renaissance structure in terra cotta (*see* Fig. 249). This dates from the time of Henry VIII and was probably intended to serve as sedilia. The church was formerly part of the Benedictine Abbey of SS. Mary and Alban; the original fabric is Norman, and chevron mouldings of this period may be noted on the arch above the sedilia. Much of the church was rebuilt in the 15th century and there were some additions in the first quarter of the century following.

THE EASTER SEPULCHRE.

Remains of the Easter sepulchre should always be looked for on the north side of the chancel, near the altar.

The rites connected with this Eastertide ceremony seem to have been observed in every English parish church, both in town and country. Explanations as to the method of carrying out this repre-

* We desire to call attention again to the very much fuller account of the variety of sedilia in Cox and Harvey's *English Church Furniture* (1907), pp. 67-74.

sentation of Our Lord's Entombment have been frequently printed; the usual custom was to place the Eucharistic Wafer within a small receptacle on Good Friday and to transfer it, together with the altar crucifix, to a tomblike structure, there to remain until daybreak on Easter Day, when it was reinstated above the high altar.

The sepulchre to which it was transferred was usually a timber framework, which was adorned with the most sumptuous hangings that the church could afford; thus the accounts of St. Edmund's, Salisbury, mention two palls of cloth of gold for the sepulchre. In many churches these timber sepulchres remained until the Elizabethan days of spoliation, when they were burnt as "monuments of superstition," or turned to secular use, as at Croxton, Lincolnshire, where the wardens testified in 1566 that it then served "as a shelfe to set dishes on."

Towards the close of the 13th century it became customary to erect a structural stone sepulchre to the immediate north of the altar; its usual form was a recess in the wall covered by a cusped and crocketed arch. Many of the finer examples are greatly enriched with tabernacle work and with appropriate figure sculpture; these are chiefly of the 14th century. Lincolnshire has various good instances of figure sculpture, the best of which is at Heckington (Fig. 250). But by far the finest Easter sepulchre in this country, or indeed in Christendom, is at Hawton, Notts (Fig. 252), where the sepulchre is combined with a founder's-tomb and a beautiful doorway opening into a former north chapel. The whole composition occupies the greater part of the north wall of the chancel; it forms a masterly piece of sculpture, 17 feet long by 12 feet high, under a well-carved cornice. The actual sepulchre portion of this elaborate imagery is divided into three compartments. In the lowest, four Roman soldiers, wearing helmets and chain-mail, are sleeping in as many niches. They are armed with swords and spears, and leaning upon shields charged with dragons and heads in profile. In the centre and largest compartment is Our Saviour in the act of rising from the tomb, with the left foot still in the sepulchre, and the drapery of the grave-clothes hanging from the left shoulder, and with uplifted right hand and arm; in the niche on the left are the three Marys, two standing with alabaster vessels in their hands, and the third in a kneeling attitude. On each side is an adoring angel. On Our Lord's right is the recessed niche where the Blessed Sacrament was placed during the three days of burial. The third or top compartment is representative of the Ascension; Our Lord's feet and a portion of the legs are shown below the clouds in the centre, with a censing angel on each side. On the finial of the intruding canopy of the central compartment are the footprints of the Risen Lord between two kneeling

Fig. 246. MILTON KEYNES, BUCKINGHAMSHIRE:
14th Century Sedilia.

Fig. 247. TILNEY ALL SAINTS, NORFOLK:
15th Century Sedilia.

Fig. 249. WYMONDHAM, NORFOLK: Renaissance Sedilia.

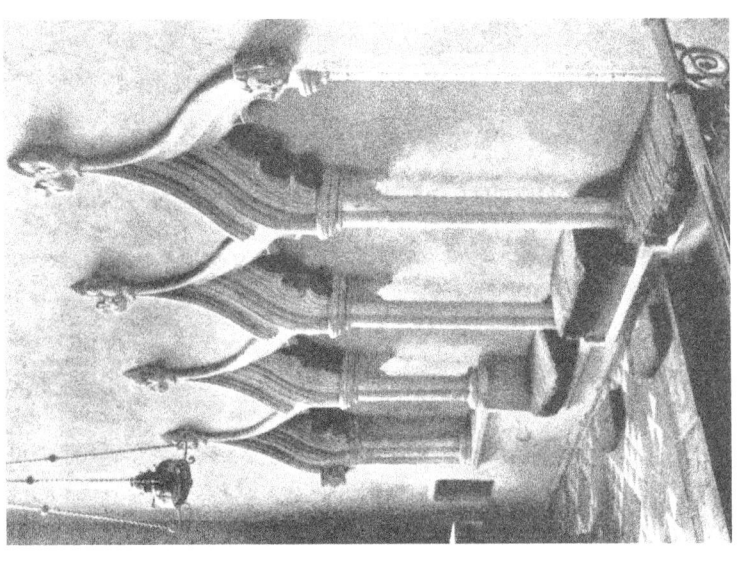

Fig. 248. SWAVESEY, CAMBRIDGESHIRE: Decorated Sedilia and Piscina.

271

FIG. 251. PATRINGTON,
EAST RIDING, YORKSHIRE.

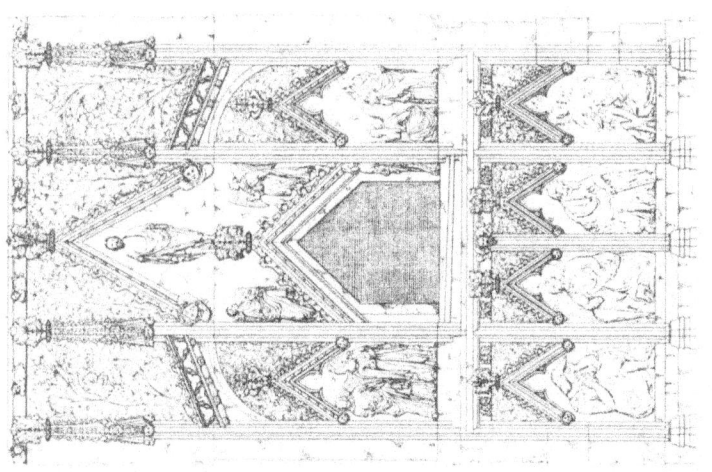

FIG. 250. HECKINGTON, LINCOLNSHIRE.

EASTER SEPULCHRES, 14TH CENTURY.

Fig. 252. HAWTON, NOTTINGHAMSHIRE: Easter Sepulchre, 14th Century.

angels, whilst three groups of the Twelve Apostles gaze upwards in amazement.

Perhaps the next most interesting sepulchre is in the chancel of the grand old 14th century church of Patrington, E.R., Yorks; it is in marvellous preservation (Fig. 251). At the foot are three sleeping soldiers. The one to the west has a lion on his shield, the one in the centre a boss, and the third the instruments of the Passion. The second compartment was for the sepulchre itself; whilst the third tier has a sculpture of the Resurrection, with angels censing the rising Lord.

Occasionally the recess, though occupied by the effigy or lettered slab of a founder or benefactor, was intended to serve for the two purposes. Thus, Thomas Windsor, of Stanwell, Middlesex, left elaborate instructions in 1485 that his recessed tomb was to serve at Eastertide as the sepulchre. Also Thomas Fiennes, Lord Dacre, directed that his tomb at Hurstmonceux, Sussex, on the north side of the chancel, was " to be there made for the placing of the Sepulchre of our Lord, with all fittinge furniture thereto, in honour of the most Blessed Sacrament."

It is as well to remember that not a few small recesses in the north wall of chancels, usually vaguely termed almeries or lockers, have sometimes served as sepulchres; this is probably always the case when such recesses have no grooves for doors, and are treated after an ornamental fashion, or are arched at the top.

A particular feature of the sepulchre was the continuous succession of watchers and worshippers during the whole period of the three days. Various parish accounts show that small sums of money were paid to certain men as watchmen, doubtless selected from the poorer of the parishioners; their services might readily be required as firemen, so great was the blazing light until the quire burst forth into the *Christus Resurgens* very early on the triumphant morn. Over the sepulchre at St. Edmund's, Salisbury, in addition to a great sepulchre taper and the expectant huge Paschal taper, there were 100 candles fixed on prickets or pins of beech-wood. The brethren and sisters of the guild of the Trinity at the church of St. Botolph, Aldersgate Without, paid a penny each to find " xiij taperes aboute ye sepulchre of Criste at Ester."

CHAPTER XVIII

ALMERIES, BREAD CUPBOARDS, COFFERS, ALMS-BOXES.

THE almery or aumbry was a mediæval cupboard; it was as necessary for the equipment of a church as were the larger chests or coffers for the storing of vestments, festival hangings and other valuables. Occasionally it took the convenient form of a chest-cupboard that went by the name of a hutch in the old inventories. This hutch differed from the chest proper inasmuch as there was no lid at the top, but it opened by one or more doors in the front. Old examples remain at Minehead, Somerset; Hambledon, Bucks; Cley, Norfolk; and at Louth; also others of rather later date, at Rossington, Yorkshire; and at Rowington, Warwickshire.*

It is as well to remember that church almeries in mediæval days were infrequently in the form of movable furniture, but were more generally recesses in the wall fitted with doors and locks. These small squared recesses are generally found in the north wall of the chancel; they were intended for the reception of altar vessels, altar books, linen, etc., as well as for the chrismatory and its holy oils. The almery in the south pier of the aspe arch of Swyncombe, Oxfordshire, is extremely ancient, and is reputed to be coeval with the church itself, c. 1020 A.D. In almost every instance of such recesses now remaining, there are plain traces of the existence of doors and locks. In many churches these have been refitted and the almery restored to its original use.

There are a fair number of instances where the old mediæval doors to almeries, or parts of them, yet remain, as at Floore, Kingsthorpe, Rotherthorpe, and Ringstead, Northants; and also at Drayton, Berks; Barrington, Cambs; Northleach, Gloucestershire; and Rattlesden, Suffolk.

A few of these wall almeries have lancet heads, as at Furneux Pelham, Herts; Eglingham, Northumberland; and Binsted and Sullington, Sussex. Occasionally these almeries in chancel walls, as on the south side of the chancel of St. Oswald's, Durham, are of an oblong shape, in which case they were probably intended for the storage of tall altar candles or of funeral tapers.

Now and again these recessed almeries occur in the east walls of chancels, usually immediately behind the high altar, as at Upton,

---

* See Mr. F. Roe's *Old Oak Furniture*.

Northants; Fishtoft, Lincolnshire; Martock, Somerset; and Burpham, Climping, Rogate, Sompting, and Wivelsfield, Sussex. In all these cases such almeries have probably been intended for the safe custody of relics. This was undoubtedly the case in the interesting church of Bibury, Gloucestershire, where the chancel was extended in the Early English period, when three large almeries were inserted in the east wall, the high altar standing clear of the wall.

In the 17th century it was customary to bequeath a sum of money to provide a Sunday dole of bread for the poor of the parish. This was a slight compensation for the loss of the constant doles of bread and other food the poor had received regularly from the monasteries before the Dissolution, but the post-Reformation usage insisted that the recipients should attend church prior to the distribution.

A later form of almery, known as a "dole cupboard," was provided in several churches as a receptacle for the loaves prior to their distribution. Some of these have disappeared under the tasteless restorations of last century, as at Ightham and Sevenoaks, Kent. In the former church a most ornamental one, with double shelves, was comparatively recently cleared away; the dole, however, continues to be distributed every Sunday after evening service; the baker's boy now deposits twelve penny loaves, in accordance with a benefaction of 1627, and six fourpenny loaves of a later bequest, every Saturday evening, in a covered basket which stands within the porch. These bread cupboards were often shallow receptacles with their fronts either fitted with slender ornamental rails or pierced apertures, so that the bread might be ventilated. There are three such almeries in a recess of the south transept of the abbey church of St. Albans, each capable of holding about a dozen loaves. The most elaborate one, carved with strap ornament, is of the reign of Charles I (1620) (Fig. 253), whilst the two plainer ones are of the reign of Charles II. In the church of St. Nicholas, Abingdon, there is a shallow recess by the tombs of John and Jane Blackwall from which a dole of loaves is still distributed. There is a 17th century dole cupboard at Kingsthorpe, Northants. In the church of All Saints, Hereford, are handsomely carved double dole shelves, 1683, with the arms of the donor as shown in the illustration (Fig. 254). At Ruislip, Middlesex, is a beautifully carved dole-cupboard of four shelves, whereon is still placed every Sunday two shillings' worth of bread, in accordance with a bequest of 1692. The church of All Hallows, Lombard Street, rebuilt by Wren in 1694, has attached to the wall in the vestibule a frame containing shelves for loaves for a Sunday distribution of bread to the poor. In the east part of the church of Christ Church, Newgate Street, are attached, both on the north and south walls, shelves to contain loaves as doles to the poor. A tablet on the south wall records that " The Bread given Weekly to the poor of St. Leonard's is from a Bequest of Sir John Trott and other Benefactors." A tablet on the north wall says that " The Bread here given to the Poor is from the Church Rate and the Benefactions of Mr. Henry Needler, Mr. Roger Harris, and Mr. Thomas Sketchley."

Coffers.

The oldest and simplest form of a large coffer or chest to be found in parish churches is a "dugout," destitute of panels, and simply constructed out of an artificially hollowed trunk of a tree, hatchet-trimmed on the exterior. The English word "dugout" carries with it its own explanation, but one or two pedantic antiquaries scorn this common word and call such a chest *monoxylon!* Such chests are almost invariably of oak, but there is a small " dugout " of elm at Eckington, Worcestershire, and two in Cambridgeshire, one of cypress at Cleveley, and one of cedar at Swaffham Bulbeck. Two or three of such chests are almost certainly pre-Conquest, whilst several others are Norman and 13th century. Two of the oldest are to be seen at Wimborne and West Grinstead. The Wimborne example, usually known as the " Relic Chest," is a dugout 6 feet long, but the interior cavity is only 22 inches by 9 inches broad and 6 inches deep. The West Grinstead dugout is somewhat similar, for it is only hollowed in the centre, leaving a solid mass at each end. We believe that the largest dugout is in the Warwickshire church of Curdworth; it is 10 feet long, iron banded, and divided into two compartments. There is another great dugout at Shustoke in the same county; it is 9 feet long and reported to weigh half a ton.

One of the most interesting of the dugouts, here depicted, is the one in Hatfield, W.R., Yorks (Fig. 255). It is of early 13th century date, and perhaps earlier in its origin; it is thickly studded with large-headed nails, as well as being stoutly bound with iron. The money slot appears to be a much later addition. Another great dugout is to be seen at West Hanningfield, Essex; it measures 8 feet 3 inches long by 2 feet 2 inches wide, and is $19\frac{1}{2}$ inches deep; it is strongly banded with iron and has lifting handles at each end. The interior is divided into two parts, and, judging from the ironwork, its date is late 13th century.

During the reign of Henry III there was a great advance in the number and finish of the church chests. Dugouts dropped out of fashion, and the chests were often clever pieces of substantial carpentry with dovetailed joints, and embellished with the graceful curves of cunningly wrought ironwork. Among the best examples of this 13th

Fig. 253. ST. ALBANS: Bread Cupboard, c. 1620.

Fig. 254. HEREFORD ALL SAINTS: Bread Shelves. 1683.

Fig. 255. HATFIELD, YORKSHIRE, W.R.: Early 13th Century.

Fig. 256. MALPAS, CHESHIRE: 13th Century.

Fig. 257. HUTTOFT, LINCOLNSHIRE: 14th Century.
COFFERS.

century iron scrollwork on chests are those of the churches of Church Brampton, Northants, of Ecklington, Suffolk, and of Tamworth, Wootton-Wawen, and Rugby, Warwickshire. Fig. 256 shows an example from Malpas, Cheshire, admirably enriched with wrought iron scrollwork. During the reigns of the first three Edwards, woodcarvers put some of their best work into the front panels and ends of church chests, usually following in design the window tracery of the period. A singularly effective instance of this kind of decoration occurs on all four sides of the panels of the chest of Huttoft, Lincolnshire (Fig. 257).

During the late Gothic and early Renaissance period, chests became more and more ornate, a well-known example of the type being that of Croscombe, Somerset, c. 1616 (Fig. 258). This is entirely covered with an intricate design of rosettes and interlacing bands in low relief. As the 17th century advanced the ornament became more restrained; an instance of this later and quieter type is shown in Fig. 259 from Frodsham, Cheshire. Good 17th century chests remain at Church Broughton, Derbyshire; Colchester St. Martin's, Essex; Burlingham St. Andrew, Norfolk; Flintham, Notts; Tilstock and Wem, Salop; and Kingston, Somerset and elsewhere.

The various uses to which these church chests or coffers were put in mediæval days is well shown by the following extracts from a 1464 inventory of the great collegiate church of Warwick. Churches of any size or importance were usually possessed of two or more chests:

It. in the lowe house under the vestry ii old ire bound coofres.
It. in the vestrye i gret olde arke to put in vestryments.
It. in the Sextry above the Vestrye i olde arke at the arters ende. i old coofre ire bonde having a long lok of the olde fasion and i large new coofre having iii loks called the tresory cofre, and contayne almaries.
It. in the inner hous i newe hie almarie with ii dores to kepe in the evidence of the Churche, and i gret olde arke and certayne old Almaries.
It. in the house afore the Chapter hous i old ire bond cofre having hie feet and rings of iron in the endes thereof to heve it bye. And therein lieth certain bokes belonging to the Chapter.

In the case of several of the largest and heaviest of the old chests, there are sometimes rings and other appliances to "heve it bye," notably at Cheshunt, Furneaux Pelham, and Hemel Hempstead, Herts; Cound, Salop; and at Upton, Notts.

The writer made an interesting discovery in June, 1903, when examining the small ancient chest at the west end of Heckfield church, Hants. He was the first to notice the then choked-up money slot. "This highly exceptional chest is just 3 feet long by $17\frac{1}{2}$ inches wide, and standing 20 inches in height. The stiles or side pieces of the front terminate in feet to keep it clear of the ground, and are slightly moulded. Within the chest at one end is a very small inner shelf or tray-box, with lid turning on wooden pivots, and in every way it corresponds to the few known examples of early 13th century larger church chests. The arrangement for the fitting of the lid and for its hinges is most ingenious. About the centre of the lid is a small money slot. There is no doubt that this chest is of early 13th century date, and that the slot is original. In the opinion of several experts, it is quite possible that it is sufficiently early to belong to the period in the reign of King John when Innocent III, confirming a similar mandate given by Henry II in 1166, ordered boxes or chests to be placed in the parish churches of England, wherein the faithful were expected to deposit money for the prosecution of the fifth Crusade."*

There are various other large chests in the top of which there is a money slot of a good deal later date than the small one at Heckfield. We have noticed these apertures in the church chests of Cheshunt, Climping, Worlingham, Hatfield, and doubtless there are several other instances. At Brading in the Isle of Wight, there is a good late Elizabethan panelled chest with a money slot. In each of these instances, including even that at Brading, it is customary for the custodian of the church to confidently claim them as constructed for the reception of Peter's Pence.

This, though a common mistake, is quite erroneous. The mediæval payment to Rome known as Peter's Pence was at no time a freewill offering, to be left to the discretion of the faithful. Certain officials were appointed for the collection of this due from each householder; it was gathered in fixed sums, on a particular date, throughout every deanery in the kingdom, on much the same principle as the church-rate was gathered in post-Reformation days. When closely examined these money slots almost invariably show traces of having been punctured in the lids at a later date than the construction of the chest. The making of these holes was probably a cheap way of complying with the general order of the 16th century for the providing of a Poor Man's Box.

Another popular blunder in connection with church coffers is to name certain cubical iron safes, with cunningly constructed elaborate locks of many bolts concealed in the lids, "Armada Chests," under the fond notion that they came out of some wrecked Spanish vessel. Such chests are known to be a product of Flemish craftsmen, and were regularly imported into this country during the 16th century, at a fixed import duty, in fairly large numbers. There are various examples of them in private or civic custody. We have noticed such iron chests in the three churches of Hythe, Oxted, and Icomb.

* *English Church Furniture* (Methuen, 1907), 295.

Although these few comments on church chests must perforce be of a superficial character, it would be wrong to pass over two of supreme interest, especially to artists and students of early painting and colour. At Newport, Essex, there is a remarkably fine 13th century chest; the inside of the lid is decorated with oil paintings in trefoil-headed niches, wherein are figures of the Rood, the Blessed Virgin, St. John, St. Peter and St. Paul. The predominating colours are red and green. Mr. Roe, in his work on *Ancient Coffers and Cupboards*, says:

> The painting on the Newport coffer proves conclusively that oil was used as a vehicle in England at this early period. It may be regarded as the earliest national specimen of that art remaining.

Mr. J. Charles Wall, in his excellent work on the chests of Essex, has been able to show that this chest was fitted up to serve as a travelling altar for a wealthy official on foreign service, the lid of the chest serving as a reredos when opened. The other, a less known instance of the same kind, is to be found in the Cambridgeshire church of Swaffham Bulbeck. This 15th century chest has the inside of the lid finely painted with the Crucifixion, flanked by roundels on which are depicted the Resurrection and the Ascension. There can be no doubt that the chest was also intended to serve as a portable altar, the opened lid forming the reredos, and the chest containing the slab of the consecrated super-altar, the necessary plate, and the vestments. It was probably used by some great lord during wartime across the seas, presumably one of the Bulbecks.

Alms Boxes.

In the highly interesting *Chronicle* by Jocelim of Brakeland, a monk of Bury St. Edmunds, wherein he described events of which he was personally cognisant between 1173 and 1202, he relates how two of the brethren constructed a certain hollow trunk (*truncum quandem concavum*) with a hole at the top and fastened with an iron lock. It was set up in the great church near the doorway into the choir, and was designed to receive the offerings of the people. The ancient order for church coffers to be provided for the receipt of offerings from the faithful in support of the Crusades has been already mentioned. There were also in various churches opportunities given for the devout to contribute for blessings received at the shrines of saints, such as St. Cuthbert at Durham, and St. Godric at Tunstall. Moreover, alms boxes for God's poor, or for other church purposes, were by no means an invention of the Reformers. There are, for instance, up-standing alms boxes of the 15th or early 16th centuries at various churches, including those of Blythburgh, Suffolk (Fig. 260); Cawston,

Loddon, and Wickmere, Norfolk; Hursley, Hants; Mears Ashby, Northants, and East Kirkby, Lincolnshire.

After the suppression of the Religious Houses, at every one of which, small and great, alms had been freely distributed, the relief of the poor became a matter of pressing necessity. The providing of poor boxes in all churches was enjoined both under Edward VI and Elizabeth, and still more definitely by Canon LXXXIV of 1603. There are dated Elizabethan boxes at Dovercourt, Essex, 1589; Bramford, Suffolk, 1591; and Hargrave, Northants, 1597. Other examples are quite frequent in the 17th century; the earliest we have noticed is at Aylestone, Leicestershire, 1613. They commonly bear the legend " Remember the Poor." Giggleswick, W.R., Yorks, is a good example (Fig. 264). There are about a dozen instances in which the boxes are quaintly carved or painted with figures of beggars or cripples. The largest example of this kind of box is at Pinhoe, Devon, where the beggar is well carved in high relief (Fig. 263). He is represented as a hale and sturdy man remarkably well dressed; under his left arm is a kind of placard on which is inscribed in small lettering, " Ye Pore Man of Pinhoe, 1700." The box itself is modern.

A plain but not unsightly post-Reformation alms box is shown in Fig. 261 from Wintringham, Yorkshire. Many of the 18th century London churches can show more or less elaborate examples of poor boxes; we have selected a well-designed specimen from St. Mary Abchurch (Fig. 262).

Fig. 258. CROSCOMBE, SOMERSETSHIRE. c. 1616.

Fig. 259. FRODSHAM, CHESHIRE: 17th Century.
COFFERS.

FIG. 262. LONDON, ST. MARY ABCHURCH.

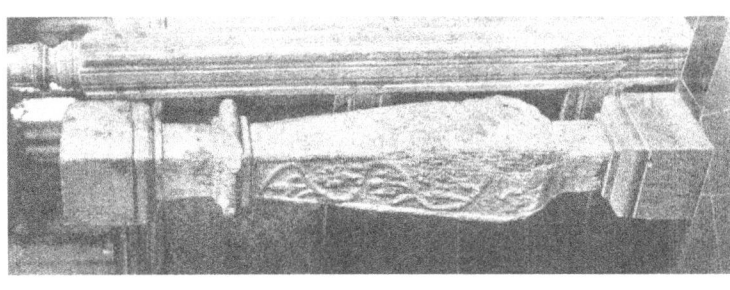

FIG. 261. WINTRINGHAM, YORKSHIRE.

ALMS BOXES.

FIG. 260. BLYTHBURGH, SUFFOLK.

285

Fig. 264. GIGGLESWICK, YORKSHIRE: Alms Box.

Fig. 263. PINHOE, DEVONSHIRE: Alms Box.

286

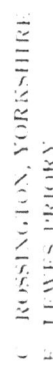

A. LITTLE MARLOW, BUCKINGHAMSHIRE.　B. CUXTON, GLOUCESTERSHIRE.　C. ROSSINGTON, YORKSHIRE.
D. HARDWICK, GLOUCESTERSHIRE. ARMS　E. BITTON, GLOUCESTERSHIRE　F. LEWES PRIORY
OF THE ABBEY OF GLOUCESTER

FIG. 265. ENCAUSTIC TILES.

CHAPTER XIX

ENCAUSTIC TILES

THE making of tiles dates back from very early days. The oldest reference to them is to be found in Holy Writ, namely, in the fourth chapter of Ezekiel: " Thou also, Son of Man, take thee a tile, and lay it before thee, and portray upon it the city, even Jerusalem." These tiles, thus referred to by the Prophet, were doubtless used for the adornment of walls, and probably resembled the *azulejos*, or Spanish-Moresco tiles, which were but comparatively rare visitors to England, or to any other part of Europe. The ecclesiastical floor tiles, with which we are familiar, were originally of the kind called tesselated, a survival of the Roman art. Floors at Ely and Westminster still survive to remind us of the precise words of old Chaucer:

> The flore and bench were pavyd faire and smooth
> With stones square of manie divers hewe,
> So well joyn'd that for to say thee scythe
> All seemed one that none the other knewe.

But ere long these floor tiles grew in size and assumed a great variety of design. Encaustic tiles, as they are now generally termed, seem to have been introduced into England from Normandy about the end of the 11th century; they soon became the favourite means of floor decoration and thus continued through the whole mediæval period. The tiles themselves were probably first imported, but this country soon became a seat of their manufacture, and more seem to have been made here than in any other country except France. Kilns for their production have been discovered at various places, notably at Great Malvern, Witton near Droitwich, Repton, Great Bedwyn (Wilts), and in the town of Nottingham.

These enriched tiles appear to have been invented on the Continent for mosaic pavements, in places where marbles suitable for the latter were rare, whilst clays were plentiful and good. The tiles, as a rule, were used sparingly, chiefly in chapels and chancels, before altars and around monuments. The rest of the floors were paved with plain tiles or slabs of stone. In a few highly elaborate buildings the floor was entirely composed of decorated encaustic tiles, as at the Chapter House (Westminster) and Prior Crauden's Chapel at Ely; but it must be remembered that the ordinary flooring of our parish churches was for a considerable time nothing more than stamped earth. English tiles are, as a rule, of two colours only, red and yellow; they usually measure from four to six inches square and about an inch in thickness, but larger specimens are occasionally found, whilst narrow border-tiles sometimes of a greenish glaze, are not uncommon.

The process of manufacture was as follows: The body of the tile was first made of the red clay, and, while soft, an embossed pattern was stamped on its face by means of a wooden die; the resulting hollows were filled in by a clay or slip which baked white, and the whole covered by a red glaze and fired. The glaze, under the influence of heat, became yellow, enriching the red and imparting a yellow tone to the white portion of the tile. In some instances the glaze has worn away, and the white portion of the tile has become detached, leaving an embossed red tile; still more rarely this form seems to have been adopted intentionally, and has an incised appearance.

Painted, or parti-coloured, tiles do not appear to have been intentionally made in this country during the Middle Ages. But in the course of firing the glazes often played a prominent part in varying the hues, mellowing down the pattern, and changing the ground-colours into divers shades of yellows, buffs, burnt-siennas, and even delicate greens, contrasted with rich browns and even chestnut blacks. Such varieties are specially to be noticed at Westleigh and Stone, Kent, and in various churches of Devon.

The subjects of these tiles are infinitely varied, and may be said to chiefly consist of architectural and geometrical figures, interspersed with human and grotesque heads, symbolical figures, and a great number of armorial bearings. Various attempts have been made by comparatively modern writers to classify these designs after a more or less arbitrary fashion; but the whole question is yet in embryo, and loudly calls for a monograph by some capable hand. At present we cannot do better than follow the classification adopted by Mr. Way many years ago when analysing the tiles of Great Malvern:

(1) Sacred symbols; inscriptions, consisting of Scriptural or pious phrases.

(2) Armorial bearings of the sovereign or individuals connected with the church by benefaction or otherwise; personal devices or mottoes.

(3) Ornaments conformable to the prevalent period of architecture, but devoid of any special import.

The earliest sacred symbol was that of the Fish. This occurs with some frequency in Worcestershire, Warwickshire, and Devon. The symbol of the Cross is naturally one of the most frequent; a good early example occurs at Little Marlow, Bucks, whereon the central equal-limbed cross is surrounded by the inscription: "*Signum sanctae crucis*" (Fig. 265a). The fleur-de-lis, a reminder of the Blessed Virgin, appears in a vast variety of forms. We illustrate a bold and simple example from Cuxton, Gloucestershire (Fig. 265b), and two elaborate composite designs from West Hendred, Berks, and Romsey Abbey (Figs. 266a and 266b respectively). The tile from the Chapel of the Bedehouse, Leicester (Fig. 266f), shows the monogram of Our Lady.

At Shelsley Walsh, Worcestershire, and also at Worcester Cathedral, are floor crosses formed of a number of encaustic tiles; single tiles which once formed part of such designs occasionally occur in churches, especially in Kent.

Of armorial bearings four examples are given. The first of these (Fig. 265c) shows the arms of Deincourt—lancette between ten billets, from the church of Rossington, Yorks. Fig. 265d illustrates the arms of the abbey church of Gloucester—the cross keys of St. Peter and the sword of St. Paul. This tile is from the church of Hardwick in Gloucestershire, which has belonged to the Abbey for many years. An encaustic tile from Hailes Abbey, also in Gloucester, is given in Fig. 266c. The Abbey was the foundation of Richard, Earl of Cornwall, brother of Henry III, and King of the Romans; the tile shows the double-headed eagle emblem of the latter dignity. The next illustration (Fig. 266d) is of a most elaborate heraldic tile from the church of Great Malvern. This tile is one of a series illustrating the descent of the Manor of Malvern from the Crown through the Clares of Gloucester to the Despensers, and then to Richard Beauchamp, Earl of Warwick. The first tile bears the arms of Clare; the second (Fig. 266d) the arms of Despenser with the scutcheon attributed to the old Earls of Warwick; the third shows the arms of Beauchamp of Warwick; and the fourth the Royal Arms (England and France quarterly), since the Manor finally reverted to the Crown.

The one instance given here of architectural ornament is of the Early English period; it is a delightful type from the church of Bitton, Gloucestershire (Fig. 265e).

It must be remembered that it frequently required a square of four or even of nine tiles to make up a complete design, and just occasionally as many as sixteen. Not infrequently only one or two tiles of an incomplete design are now extant in a village church.

In addition to the four divisions here mentioned, there are a certain number of what Mr. Way has termed pictorial tiles. Such designs on a large scale are very rare, but a fine 14th century example is in Prior Crauden's chapel at Ely, where the Temptation of Adam and Eve is represented. In the Early English pavement of the Chapter

House, Westminster, subjects from the life of the Confessor are found, whilst good tiles illustrating the secular legend of Tristram and Iseult were uncovered on the site of Chertsey Abbey. These latter have now found their way to the British Museum. At Lingfield, Surrey, there is a unique instance of a portrait effigy in tiles, representing a priest, and forming a sepulchral monument.

The simple example here given of what may be included in the humbler form of pictorial tiles consists of an effectively drawn stag and hound (Fig. 265f). It came from Lewes Priory and is now in the British Museum. In this class, unless it be considered perhaps as a badge or a symbol, is the unusually well-drawn and spirited lion rampant from Newnham Murren, Oxon (Fig. 266e).

The employment of tiles as a mural decoration is almost unknown, but some large architectural tiles of the 15th century are used as a reredos at Great Malvern, bearing the precise date of 1457-8.

About the earliest known pattern tiles extant in England are those of Castleacre, Norfolk, which are semi-Norman in date and quite rude in design and execution. Tiles of the Perpendicular period are of quite frequent occurrence, more especially in Worcestershire, as well as in the midland counties of Derby, Leicester and Nottingham. It is not generally known that between the years 1816 and 1821 four separate kilns were discovered in the town of Nottingham near George Street, where an immense quantity of tiles were discovered, and for the most part carelessly dispersed, of exactly the same type as the more celebrated later discovery at Repton.

The study of our English and Welsh ecclesiastical tiles had best be carried out in the Cathedral and Monastic church, where they have mostly been systematically investigated, but apart from these it may be pointed out that the present writer has personally noted their occurrence in 150 parish churches, and they probably yet remain, in small numbers, in about 250 all told, so that there is ample material, in almost every county, for the student interested in these remains.

About forty years ago, when a slight examination was made of the site of the quire of the once great church of Meaux Abbey, E.R., Yorks, four remarkable and beautiful tiles came to light. These were eventually presented to the present writer, who gave them to the Hull Museum. These varnished and enamelled tiles, termed *azulejos*, proved to be the work of Moors, who founded the kingdom of Granada in Spain in 1235, and held it till their final surrender in 1492. The Moorish potters, however, carried on their work in these tiles under their Christian masters for some thirty or forty years, to which period, c. 1500, these tiles belong. About this period these *azulejos*, or Spanish-Moresco tiles,

A. WEST HENDRED, BERKSHIRE. B. ROMSEY ABBEY, HANTS.
C. HAILES ABBEY, GLOS. D. MALVERN PRIORY, WORCS.
E. NEWNHAM MURREN, OXON. F. LEICESTER, CHAPEL OF THE
BEDEHOUSE.

FIG. 266. ENCAUSTIC TILES.

FIG. 267. GT. BIRCHAM, NORFOLK: LATE 15TH CENTURY EMBROIDERED COPE.

FIG. 268. GT. BIRCHAM, NORFOLK: DETAIL OF COPE.

reached England, and were possibly used as ballast in the vessels which brought wine to the ports of Bristol and Hull. They still remain in the Poyntz Chapel of St. Mark's Church, Bristol. One was found in the church of Haccombe, Devon, and there are several fragments in the church of Canons Ashby, Northants.*

With the destruction of the monasteries the English art of making encaustic tiles died out. Such tiles as are found in England of the 17th and 18th centuries came from abroad. A remarkable instance of this occurs in the costly chapel to Sir John Willoughby, erected in 1624 by the extension eastward of the south aisle of the church of Wilne, Derbyshire. The floor is paved with glazed tiles of bright colour, showing an effective rose pattern formed from four tiles.† This pavement was undoubtedly imported from the Netherlands. Most of the other occasional tiles of this and the following century are to be found in private houses.

The use of ornamental tiles for church floors was revived by a potter, J. Sheldon, near Stoke-on-Trent, in 1830. Messrs. Minton of that town bought up his patent in 1844; these tiles were largely and often tastelessly used in the earlier Gothic revivals of the Victorian era.

Students of the fascinating but much neglected study of our mediæval encaustic tiles will be glad of the following list of books and good articles of reference:—

Examples of Decorative Tiles sometimes termed Encaustic. By John Gough Nichols, 1845. With 100 plates engraved in facsimile.

Specimens of Tile Pavements. By Henry Shaw, 1830. Forty-seven plates.

Church Furniture and Decoration. By Rev. E. S. Cutts, 1854. Pp. 106-186.

Also various articles in the *Archæologia* and *Gentleman's Magazine*.

On Encaustic Tiles, a learned paper of 1867, by Revd. George Rowe, in *Associated Architects' Reports.*

The Ancient Encaustic Tiles of Worcestershire and *Four Notes on the Ancient Encaustic Tiles in Tewkesbury Abbey,* papers of 1888 and 1896 in the *Associated Architects' Reports,* by the late Canon Porter.

A general paper of much value on these tiles by Dr. Renaud in the ix vol. of the Lancashire and Cheshire Antiquarian Society.

But by far the best article yet written on this subject, admirably illustrated, is in vol. xiv (1892) of *Derbyshire Archæological Society's Journal,* by Mr. John Ward, pp. 119-140.

* See illustrated paper by Dr. Cox in vol. ii. of the *East Riding Antiq. Society.*
† Dr. Cox's *Notes on the Churches of Derbyshire,* vol. iv., pp. 403-4.

CHAPTER XX

VARIA

Dog Tongs.

VISITORS to Welsh and Scottish churches may have met with survivals of those curious implements, the dog-tongs, formerly used for ejecting disorderly dogs from the church during service. It seems extraordinary to our modern notions of seemliness that dogs should be brought within the precincts at all, but nevertheless they commonly attended with their masters even so late as the first half of the 19th century, certainly in Wales and Scotland, and probably in some of the more remote and mountainous parts of England. In the sheep-farming districts aforementioned the great sheep-dogs accompanied their masters everywhere, and it would have been considered most arbitrary and unfriendly for any incumbent to refuse to admit them to church, provided their conduct was moderately decent. But it is sadly apparent from evidence that the behaviour of the dogs was no more seemly in church than elsewhere, so that the office of expeller of disorderly dogs became a pressing necessity.

In an interesting article in the *Reliquary*, the late Rev. Elias Owen quotes a number of extracts from Welsh churchwardens' accounts of the 17th and 18th centuries which go to prove that the office was recognized and paid for by the church officials. Sometimes the remuneration is quite considerable, which would indicate that the office was no sinecure.

The actual implements of expulsion were powerful and effective weapons, to judge from the examples remaining. They are either of stout oak or of iron, but invariably they consist of bars crossed to form a lattice with handles and forceps, a fashion revived as a toy sold in the streets. The latter are occasionally provided with spikes, and this kind must have been cruel and painful, although in fairness to our ancestors we must add that the nuisance seems to have been considerable ; the sheep dog is a powerful animal and there are not wanting such evidences as teeth marks to show that the dogs often gave a good account of themselves before ejection ! Examples of dog tongs remain at Llaniestyn and Clynnog Fawr, Carnarvonshire

(Fig. 271); Llanynys, Denbighshire; Pemmyrydd, Anglesey; Cloddock, Herefordshire (Fig. 270); and at Bangor Cathedral.

In England it was not apparently the custom to bring dogs within the church, but presumably they strayed in occasionally, while waiting for their masters in the churchyard or the porch. At any rate individuals were appointed to chase them out and were provided with a whip for that purpose. The ancient dog-whip may still be seen at the church of Basford, Derbyshire, and at Youlgreave in the same county the dog-whipper's pew remained until 1868. References to payments made to dog-whippers are not infrequent in English churchwardens' accounts.

Embroidery.

During the Middle Ages the ecclesiastical embroidery of England was renowned throughout Christendom. Even in Anglo-Saxon times much beautiful needlework was produced, and from the 11th century to the close of the mediæval period, English work, known as "Opus Anglicanum" in contemporary records, was universally esteemed for its beauty and richness. The most beautiful and elaborate examples are naturally to be found in Cathedrals or Abbey Churches, and many of the finest specimens are to be found abroad, for in addition to the work commissioned by foreign dignitaries, a fair amount was sent abroad to avoid destruction at the time of the Reformation. A well-known instance of this is the celebrated Syon Cope. Originally belonging to the Monastery of Syon, near Isleworth, this masterpiece of needlework was taken abroad by the nuns at the Dissolution, and after many vicissitudes it was brought back to this country in 1830. Subsequently it was acquired for the nation and is now in the Victoria and Albert Museum, South Kensington. The cope, which dates from the end of the 15th century, is of linen, the ground entirely covered with em- broidery in gold, silver, and silks of many colours. The cope is patterned with interlacing quatrefoils, within which are beautifully executed figures of Apostles and Saints surrounding Our Lord seated upon a throne. The cope has suffered some little damage and remodelling, but is on the whole in a fairly good state of preservation.

The quantity of splendid embroidery possessed by our churches before the Spoliation must have been amazing indeed. It will be remembered that the priestly vestments—especially the cope and chasuble—were always of the finest materials richly embroidered; altar cloths and frontals were of silk or velvet embroidered with silver and gold, and every church boasted beautiful embroidered banners for processional use in festivals. An examination of mediæval wills and inventories proves that these things were common even to the humblest of village churches; and although a vast amount has been mutilated and converted to secular usage, and a great quantity totally destroyed, there is yet a far larger amount of ancient embroidery extant in churches than is commonly imagined.

It may not be out of place to indicate here a few of the characteristics of this "Opus Anglicanum." The work reached its greatest excellence in the years between 1270 and 1330; after that there is a distinct decline both in design and workmanship, although there is a revival towards the close of the 15th century. The work of the best period is distinguished by the great beauty of the figure work, generally Saints and Angels boldly embroidered on a ground often entirely worked over in gold thread. By the early 14th century the work is almost completely emancipated from the stiff conventionality of early art, the figures have dignity and grace and fit perfectly into the design of the whole, while the technique of the needlecraft is beyond criticism. The materials used are always of the finest, velvet being especially favoured, and great quantities of metal thread, always of pure gold or silver, were employed. A very favourite motif with the English embroiderers is the cherub mounted on a wheel; our illustration (Fig. 267) shows an instance. Architectural ornament—canopies, arcades, quatrefoils, crockets, etc.—was of course employed, and the vine trail foliage was as beloved of the needleworkers as of the wood and stone carvers. Two other forms occurring frequently are the lion mask and the leopard's head with protruding tongue.

Naturally our parish churches cannot show anything even approximating in splendour to the Syon cope, or some of the magnificent examples possessed by certain Italian and Spanish cathedrals. But many of the remains are nevertheless of very considerable beauty, although in the majority of cases the original design is somewhat injured by the conversion of the embroidery—if a vestment—from its intended use. At the church of Chipping Camden, in Gloucestershire, is a beautiful early 14th century cope which has been turned into an altar frontal. The orphreys are embroidered with a most unusual design, introducing angels mounted on horseback. There is also a very fine cope of embroidered red velvet at East Langdon, Kent; another at Skenfrith in Herefordshire, while other churches possessing notable embroideries include Littledean, Gloucestershire; Buckland, Worcestershire; Hullavington, Wiltshire; Wool, Dorsetshire; and Great Bircham, Norfolk (Figs. 267 and 268). At the latter church is an ancient cope of the 13th century, of crimson velvet, embroidered with a series of four-winged cherubims on wheels alternating with double-headed eagles. This cope now serves as an altar cloth. Fig. 248 shows an enlargement of the eagle motif.

The use of embroidery within churches died out with the Reformation and has only been revived of recent years. There are, however, a few instances of embroidered church hangings worked in the intervening period. A curious instance, not hitherto chronicled, occurs at Hedgerly, Bucks, where is an old piece of red velvet in a frame on the chancel wall. When visiting the church in 1873 we were assured that it was a portion of the cloak wherein Charles I suffered execution, and that it had been given to the church by a staunch royalist in 1660 to serve as an altar cloth. We fear that this story is a picturesque fable, for it can be easily proved that the king wore no such garb on the day of his beheading. Another story is that Charles II when visiting the church noticed that the Communion Table was destitute of covering, whereupon he took off his cloak of state and laid it thereon. This version is no more feasible than the earlier one; the probability is that this piece was executed for the church by some pious benefactor about the middle of the 17th century.

Acoustic Jars.

The ancient jars and vases that have been found, and are still occasionally being found, in different parts of our old English parish churches are now universally regarded, by experts in such matters, as placed there for the purpose of improving the resonance of the building. These so-called acoustic jars of our mediæval church buildings are but a reflection of an old classical custom. "It is certain," says Sir E. Beckett, "that the ancients had devices for improving the acoustics of large buildings, . . . for in the days of the past ancient theatres, such as the Coliseum of Rome, ten times as many people could hear as in our modern churches. They had a peculiar contrivance of horizontal pots along the seats, which are understood to have all generated the sound in the same way as a short and wide tube presented to a hemispherical bell when struck augments its sound."*

In addition to the large earthenware vessels discovered in the basement of the quire of Fountains Abbey and at two or three other large conventual churches, such things have come to light in similar positions in several of our parish churches. Especially is this the case at Norwich, where jars have been found beneath the quire stalls of the churches of All Saints, St. Peter Mancroft and St. Peter Parmentergate.†

* Book on *Building* (1880), 281.
† These jars are figured in *Norf. Arch.*, vol. vii.

These vessels have been found far more frequently embedded in the tops of chancel walls, and occasionally of nave walls, as at Lyddington, Rutland; Upton, Notts; Leeds, Kent; East Harling, Norfolk; Fairwell, Staffordshire; Denford, Northants; Rushton Tarrant, Dorset; Ashburton and Luppitt, Devon; St. Nicholas, Ipswich; St. Clement, Sandwich; St. Olave's, Chichester; as well as in two or three cases in Yorkshire village churches. Usually the jars are found lying on their sides, with mouths directed to the inside of the churches, partly covered by pieces of slate or plaster.

Horses' skulls have also sometimes turned up, obviously used with similar intent; thus in the bell turret of Elsdon, Northumberland, three skulls of horses were found in 1856, built into the masonry.

Confessionals and Low Side Windows.

It used to be the custom for the inspector of old churches to exercise his ingenuity in the discovery of apertures supposed to be suitable for penitents to breathe their confessions into the ears of the priest-confessor. Such holes or openings are all contradictory to the known facts about auricular confession in our own country in mediæval days, and are obviously absurd to those who nowadays make use of private confession, whether as penitents or confessors.

Compulsory auricular confession was established about the time of the Fourth Lateran Council of 1215. The Council of Durham laid down, in 1217, that the confessions of women were to be heard without the veil, openly (*in propatulo*), but none was to be overheard. A like ordinance was enjoined by the Synod of Exeter in 1287. The constitutions of Archbishop Reynold of Canterbury, 1322, ordered that the priest when about to hear confessions was to select some common place in the church, where he would be seen of all indifferently, and was not to be allowed to exercise that rite in any obscure place.

A wooden erection used to be pointed out at Tavistock as a confessional, and a curious chair at Bishop's Canning was known as a "confessional chair." A small chamber of stone in the Yorkshire church of Tanfield is still pointed out as a "confessional" (an illustration is given in Fig. 269). It is entered behind a pier on the north side of the chancel; it has on the east side three small lights, one above the other two; and on the south two small lights; it is of 15th century date, and has probably served as the base of the stairway to the rood loft, combined with a squint or squints as found in several Cornish churches.

The usual place for the priest to hear confessions, as is shown by various illuminations and woodcuts, was at the entrance of the chancel.

It used to be supposed that the small pierced openings in the panels of some rood screens, found in upwards of thirty churches,* were for the accommodation of penitents; but after testing the possibility of using them for this purpose, the impossibility of thus communicating with the priest has proved the complete fallacy of such a notion. The best surmise as to the use of these little pierced apertures in the bases of various screens is that they were made to enable kneeling folk to see the altar beyond, and more particularly the elevation of the Host; whilst the lower openings would serve for children.

There is little doubt that confessional boxes such as are now known throughout Western Christendom are of comparatively modern invention, and were utterly unknown in pre-Reformation England. The only thing which at first sight militates against this statement are certain entries which appear in a few churchwarden accounts of the close of the 15th century and throughout the first half of the succeeding century relative to shriving pews, which at first sight seem to point to what might be called confessional boxes. They chiefly occur in the parish accounts of the City of London, but are also found in early accounts of two or three churches in Cambridgeshire, Dorsetshire, Norfolk and Bristol.

Here are some of those of the city churches :—

1493-4.—(*St. Mary-at-Hill*). For a matte for the shryvyng pewe, iiij*d*.
1499-1500.—(*St. Andrew Hubbard*). For a matte for the Shryvyng pewe, 1*d*.
1511.—(*St. Margaret Patterne*). A clothe for Lent to hang before the Screvyng pewe, ——
1515.—Dressyng ye yrons of the shrevyng pew, 1*d*.
1548.—(*St. Michael, Cornhill*). To the joyner for takynge down the shryvyng pew & making another pew in the same place, iij*s*.

It is, however, highly unlikely that such entries as these indicate the use of pews as confessionals. It is far more probable that they refer to pews that were reserved for penitents waiting to take their turn to confess, especially during obligatory seasons such as Lent, preparatory to making their Easter Communion. Such a custom as this now prevails in many Catholic churches throughout Christendom.

Finally the supposition is still upheld by a few, including two antiquaries of repute, that the chief use of low side windows of our chancels was for the purpose of hearing confessions, the penitent outside the church and the confessor within. But this notion is to our mind hopelessly wrong. It requires us to believe that penitents some-

* See Cox and Harvey's *English Church Furniture*, 100.

times mounted a ladder to confess! Also the confessor would in most cases be altogether excluded from the sight of the people. Moreover, what position can be considered more awkward for the penitent than kneeling, in our ever wet climate, on the damp grass of the churchyard, frequently within a yard or two of the chief road through the village? Those who argue for the confessional use of these once shuttered windows usually show themselves ignorant of the usage of private confession. Thus one wiseacre, who had diligently studied every low-side window throughout an important Midland county, gives it as his opinion that the priest when hearing the confession of any very bad sinner directed him to confess from the outside of the church as an extra act of humility! It did not occur to this writer that the priest could not possibly know whether the sins were venial or deadly until after the confession was completed. The only basis for this extraordinary theory, which fairly bristles with difficulties, is a sentence in a letter from Thomas Bedyll, Clerk of the Council of Henry VIII, who, in a letter to Vicar-General Cromwell, wrote of walling up the place where friars were wont at certain times of the year to hear the outward confessions of all comers. To our mind it is a complete misconception to apply this sentence to parish churches; it only affected houses of friars.

This *questio vexata* among some ecclesiologists has given rise to a strange number of queer theories. The once popular leper theory is now rapidly dying out; the answer to this is very simple—lepers were forbidden to enter churchyards, and they had their own chapels and their own priests in every county. The lychnoscope idea has been recently given a fresh start by a speculative antiquary who has given them the name of "speculatories" for outside viewing of the sepulchre lights; this is a distinct absurdity, for the hinges of the shutters were on the east side and effectually shut out all view of either sepulchre or altar from the exterior. Whilst possibly the most untenable of all the theories is that of a northern antiquary who argues that they were to show forth lights to scare away evil spirits from the graves! One of half-a-dozen answers to this suggestion is that all outside windows are placed at angles where the light thrown on a graveyard is reduced to the greatest possible minimum; moreover, how would a light be kept burning when the shutter was opened?

The one explanation which it is difficult to controvert, and which has the support of most competent ecclesiologists, including the late Sir W. H. St. John Hope, is that these low side windows were for the ringing of a sanctus bell at the most solemn periods of the Mass by the altar-clerk to warn outsiders of the Holy Mysteries, before sanctus

Fig. 269. TANFIELD, YORKSHIRE: Stone "Confessional."

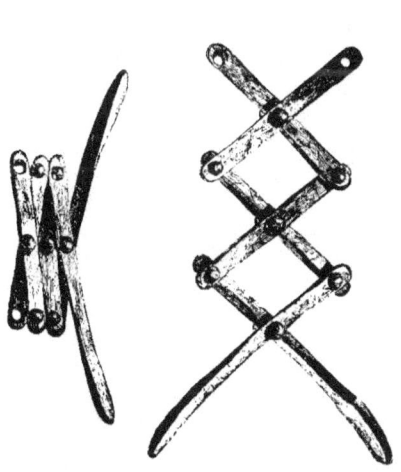

Fig. 270. CLODOCK, HEREFORDSHIRE: Wooden Dog Tongs, Closed and Extended.

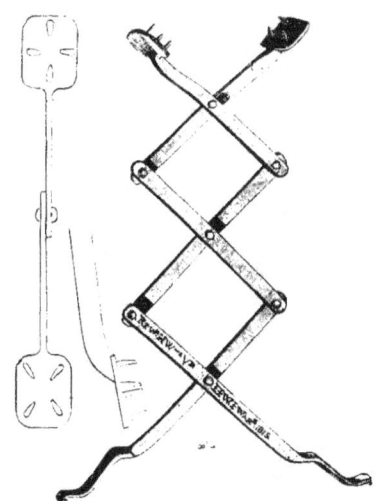

Fig. 271. CLYNNOG FAWR, CARNARVONSHIRE: Iron Dog Tongs.

Fig. 272. MINSTERLEY CHURCH, SHROPSHIRE.

Fig. 273. ABBOTTS ANN, HANTS.

Fig. 274. ILAM, STAFFORDSHIRE.

MAIDENS' FUNERAL GARLANDS.

bell-cotes on the nave gable came into use. Many pages could be written in support of this reasonable theory from various aspects.*

BIERS AND COFFINS.

During the mediæval period it was customary to bury the humbler folk without a permanent coffin, and this custom lingered on until the dawn of the 18th century. The body was carefully shrouded and deposited within a common lidless coffin, wherein it was conveyed to the graveside on the common or parish bier. The body was then placed in the grave simply wrapped in the shroud.

Burial in a coffin which remained in the grave was looked upon as a luxury, and usually incurred an additional fee. In a "Table of Dutyes," drawn up in 1664 for Shoreditch, London, it is stated that:

> For a burial in ye new churchyard without a coffin, eight pence.
> For a burial in ye olde churchyard without a coffin, seven pence.
> For the gravemaking and attendance of Vicar and Clerke, on ye interment of a corps uncoffined, the churchwardens to pay the ordinary duteys and no more of this table.

There are several like entries of burial fees for the uncoffined throughout the 17th century.

In Mr. White Watson's, of Bakewell, *Common Place Book*, beginning in May, 1774, is the following quaint entry:

> The custom of Interment in Wooden coffins (wooden Josephs) was on the Revd. Mr. Monks coming to reside here. A corpse from Sheldon was brought here in swaddling clothes (which was abolished in 1797) and was detained in the Church until a coffin was made, and the wife then took off the flannel for her own use.†

The wording of the burial service in the Book of Common Prayer clearly expects uncoffined interment. The word coffin is not mentioned, it is always the "corpse" or the "body," as in the rubric, "the earth shall be cast upon the body." Wheatley's work on the Common Prayer, first printed in 1710, says: "When the body is stripped of all but its grave-clothes, and is just going to be put into the grave," etc.

References to parish coffins are by no means infrequent in early churchwardens' accounts, such as Louth, in 1521. The larger parishes usually provided one or more shells or coffins for placing on the biers.‡

---

* See *The English Parish Church*, pp. 106-7. The present writer has given much space to this matter in various books during the last quarter of a century; he was editor of the *Antiquary* in 1892, where a "Conference" appeared on this subject, vol. xvi., pp. 327-9, wherein Mr. C. E. Ponting, F.S.A., argued strongly for the hand bell-ringing use.

† *Derb. Arch. Journ.*, vol. xi. (1889), 159. The local name of "Wooden Joseph" for a coffin was obviously taken from the last verse of the Book of Genesis.

‡ See Dr. Cox's *Parish Registers* (1910), 121-2; and *Churchwardens' Accounts* (1913), 172-3.

E.C.

The following are among entries relative to such coffins in the accounts of London churches:

1501.—(*St. Margaret's, Westminster*). For a new bere and a coffyn for chyldren, vis. viiid.
    For mending of the olde beres, three in number, each with its own coffin, iiid.
1554.—(*St. Michael, Cornhill*). For mendynge of the coffin that carrys the corses to the churche, xiid.
1568.—(*St. Michael, Friday Street*). For ii coffyns bought to carry corses to the church, vs. viiid.

There are remains of an old parish coffin in the room over the south porch of the fine old church of Howden, E.R., Yorks. In the tower of Easingwold Church, N.R., Yorks, is an old parish coffin with a lid, of early 17th century date. The present writer remembers, in the days of his youth, the remains of two parish coffins amid lumber in the tower of Porlock Church, West Somerset.

There are at least a dozen instances of 17th century parish biers of oak, mostly with jointed handles, as at Bledington, Gloucestershire. In two or three cases they are still in use. The example at Weston-on-Trent, Derbyshire, is precisely dated 4th November, 1653. The oak bier in Broughton Church, Bucks, is also dated 1653. In the ancient historic church of Lastingham, N.R., Yorks, the bier is claimed to be of pre-Reformation date, and the six circular holes bored in the top of the carrying poles on each side are supposed to have been for tapers. But the latter suggestion is improbable; they were more likely for circular supports for the pall.

In post-Reformation days, when the coffin was brought into the church, it was usually supported at the east end of the nave on low coffin-stools. These were usually, in Jacobean and Carolean days, well-turned pieces of carpentry, and they have often found their way into curiosity shops, and hence readily enough into the drawing-rooms of ladies, who would be shocked if they knew that they were asking their friends to have afternoon tea off a coffin-stool. These pairs of coffin-stools are still fairly often to be seen in parish churches, but are rarely, if ever, reserved for their proper occasional use. We have noted them, or a single one, in the Notts churches of Bole, West Drayton, Eakring, Granby, Kilham, Langar, North Muskham, Shelton, and Sutton-on-Trent. At Great Broxted, Essex, a pair of these stools have lately been utilised after a strange and unseemly fashion; one serves for a litany foldstool and the other has had its legs raised to supply the place of a credence-table. At Upper Snell, Gloucestershire, one of a pair of these stools serves, inappropriately, as a seat for the harmonium player, and the like is the case with another one in the church of Carisbrooke, Isle of Wight, as well as in the tiny Somerset church of

Culbone. The good pair that once stood in the fine old church of Branscombe, south-east Devon, have now found their way into the lobby of the village inn.

Maidens' Funeral Garlands.

An old and picturesque custom once widely prevalent in England was the bearing of a garland of real or imitation flowers in the funeral procession of a maiden. These garlands were afterwards suspended in the church, usually over the empty seat of the departed girl. This was doubtless done in remembrance of " The radiant coronet prepared for virgin souls," about which Keble sings on the Wednesday before Easter in the *Christian Year*; an idea as to which there were several pretty legends of the virgin saints current in mediæval times.

This custom did not, however, meet with universal approval. For instance, good Bishop Wren of Ely inquired in 1662, at his visitation:

> Are any mean toys or childish gewgaws, such as the fonder sort of people prepared at some burials, suffered to be fastened up in your church at any one's pleasure? or any Garlands and other ordinary funeral ensigns to hang where they hinder the prospect, or until they grow foul and dusty, withered and rotten?

The suspension of such garlands in churches lingered longest in Derbyshire. The following notes were chiefly taken in the seventies of last century, but are in many cases supported by much later visits.*

At Ashford-in-the-Water five of these garlands still hang within the church. They are all constructed of white paper cunningly cut into flowers, rosettes, and other designs, whilst within each hangs a single glove, a collar, or kerchief. On the glove or collar of each has been written a verse of poetry, together with the name, age, and date of the death of the virgin commemorated. These writings are now wholly illegible, but in 1874 I managed, after considerable difficulty, to decipher the date of April 12th, 1717, on one, and the name of Anne Howard, who died at the age of 21, whilst a third of much later date bore the following :—

> Be always ready, no time delay,
> I in my youth was called away
> Great grief to those that's left behind.
> But I hope I'm great joy to find.
>   Ann Swindel.
>   Aged 23 years.
>   Dec. 9th 1798.

In the vestry of the old church of Matlock there still hang, I believe, six of these white paper garlands; there used to be eight, but that omnivorous collector and despoiler of churches, the late Mr. Bateman,

* See Dr. Cox's *Churches of Derbyshire*, i, 21, 440-5; ii., 51, 521; iii., 302, 340; iv., 532.

was suffered to remove two to his museum at Lomberdale House, where I once saw them hanging. In South Wingfield there yet hangs (or hung) a single garland, in its original position, commemorating the sad end of Ann Kendall of the Peacock Inn, who died on May 14th, 1715. At Trusley I used to see a solitary survivor of these garlands, but I could not detect it on a visit in the present century. I have talked with old people who had vivid recollection of these garlands hanging in the churches of Ashover from the chancel screen (up to 1843), Alvaston, Bolsover, Eyam, Fairfield, Glossop, Heanor, Hope, Tissington, and West Hallam. At the last of these churches my informant remembered at least thirty hanging from the piers. At Heanor they were very numerous, but they disappeared during a vigorous cleaning to signalise the advent of a new incumbent.

Anna Seward, writing a poem in honour of the romantic village of Eyam, about the beginning of last century, said :

> The gloves suspended by the garland's side,
> White as its snowy flowers with ribands tied,
> Dear village ! long these wreaths funereal spread,
> Simple memorial of the early dead.

But the best surviving examples of these expressive tokens of the virgin life are to be seen in the Shropshire church of Minsterley (*see* Fig. 272). Projecting from the north and south walls of the nave are a number of short vine rods, capped by small escutcheons, to all of which maidens' garlands were once attached. Seven of them remain, recently removed to the gallery over the west entrance. They are of considerable size, as each of them is over a foot in length. They vary in date from 1726 to 1794. The framework has been covered with linen on which are fastened roses of white and pink paper, and within are hung pairs of white paper gloves, whilst from the bottom depend short streamers of blue and white paper.

At Acton Burnell and at Astley Abbots, in the same county, there are also single garlands ; at the latter church it is dated 1709.

Amongst other places where I have personally noted single examples of these paper garlands may be mentioned Alfriston, Sussex, and Alne, N.R., Yorks. In the former case an old man assured me that he could remember at least fifty hanging in the church when he was a youngster. At Alne the garland is deposited in a niche to the north of the chancel arch. Examples remain also, or did at least until recently, at Abbotts Ann in Hampshire and at Ilam, Staffs (*see* Figs. 273 and 274).

INDEX

The figures in black type indicate the page number on which an illustration is to be found.

A.

Abbot's Langley, Herts., 170
Abbotts Ann, Hants: Maidens' Garlands, **302**, 306
Abbey Dore, Hereford: Jacobean Pulpit, **124**, 128
—— —— Screen, 148
—— —— Stone Altar, 245
Aberedw, Radnor, 239
Abingdon St. Helen, 229
—— St. Nicholas, 275
Acton, Cheshire: Altar Rails, 225, **257**
—— —— Screen, 148
—— Burnell, Salop, 306
Adderley, Cheshire: Organ, 234, **236**
Aldbrough, Yorks: Effigy in Churchyard, 31
Aldermaston, Berks, 200
Aldwinckle St. Peter, Northants: Stained Glass, **201**, 203
Alfriston, Sussex, 306
Allen, Romilly, 231
Almondbury, N.R. Yorks: Glass in Kaye Chapel, 206, **208**
Alne, Yorks, 306
Altars, Ancient Stone, 18
Alvaston, Derby, 306
Archæologia Cantiana, 14
Archery in Churchyards, 41
Arderne, Sir Thomas and Lady, **55**, 58
Arksey, Yorks: Font Cover, **96**, 99
Armour in Effigies, **52**, **55**, **56**, 57-60
Arundel, Sussex: Mural Painting, 213
—— —— Tomb, **64**, 66
Ashbocking, Suffolk, 167
Ashburton, Devon, 36, 298
Ashby-de-la-Zouch, Leicester, 260
Ashby St. Ledgers, Northants: Screen, 143

Ashford-in-the-Water, Derby, 305
Ashington, Somerset: Bell Turret, **84**
Ashover, Derby: Font, 88, **89**
—— —— Maidens' Garlands, 306
Astbury, Cheshire, *Frontispiece*, 8
—— —— Lectern, **129**, 131
Astley Abbots, Salop, 306
Atherington, Devon: Roodloft, 144, **145**
Attleborough, Norfolk: Roodloft, 144, 147
Awliscombe, Devon: Screen, 133
Axbridge, Devon: 214
Aylestone, Leicester, 282
Aylmerton, Norfolk, 169
Aymestrey, Hereford: Screen, 143
Azulejos (Spanish Moresque Tiles), 287, 290, 293

B.

Badderley, Cheshire, 170, **175**
Badley, Leicester, 223
Bakewell, Derbyshire: Cross 29
—— Pre-Norman Tomb, **46**, 48
—— Robert Smith, 158, 163
Ball Games in Churchyards, 42
Banwell, Somerset: Pulpit, 121
Bardolph, Sir William Phelipp, Lord and Lady: Effigies, 58
Barrington, Cambs, 274
Barton Bendish, Norfolk, 266
Barton Turf, Norfolk: Screen, 138
Basford, Derbyshire, 295
Basingstoke, Hants, 166
Bass Fiddle, 241, **243**
Bassoon, 240, 241, **243**
Bawburgh, Norfolk, 203
Beauchamp, Richard, Earl of Warwick: Tomb, 66
Beckenham, Kent: Lychgate, 14, 24, **27**

Beckington, Wilts, 166
Bedfont, Middlesex: Churchyard Yews, 38
—— —— Painting of "Doom," 214
Belper, Derby, 245
Bengeworth, Glos, 170
Beresford, Thomas and Wife: Effigies, 60
Bethell, Slingsby, Lord Mayor (1755) 158
Bibles in Churches, 195
Bickington, Devon: "Church House," 26
Binfield, Berks, 187
Binsted, Sussex, 274
"Bishop's Bible," 187
Bishop's Lydeard, Somerset: Benches, 110, **111**
—— —— Churchyard Cross, **28**, 30
Bitton, Glos: Tiles, **286**, 289
Bledington, Glos, 304
Bletchingley, Surrey: Clayton Monument, 68
Blisland, Cornwall, 167
Blithfield, Staffs, 203
Bloxham: *Companion to Gothic Architecture*, 31, 223
Blyford, Suffolk: Holy Table, 245, **247**
Blyth, Notts: Sepulchral Slab, 53
Blythburgh, Suffolk: Alms Box, 281, **284**
—— —— Striking Jack, 181, **185**
Boldre, Hants: Maple in Churchyard, 36
Bolsover, Derby, 306
Bolting, John: Slab, 163
Bolton-le-Moors, Lancs, 197
Bottisham, Cambs: Screen, 133
Boughton, Lincs, 222
Bradbourne, Derbyshire: Cross, 29
Bradbrook, Northants, 239
Brading, I. of W., 280
Bramfield, Suffolk: Screen, 137, **140**, **142**
Bramford, Suffolk: Poor Box, 282
—— —— Stone Screen, 133, **135**
Brancepeth, Durham: Post-Reformation Screen, 148
Branscombe, Devon: Altar Rails, 255, **257**
—— —— Coffin Stools, 305

Brasses, **72**, 73–75
Bray, Berkshire: Churchyard approach, 26
Breadsall, Derbyshire, 196
Brent, Sir Nathaniel, 250
Brett Collection of Armour, 164
Brightlingsea, Essex, 223
Brigstock, Northants, 131
Brilley, Hereford, 163
Brimpton, Somerset: Screen, 133
Bristol, Christchurch: Sword Rests, 158, **162**
—— St. John Baptist: Sand Glass, 187, **189**
—— St. Mary Redcliffe: Canynges Effigies, **56**, 59
—— —— Library, 193
—— St. Nicholas: Iron Screen, 158, **160**
—— St. Philip's: Sword Rests, 158, **162**
—— Temple Church: Candelabra, 220, 224, **225**
—— —— Royal Arms, 167, **173**
British Museum, 290
Broadfield, Somerset: Churchyard Cross, 30
Broughton, Bucks, 304
—— Oxon: Screen, 133
Buckland, Glos: Table Tomb, 31
Bunbury, Cheshire: Iron Grille, **154**, 155
—— —— Musical Instruments, 240, 241
Burgh, Lincs: Finial to Font Cover, **94**, 99
—— —— Pulpit, 128
Burlingham St. Andrew, Norfolk, 279
—— St. Edmund, Norfolk, 213
Burnham Norton, Norfolk: Pulpit, **123**, 127
—— —— Screen, 138
Burpham, Sussex, 275
Burstwick, E.R. Yorks: Royal Arms, 167
Burwash, Sussex: Iron Slab, 163
Bury, Hunts: Desk Lectern, **130**, 132
—— St. Edmunds, St. James, 205
Butterwick, Lincs: Sycamore in Churchyard, 35

C.

Cambridge, Great St. Mary's: Cartouche Cover, **96**, 99, 100
—— St. Botolph: Font Tablet, **71**, 73
Campsall, Yorks: Seating, **101**, 103
Canons Ashby, Northants, 177, 293
Canopied Tombs, 60, **61**, 65
Canterbury Cathedral: Mural Painting, 212
—— Stained Glass, 13, 199, 200
Canynge Effigies, Bristol, **56**, 59
Carey, Lady Elizabeth: Tomb, **65**, 67
Carisbrooke, I. of W., 304
Cartmel, Lancs: Library, 197
Cartmell Fell, Lancs: Rood Fragment, 147
Cartouche Tablets, **71**, 73
Castleacre, Norfolk, 290
Catlyn, John, 167
Cave Family Hatchments, 177
Cawston, Norfolk: Alms Box, 281
—— —— Benches, 109
—— —— Screen, 138
Chaldon, Surrey, 212
Chalfont St. Giles, Bucks: Churchyard Approach, 26
Chalice and Paten, 256, **258**
Change Ringing, 86
Chapel-en-le-Frith, Derby: Cockpit in Churchyard, 43
Charing, Kent, 239
Charlton-on-Otmore, Oxon: Screen, **4**, 13
Charlton, Wilts: Stone Screen, 133
Chartres, 199
Cheam, Surrey: Cartouche, **71**, 73
Cheddar, Somerset: Pulpit, 127
—— —— Stained Glass, 206, **207**
Chediston, Suffolk: Pulpit, 128
Chelmorton, Derby: Screen, 133
Cherry Hinton, Cambs: Piscina, **263**, 266
Cheshunt, Herts, 279
Chester, St. John's: Warburton Chapel Screen, **156**, 157
Chetham, Humphrey, 198
Chichester, St. Olave, Sussex, 298
Chiddingstone, Kent: Iron Slab, 163

Chilthorn, Somerset: Bell Turret, **84**
Chilton Trinity, Somerset: Churchyard Cross, 30
Chipping Camden, Glos, 296
Chipping Norton, Oxon, 223
Chirbury, Salop: Chained Library, 197
Cholmondeley, Cheshire: Screen, 148, **151**
Church Brampton, Northants, 279
—— Broughton, Derbyshire: Bassoon, 240, **243**
—— —— Chest, 279
—— Marks, 38, 41
Churchyard Tombs, 30–35, **33**, **34**
Clapton-in-Gordano, Somerset: Seating, **106**, 109
Clarinet, 241, 242
Claughton St. Chad, Lancs: Dated Bell, 78
Claverley, Salop: Mural Painting, 213, **217**
Clayton, Sussex: Mural Painting, 213, **217**.
—— Sir Robert and Lady: Tomb, 68
Cleve, Somerset: Bell Tower, **84**
Cleveley, Cambs, 276
Cley, Norfolk, 274
Climping, Sussex, 275
Cloddock, Hereford: Dog Tongs, 295, **301**
Clun, Salop: Bells and Belfry, 80 82
—— —— Lychgate, 25, **27**
Clynnog Fawr, Carnarvon: Dog Tongs, 294, **301**
Cobham, Kent: Brasses, **72**, 74, 75
Cock-fighting in Churchyards, 43, 44
"Coffin Lids," 31. (*See also Incised Slabs.*)
Coffin Stools, 304
Coke Hatchments, Trusley Church, 177
Colchester St. Martin's, 279
Cold Ashby, Northants: Dated Bell, 78
Coleridge, Devon: Pulpit, 122, 127
Coline, Thomas: Slab, 163
Collumpton, Devon: Rood Fragment, 147
Combe Martin, Devon: Royal Arms, 169

Comboyne, Devon, 170
Commandments, Creed, etc.: Tablets, 169, 170, **174-176**
Compton Bassett, Wilts: Sandglass, 187, **189**
—— —— —— Stone Screen, 133, **135**
—— Family Hatchments, 178
—— Wynyates, Warwick, 177
Cooksey, Suffolk, 128
Copdock, Suffolk: Font Cover, **95**, 99
Copford, Essex: Mural Painting, 213, **217**
Cotes-by-Stow, Lincs: Roodloft, **142**, 147
Cound, Salop, 279
Courtenay, Bishop, 184
Cowden, Kent: Iron Slab, 163
Cowfold, Sussex: Church Marks, 41, 222
Cranbrook, Kent: Georgian Royal Arms, 168, **172**
Crediton, Devon: Armour, 165, **171**
Croscombe, Somerset: Chest, 279, **283**
Crosses in Churchyards, 14, 26, 29, 30, **7, 9, 28**
Croughton, Northants: Churchyard Elm, 35
Crowhurst, Surrey: Churchyard Yew, 38, **45**
—— Sussex: Churchyard Yew, 38
—— —— Iron Slab, 163
Croxton, Lincs, 268
Culbone, Somerset, 305
Cumberland, Neglect of Churches in, 43, 250
Curry Rivell, Somerset, 110, **111**
Cuxton, Glos, **286**, 289

D.

Dance, George, 185
Darley Dale, Derbyshire: Churchyard Tombs, 32, **34**
—— —— Effigies, 53, 54
—— —— Yew Tree, 37
Dartmouth, Devon: Pulpit, 127
D'Aubernoun, Sir John: Brass, 57, 74
Dearham, Cumberland, **231**
Denbigh, St. Marcella: Altar Rails, 250, **253**

Denford, Northants, 298
Dennington, Suffolk: Effigies, 58
—— —— Parclose Screen, **141**, 143
Derby, All Saints: Library, 194, 195
—— —— Pulpit, 128, 131
—— —— Wrought Iron Screens, 163
—— —— Wooden Effigy, 66
Devizes, St. Mary, 169, 187
Doddington, Kent: Sedilia, 19
Dodford, Northants: Keynes Effigy, **52**, 54, 56
Donchester Abbey, Oxon, 32, 199, 205, **209**
"Doom," Paintings of, 214, **218**
Dovebridge, Derbyshire: Churchyard Yew, 37
Dover, St. Mary's, 169
Dovercourt, Essex, 282
Drayton, Berks: Almery, 274
—— —— Reredos, **244**, 246, 249
Dronfield, Derbyshire, 256, **258**
Dryden Family Hatchments, 177
Dunchideock, Devon: Screen, **136**, 137
Dundon Compton, Somerset: Screen, 133
Dunsfold, Surrey: Seating, 109
Dunster, Somerset: Churchyard Cross, 30
Durham, St. Oswald's: Incised Slab, 49, **51**
—— —— Wall Almery, 274
Dyserth, Flintshire, 205

E.

Earl Stonham, Suffolk: Sand Glasses, 188, **190**
East Allington, Devon: Pulpit, 122
—— Bridgeford, Notts, 203
—— Harling, Norfolk, 298
—— Kirkby, Lincolnshire.
—— Langdon, Kent, 296
—— Leake, Notts, 223, 239
Eaton Bray, Beds: Font, 88, **92**
Eckington, Worcs, 276
Ecklington, Suffolk, 279
Edenbridge, Kent, 200
Edington, Wilts: Roodloft, 147
Edlaston, Derbyshire, 158
Edlesborough, Bucks: Misericord, 104, **106**

INDEX

Edlesborough, Bucks: Pulpit and Tester, **120**, 127
Edney, William, Smith, 158
Effigies, **52**, 53, 54, **55**, **56**, 57, 58, 59, 60, **62**, **63**, **64**, 65–68, **69**
Egerton, Sir Ralph, 154
Eglinham, Northumberland, 274
Elford, Staffs: Arderne Effigies, **56**, 58
Ellingham, Hants: Painted Tablets, 169, **174**
Elmstead, Essex: Wooden Effigy, **63**, 66
Elsdon, Northumberland, 298
Elsing, Norfolk, 203
Ely, Bishop Alcock's Chapel, 157
——— Bishop West's Chapel, **156**, 157
——— Prior Crauden's Chapel, 289
Emneth, Norfolk: Bell Turret, **84**, 86
Enstone, Oxon: Altar, **244**, 245
Erdeswike, Hugh and Cecile: Effigies, 54
Ewelme, Oxon: Font and Cover, 8, **21**, 99
——— ——— Tomb of Alice Chaucer, Duchess of Suffolk, 65
Exeter, Cathedral Clock, 183-184, **186**
——— St. Mary Steps: Clock, 181, **185**
——— St. Petrock, 148
Eyham, Derby: Pre-Norman Cross, 29
——— ——— Maidens' Garlands, 306
Eye, Suffolk: Roodloft, 147
——— ——— Screen, **16**, 138, **140**

F.

Faceless Clocks, 182
Fairfield, Derby, 306
Fairford, Glos: Parclose Screen, **141**, 143
——— ——— Stained Glass, 203
Fairs in Churchyards, 25
Fairwell, Staffs, 298
Faringdon, Hants: Churchyard Yew, 37
Farleigh, Hungerford, Somerset: Gates, 157, **159**
——— ——— Tombs, 66
Farndon, Cheshire, 240, 241

Farningham, Kent: "Seven Sacraments Font," 19
Faversham, Kent: Archer's Loophole, 18
Fenny Bentley, Derbyshire: Beresford Effigies, 60
Fettiplace Effigies, Swinbrook, 59, **69**
Fiennes, Thomas, Lord Dacre, 273
Filey, Yorks, 267
Finningham, Suffolk: Font Cover, **95**, 99
Fishlake, Yorks: Screen, 143, **146**
Fishtoft, Lincs, 275
Fitzherbert, Sir Ralph and Lady Effigies, 58, 59
Flamborough, E.R. Yorks.: Roodloft, 144, **149**
Fledborough, Notts, 203
Flintham, Notts, 279
Floore, Northants, 274
Folkestone, Kent: Churchyard Steps, 14
Folkestone, Kent: Tomb, **10**, 17
Forster, Anne: Slab, 163
Foxe's Book of Martyrs, 196
Framlingham, Suffolk: Howard Effigies, 60, **62**
——— ——— Organ Case, 234, 236
Frodsham, Cheshire: Chest, 279, **283**
Fryer, Dr. Alfred C., 231
Furneaux Pelham, Herts, 168, 274, 279

G.

Games and Sports in Churchyards, 41-44.
Garrett Ironworks, 163
Garsington, Oxon: Lychgate, 25
Gateley, Norfolk, 169
Gedling, Notts, 229
Gibbs, James, 131, 163
Giggleswick, Yorks: Bass Fiddle, 241, **243**
——— ——— Poor Box, 282, **285**
——— ——— Royal Arms, 168
Godmanchester, Hunts: Headstone, 32, **40**
Glastonbury Abbey, 183
Glossop, Derby, 306
Grantham, Lincs: Chained Library, **191**, 197

Great Bardfield, Essex : Screen, 133
—— Bircham, Norfolk : Ancient Cope, **292**, 296
—— Brington, Northants : Armour, 165, **171**
—— —— —— Hatchments, 177
—— —— —— Spencer Tomb, **61**, 65
—— Broxted, Essex, 304
—— Budworth, Cheshire : Stalls, **102**, 103
—— Chalfield, Wilts : Screen, 133
—— Gonerby, Lincs, 203
—— Gransden, Hunts : Piscina, **263**, 266
—— Malvern, Worcs : Tiles, 287, 289, 290, **291**
Greens Norton, Northants, 166
Grisaille Glass, 200, **201**, 205, 206
Grundisburgh, Suffolk : Bench End, **108**, 110
—— —— Screen, **5**
Guildford, Surrey Archæological Museum, 240, **243**

H.

Haccombe, Devon, 293
Hadley, Herts : Cresset in Tower, 78
Hailes Abbey, Glos : Heraldic Tiles, 289, **291**
Hallow, Hatchment to Mrs., **179**
Halston, Salop, 223
Haltham, Lincs, 169
Halton, Lancs : Pre-Norman Cross, 29
Hambledon, Bucks, 274
Hampstead, St. John's, 260
Handborough, Oxon : Screen, 13
Harberton, Devon : Pulpit, 122
Harbledown, Kent, 200
Hardham, Sussex, 212
Hardwick, Glos : Heraldic Tiles, **286**, 289
Harefield, Middlesex : Reredos, 249, **254**
Hargrave, Northants, 282
Harlton, Cambs : Screen, 133
Harptree, Somerset : Churchyard Cross, 30
Harrington, Northants, 239
Harris, Renatus, 234

Hartfield, Sussex : Churchyard Approach, 26
Hartshorne, Derby, 241
Harty, Sheppey : Coffer, 20, **15**
Hastings, All Saints. 223
Hatfield, W.R. Yorks, 276, **278**
Hautboys, 241, 242
Hawstead, Suffolk : Lectern, **12**, 19
Hawton, Notts : Easter Sepulchre, 268, **272**
Hayes, Kent : Lychgate, 24
Hayfield, Derbyshire, 240, 241
Headstones, 32, **39**, **40**
—— Wooden, 35, **34**
Heanor, Derby, 306
Heckfield, Hants, 279
Heckington, Lincs : Easter Sepulchre, 268, **271**
Hedgerley, Bucks, 297
Helmingham, Suffolk : Tollemache Effigies, 67, 68
Helpringham, Lincs, 223
Hemel Hempstead, Herts, 279
Heraldic Glass, **202**, 206
Hereford, All Saints : Bread Shelves, 275, **277**
—— —— Jacobean Pulpit, 127
—— —— Library, **192**, 197
—— Cathedral Library, 197
Herse, **64**, 65, 66
Heston, Kent : Lychgate, 24
Hexham, Northumberland : Roodloft, 147
Heydour, Lincs, 203
Higham Ferrers, Northants : Misericord, 104, **106**
Hilmarton, Wilts : Screen, 133
Hilyard, Sir Christopher : Effigy, 59, **62**
Hitchin, St. Mary, Herts : Screen, 143, **146**
Holcombe Rogus, Devon : Bluett Pew, **113**, 115
Holdenby, Northants, 177
Hollingbourne, Kent : Embroidery, 20
Holme, Norfolk, **30**
Homilies, Books of, 196
Hope, Derbyshire : Incised Slabs, 50
—— —— Maidens' Garlands, 306
Horsmonden, Kent : Candelabra, **226**, 229
Howden, E.R. Yorks, 304

INDEX

Hubberholme, W.R. Yorks: Rood-loft, 144
Hugutin's Vocabularium, 194
Hull, Holy Trinity: Font, 11, 19
—— —— Ledger Stones, 70, 73
Hullavington, Wilts, 296
Hungerford, Sir Thomas and Wife: Tomb, 66
Hursley, Hants, 282
Hurst, Berks, 187
Huttoft, Lincs, 278, 279

I.

Ightham, Kent, 229, 275
Ilam, Staffs: Maidens' Garlands, 302, 306
Ilkeston, Derby: Screen, 133
Incised Effigies, 53, 54
Incised Slabs, 48, 49, 50, 51, 52, 53. See also *Coffin Lids*.
Insula, Sir Gerard de: Effigy, 52, 57
Ipplepen, Devon, 260
Ipswich, St. Nicholas, Suffolk, 298
—— St. Peter: Tournai Font, 11, 19
Iron Slabs, 163

J.

Jesse, Tree of, 204, 205, 209
Jewel's Defence of the Apology, 195
Jocelin of Brakelond, 281
Johnson, Abraham, 234
Johnston, P. M., 35, 212
Jones, E. A.: *Church Plate of Carnarvonshire*, 256

K.

Kedington, Sussex: Pew, 113, 115
Kedleston, Derbyshire: Incised Slab, 49
Kellington, Yorkshire: Churchyard Tomb, 31
—— —— Lychgate, 24
Kelmscott, Oxon: Bell Turret, 83
Kelston, Somerset: Pre-Norman Cross, 30
Kensey, Cornwall: Cresset Stone, 228, 231
Kenton, Devon: Pulpit, 119, 122
—— —— Screen, 138, 139
Kewstoke, Somerset: Pulpit, 122

Keynes, Sir Robert de: Effigy, 52, 54, 56
Keynsham, Somerset: Royal Arms, 167, 172
Keyser: *Mural Paintings*, 221
Keysoe, Beds: Inscription on Font, 97
Kingerby, Lincs, 203
Kingsclere, Hants, 229
King's Nympton, Devon: "Bowling Green," 44
Kingsthorpe, Northants, 274, 275
Kingston, I. of W., 240
—— Somerset, 279
Kirk Sandall, Yorks: Screen, 143
Kirkstead, Lincolnshire: Bell, 80, 83
Knotting, Beds: Cockfighting in Church, 43

L.

Laleston, Glam: Cross, 9, 14
Lanchester, Co. Durham, 199
Laneast, Cornwall, 204
Langdon, A. G., F.S.A., 231
Lanhydrock, Cornwall, 167
Lanteglos-by-Fowey, Cornwall, 169, 204
Lastingham, Yorks, 304
Laud, Archbishop, Visitation, 250
Launcells, Cornwall: Bench-ends, 110
Laxfield, Suffolk: Font, 93, 97
Lead Fonts, 9, 87, 88, 91
Lecterns, 19
Ledger Stones, 68, 70, 73
Lee, Bucks, 200
Leeds, Kent, 298
Leicester, Chapel of the Bedehouse: Tiles, 289, 291
—— St. Martin's, 169
—— St. Mary's, 267
Leiston, Suffolk: Iron Headstones, 163
Lenham, Kent: Lychgate, 25
"Leper Windows," 299-300
Lessingham, Norfolk: Screen, 138
Lettering on Bells, 79, 81
—— on Headstones, 32, 40
Leverington, Cambs, 205
Lewannick, Cornwall: Cresset Stone, 228, 231

Lewes Priory, Tile from, **286**, 290
Lew Trenchard, Devon, 229
Leyland, Lancs: Chalice, 20
Lightfoot, Peter, 183
Lincoln Minster: Stained Glass, 199, 200
Lingfield, Surrey, 229, 290
Little Casterton, Rutland, 266
Littledean, Glos, 296
Little Marlow, Bucks: Tiles, **286**, 288
Llananno: Roodloft, 144
Llanarmon-yn-Ial, Denbigh, 224
Llandegla, Denbigh, 224
Llandudwen, Carnarvon: Chalice, 256, **258**
Llanegryn: Roodloft, 144, **149**
Llanelian, Denbigh, 256
Llaniestyn, Carnarvon, 294
Llanmaes, Glamorgan, 256
Llanrhaidr, Denbigh, 205
Llanrwst: Roodloft, 144
Llanwnog: Roodloft, 144
Llanynys, Denbigh, 295
Local Types in Church Architecture, 13
Loddon, Norfolk, 282
London, All Hallows, Barking: Sword Rests, 158, **162**
—— —— —— Organ, 234
—— —— Lombard Street: Bread Shelves, 275
—— —— —— Organ, 234, **237**
—— —— Thames Street: Screen, **152**, 153
—— Bermondsey Parish Church, 230
—— Charterhouse Chapel: Founder's Tomb, 17
—— Christchurch, Newgate, 275
—— Lambeth Parish Church, 184
—— St. Alphege, Greenwich: Altar Rails, 158, **161**
—— —— —— Benefaction Tablet, 170, **176**
—— —— —— Sand Glasses, 188, **190**
—— St. Andrew, Holborn: Organ, 234
—— —— Hubbard, 26, 299
—— —— Undershaft: Library, 195, 196
—— —— —— Organ, 234

London, St. Botolph, Aldersgate Without, 273
—— St. Catherine Cree: Altar Table, 246, **248**
—— St. George's, Hanover Square, 205
—— St. Giles, Cripplegate, 234
—— St. James, Garlickhithe: Font Cover, **96**, 99
—— —— —— Pulpit, **126**, 131
—— St. Leonard, Shoreditch: Clock, **180**, 185
—— —— —— Wardens' Accounts, 303
—— St. Magnus-the-Martyr: Organ, 234, **238**
—— —— Reredos, 249, **252**
—— St. Margaret, Lothbury: Screen, **152**, 153
—— St. Margaret Pattens: Pew, 116, **117**
—— —— Wardens' Accounts, 303
—— St. Martin's-in-the-Fields, 169
—— St. Mary Abchurch: Poor Box, 282, **284**
—— —— Reredos, 249, **251**
—— St. Mary Woolnoth: Altar Rails, 158, **161**
—— St. Michael, Cornhill, 194, 303, 304
—— —— Friday Street, 304
—— St. Paul's Cathedral, 157, 183
—— St. Stephen, Walbrook, 148
Long Coombe, Oxon: Painting of "Doom," 214, **218**
—— —— Stone Pulpit, **118**, 121
—— Melford, Suffolk, 8
—— Stanton, Cambs, **84**
Loversall, Yorks: Churchyard Tomb, 30, **33**
Lower Halstow, Kent: Lead Font, 18
Lowick, Northants: Effigy, 67
Luccombe, Somerset, 177, 181, 241
Ludham, Norfolk: Royal Arms, 166, 167
—— Screen, 138
Ludlow, Salop, 169, 205
Luppitt, Devon., 298
Lychgates, 13, 14, 24, 25, **27**
Lyddington, Rutland, 298
Lydiard Tregoze, Wilts.: Communion Rail, 158, **161**

INDEX 315

Lymington, Hants: Royal Arms, 168, **173**
Lyndwood, William, Bishop of St. David's, 193
Lyttelton, Sir Thomas: Will, 1481, 194

M.

Maidstone, Kent, Museum, 14
Malpas, Cheshire: Chest, **278**, 279
Mancetter, Warwick: Jesse Window, 205
Markham's *Essay on Hatchments*, 177
Marmion, John and Wife: Tomb, 66
Marston Magna, Somerset, 182
Marton Cheshire, 223
Matlock, Derby, 305
Matterdale, Cumberland, 239
Mayfield, Sussex, 229
Mears Ashby, Northants, 282
Meaux Abbey, E.R. Yorks, 290
Mellis, Suffolk, 167
Mellor, Devon: Pulpit, **119**, 122
Melton Mowbray, 260
Melton-on-the-Hill, W.R. Yorks: Stained Glass, 206, **210**, 211
Mensæ or Altar Slabs, 255
Mere, Wilts, 8
Merevale, Warwick: Stained Glass, 203, **207**
Merrington, Durham: Post-Reformation Screen, 148
Merton, Surrey, 178
Milton Keynes, Bucks: Piscina, **263**, 266
—— —— —— Sedilia, 267, **269**
Milverton, Somerset: Bench Ends, 110, **112**
Minchinhampton, Glos, 170
Minehead, Somerset: Almery, 274
—— —— Canopied Tomb, 65
—— —— Striking Jack, 181
Minster Lovell, Oxon: Table Tomb, 17
Minsterley, Salop: Maidens' Garlands, **302**, 306
Minton, Potteries, 293
Misericords, 104, **106**
Mitcham, Norfolk, 203
Mobberley, Chester: Communion Cup, 259, **261**
—— —— Screen, 143

Mochdre, Montgomery: Rood Fragments, 147
Monk, William, 182
Monksilver, Somerset: Bench Ends, 110, **112**
Monyash, Derbyshire: Sedilia, **264**, 267
Mordaunt, Lady Mary: Effigy, 1705, 67
Morpeth, Northumberland, 205
Morton Morrell, Warwick, 239
Moses and Aaron: Mural Paintings, 223

N.

Nantwich, Cheshire: Stalls, 104, **105**
Nelson, Dr., *Ancient Painted Glass in England*, 198, 199, 203
—— Hatchment to Lord, 178
Newcastle, Castle Chapel: Incised Slab, 49, **51**
Newcastle-on-Tyne, All Saints, 187
Newington, Kent, 214
Newland, Glos: Table Tomb, 31
Newnham Murren, Oxon: Tile, 290, **291**
Newport, Essex, 281
—— I. of W.: Carolean Pulpit, **125**, 128
Norbury, Derbyshire: Effigies, 58, **59**
—— —— Stained Glass, 203
Northampton, St. Giles, 241
North Crawley, Bucks: Wooden Headpost, **34**, 35
—— Denchurch, Berks, 197
Northiam, Sussex: Candelabra, **227**, 229
Northleach, Glos, 245, 274
North Luffenham, Rutland, 266
—— Walsham, Norfolk: Royal Arms, 168
—— Wingfield, Derbyshire, 232
Northwold, Norfolk: Easter Sepulchre, **22**, 23
Norwich, All Saints, 297
Norwich, St. Peter Mancroft, 260, 297
—— —— Parmentergate, 297
Notes and Queries, 165
Nottingham, 287, 290

O.

Oboe, 241, 242
Oddington, Oxon: Shrouded Effigy, 60
—— Glos.: "Doom" Painting, 214
Oldfield, Humphrey, 197, 198
Old Radnor, St. Stephen: Church Organ, 234, **235**
—— —— Fortified Tower, 76, 77
Opus Anglicanum, 295, 296
Ormonde, Thomas, Earl of: Will (1515), 194
Oswestry, Salop: Lychgate, 26
Otford, Kent, 230
Ottery St. Mary, Devon, 267
Over Stowey, Somerset, 229
Owen, Rev. Elias, 43, 294
Oxford, All Souls' Chapel: Stained Glass, 13

P.

Painswick, Glos: Yews in Churchyard, 38, **45**
Painted Decoration, **16**, **123**, 127, 138, **140**
Palimpsest, Royal Arms, 168, **173**
Parclose Screens, 115, **141**, 143
Parish Armouries, 164, 165
—— Coffins, 303, 304
Parwich, Derbyshire, 223, 232
Patcham, Surrey, 212
Patricio, Brecon: Roodloft, **6**, 144
Patrington, E.R. Yorks: Easter Sepulchre, **271**, 273
—— —— Font, **92**, 97
Pemmyrydd, Anglesey, 295
Penrith, Cumberland, 229
Penshurst, Kent: Churchyard Approach, 26
Peter's Pence, 280
Petsey, Salop, 205
Pews, **113**, **114**, 115, 116, **117**
Pickering, N.R. Yorks: Mural Paintings, 214, **218**, 221-2.
Pinhoe, Devon: Poor Box, 282, **285**
Piscina, 19
Pitch-pipe, 234, 239
Pittington, Durham, 170
Pleasley, Derbyshire, 188
Poppyheads, **107**, 109
Porchester, Hants, 166

Porlock, Somerset, 223, 304
Poughill, Cornwall, 167
Powysland Museum, 147
Prestbury, Cheshire: Sand Glass, 187
—— —— Screen, **151**, 153
Preston, Glos: Bell Turret, **84**, 86
Purbeck: Marble Effigies, **52**, 54, 57
Purey-Cust, Dr. Arthur, 212

Q.

Quethiock, Cornwall, 204

R.

Radcliffe-on-Trent, Notts, 67
Ranworth, Norfolk, 8, 138
Rattlesden, Suffolk: Almery, 274
—— —— Poppyhead, **107**, 109
Raunds, Northants, 184, 216
Reading St. Laurence, 182
Reighton, E.R. Yorks: Font, 88, **90**
Repton, 287, 290
Richardson, C. J., 187
Ringer's Rhymes, 80, 85
Ringstead, Northants, 274
Rivenhall, Essex, 199
Roberts, The Brothers, Smiths, 158
Rodmersham, Kent: Sedilia, 19
Roe, *Ancient Coffers and Cupboards*, 281
Rogate, Sussex, 275
Rolleston Effigies, Darley Dale, 53, 54
Romsey Abbey: Tiles, 289, **291**
Romsey, Hants: Desk Lectern, **130**, 132
Roodlofts, **6**, **143**, 144, **145**, 147, 148, **149**
Rossington, W.R. Yorks: Almery, 274
—— —— Pulpit, **123**, 127
—— —— Tiles, **286**, 289
Rotherthorpe, Northants, 274
Rowberrow, Somerset: Pre-Norman Cross, 30
Rowington, Warwick: Almery, 274
—— —— Pulpit, 122
Rowlestone, Hereford: Iron Bracket, 154, **155**, 229
Ruislip, Middlesex, 275
Rugby, Warwick, 77, 279
Rushden, Northants, 205

INDEX

Rushton Tarrant, Dorset, 298
Ruston Parva, Yorks : Font, 88, **90**
Ruyton, Salop, 170
Rycote, Oxon : Altar Table, 245, **247**
—— —— Pews, **114**, 115
Rye, Sussex : Altar, 245, **248**
—— —— Clock Jack, 181
Ryton, Durham : Post-Reformation Screen, 148

S.

St. Alban's Abbey : Bread Cupboard, 275, **277**
St. Alban's, St. Michael : Pulpit, **124**, 128
—— —— Royal Arms, 168
St. Austell, Cornwall, 184
St. Breock, Cornwall, 167
St. Breward, Cornwall, 167
St. Christopher, 215, **219**
St. Dennis, Cornwall, 167
St. Endellion, Cornwall : Ringers' Rhymes, 85
St. Ewe, Cornwall : Royal Arms, 166
St. Feack, Cornwall : Royal Arms, 167
St. John Hope, Sir William, 20, 300
St. Kea, Cornwall : Font, 88, **91**
St. Kew, Cornwall : Stained Glass, 204
St. Keyne, Cornwall, 204
St. Leven, Cornwall : Lychgate, 26
St. Mellion, Cornwall : Stained Glass, 204
St. Mylor, Cornwall, 167
St. Neots, Cornwall : Stained Glass, 203, 204
St. Newlyn, Cornwall : Royal Arms, 167
St. Perran Zabuloe, Cornwall : Seating, 103
St. Sampson, Cornwall, 167, 204
St. Teath, Cornwall, 204
St. Winnow, Cornwall : Bench Ends 110
—— —— Gateway, 26
—— —— Stained Glass, 204
Salford, Lancs., 197
Salisbury Cathedral, Library, 193
Salisbury, St. Edmunds, 194, 273
—— St. Thomas, 166, 214

Saltfleet-by-All Saints, Lincs, 246
Samwell, Sir Thomas, Hatchment, 178, **179**
Sandon, Staffs : Erdeswike Effigies, 54
Sandridge, Herts : Screen, 133
Sandwich, St. Clement, 298
Sarum, St. Edmund, Wilts, 187
Saxton, Yorks : Dacre Tomb, 30
Sedgefield, Durham : Post-Reformation Screen, 148
Sedilia, 19
Segrave, Sir John de : Tomb, **10**, 17
Selbourne, Hants : Churchyard Yew, 37
Selworthy, Somerset, 241
" Serpent," 240, **243**
Sevenoaks, Kent, 275
" Seven Sacraments " Fonts, 19, **93**, 97
Shaw, Henry, 224, **225**
Shawms, 239, 240
Sheldon, J., 293
Shelsley Walsh, Worcs, 289
Shipdham, Norfolk, 170
Shorwell, I. of W. : Mural Painting, 215, **219**
Shotteswell, Warwick, 245
Shouldham, Norfolk : Incised Slab, **51**, 53
Shrewsbury, St. Mary : Jesse Window, 205
Shute, Devonshire : Pole Effigy, 68
Siddington, Glos : Stained Glass, **202**, 206
Skenfrith, Hereford, 296
Skirbeck, Lincs : Stone Seating, **101**, 103
Slabs, Altar, 255
—— Incised, 48, 49, 50, **51**, **52**, 53
—— Iron, 163
—— Semi-effigal, 54
Sleaford, Lincs, 196
Smith, Father, 234
Somerby, Lincs : Dated Bells, 79, **81**
Somercotes, Lincs : Dated Bells, 79, **81**
Somerleyton, Suffolk : Screen, 138
Somerton, Oxon : Reredos, **244**, 249
Sompting, Sussex, 275
Sotterley, Suffolk : Screen, 138
Southampton, St. John, 188

South Carney, Glos: Rood Fragment, 147
—— Molton, Devon: Pulpit, 122
—— Petherwin, Cornwall, 167, 204
—— Wingfield, Derby, 306
Southwold, Suffolk: Roodloft remains, 147
—— —— Screen, 138
—— —— Stalls, 102, 104
—— —— Striking Jack, 181, **185**
Spanish Moorish Tiles, 287, 290, 293
Spencer, Sir John and Lady Isabella, Tomb, **61**, 65
Spilsby, Lincs: Willoughby Effigies, **55**, 58, 68, **69**
Spratton, Northants: Swynford Effigy, 55, **58**, 66
Staines, All Hallows, 187
—— St. Peter's, 187
Stalls, **102**, 103, 104, **105**
Stamford St. John's, Lincs: Roodloft, 147
Stanford, Northants, 177
Stanstead Abbots, Herts, 166
Stanton Harcourt, Oxon: Iron Gates, 158, **159**
—— —— Screen, 13
Staple, Kent: Lychgate, 25
"Statas Armys," 167
Stebbing, Essex: Stone Screen, 133
Steeple Aston, Oxon: Mediæval Cope, 20
Stoke Bruern, Northants: Hatchment, 177, **179**
—— d'Abernon, Surrey: Brass, 57, 74
Stokesay, Salop: Patron's Pew, 116, **117**
Stone, Kent, 288
—— Pulpits, **118**, 121, 122
—— Screens, 133, 134, **135**
Stow-nine-Churches, Northants: Effigies, 52, **57**, 64, **67**
—— —— Screen, 148
Stratford-on-Avon, 267
Stratton-on-the-Fosse, Somerset: Pulpit, 122
Streatfeilde, Richard: Slab, 163
Striking Jacks, 181, **185**
Sturminster Marshall, Dorset: Pulpit, 131
Suffolk, Alice (Chaucer), Duchess of, Tomb, 65

Sullington, Sussex, 274
Surrey Archæological Society Collections, 38, 41
Sussex Collections, 41
Sutton, Lincs: Ringers' Rhymes, 85
Swaffham Bulbeck, Cambs, 276, 281
Swavesey, Cambs: Sedilia, 267, **270**
Swinbrook, Oxon: Churchyard Tombs, 32, **39**
—— —— Fettiplace Effigies, 59, **69**
Sword Rests, 158, **162**
Swymbridge, Devon: Screen, **136**, 137
Swyncombe, Oxon, 274
Syon Cope, 295, 296

T.

Tablets, Commandments, Creed, etc., 169, 170, **174**, **175**, **176**
—— Memorial, **71**, 73
Tamworth, Warwick, 279
Tandridge, Surrey: Churchyard Yew, 38
Tanfield, Yorks: Marmion Tomb, 66
—— —— Stone "Confessional," 298, **301**
Terrington, St. Clements, Norfolk, 170, **176**
Teynham, Kent, 14
Thaxted, Essex, **3**
Theddlethorpe, Lincs, 246
Thornhill, Yorks: Saville Tomb, 17
—— W. R. Yorks: Stained Glass 205, 206
Throwleigh, Devon, "Church House," 26
Thursley, Surrey: Chestnut Tree in Churchyard, 35
Tijou, Jean, 157
Tilney, All Saints, Norfolk, 148, 266
Tilstock, Salop, 229, 279
Tilston, Cheshire: Churchyard Cross, **28**, 30
Tintagel, Cornwall, 245
Tissington, Derby, 306
Tollemache Effigies, Helmingham, 67, 68

Torksey, Lincs: Churchyard Tomb, 31
Tortworth, Glos: Chestnut Tree in Churchyard, 35
Totnes, Devon: Screen, 133
"Tournai Fonts," 11, 19
Trees in Churchyards, 35-38, 45
Trumpington, Cambs: *Grisaille Glass*, 201, 206
Trunch, Norfolk: Screen, 138
Trusley, Derbyshire, 177
Tunstead, Norfolk: Rood beam, 144
—— —— Screen, 138
Turton, Lancs, 198
Twycross, Leicester, 200
Twyford, Hants: Churchyard Yew, 37-38

U.

Uffington, Berks: Sedilia, 264, 267
Ufford, Suffolk: Font Cover, 94, 98
—— Poppyheads, 107, 109
Ugborough, Devon: Screen, 137, 138, 139
Upper Snell, Glos, 304
Upton, Northants: Hatchment, 178, 179
—— —— Wall Almery, 274
—— Notts, 279, 298

V.

Vamping Horns, 239
Victoria and Albert Museum — South Kensington: 17th century Communion Cup, 259, 260, 261
—— —— Syon Cope, 295

W.

Wall, J. Charles, 281
Walsoken, Norfolk: Bench End, 108, 109, 110
—— —— Font, 93, 97
—— —— Screen detail, 134, 140
Walton-on-the-Hill, Surrey: Font, 88, 91
Warburton Chapel, St. John's, Chester, 156, 157
Wareham, Dorset, 231
Warkworth, Northumberland, 158

Warwick St. Mary's: Beauchamp Tomb, 66
—— —— Beauchamp Chapel, 215
Washfield, Devon: Carolean Screen, 148, 150
Watson, White, of Bakewell, 303
Watton, E. R. Yorks, 232
Weddington, Warwick, 245
Wedmore, Somerset, Candelabra, 226, 230
Wells, Cathedral Clock, 183, 186
—— Cathedral Library, 198
Wem, Salop, 279
West Chantry, Ely: Iron Gates, 156, 157
—— Chiltington, Sussex, 213
—— Grinstead, Sussex, 276
Westhall, Suffolk: Poppyhead, 107, 109
—— —— Screen, 16, 138
West Hallam, Derby, 306
—— Hanningfield, Essex, 276
—— Hendred, Berks: Tiles, 289, 291
—— Horsley, Surrey: 13th Century Glass, 200, 201
Westlake: *Stained Glass*, 199
Westleigh, Kent, 288
Weston, E.R. Yorks: Cresset Stone, 228, 232
Weston-on-Trent, Derby, 304
Westwell, Kent: Jesse Window, 205
Westwick, Norfolk: Screen, 138
West Wickham, Kent: Lychgate, 25
Whalley, Lancs: Pre-Norman Cross, 29
Wheatley, *Common Prayer*, 303
Whitchurch, Salop, 229
Wickmere, Norfolk, 282
Wigginhall St. Mary, Norfolk: Lectern, 129, 131
—— —— Poppyheads, 107, 109
Willoughby Effigies: Spilsby, 55, 58
Willoughton, Lincs, 239
Wilne, Derby: Font, 87, 89
—— Tiles in Willoughby Chapel, 293
Wilton, Wilts, 199
Wimborne Minster: Chained Library, 191, 198
—— Relic Chest, 276
Winchester, St. John's, 214

Winchfield, Hants, 214
Windsor, Thomas, of Stanwell, 273
Winestead, E.R. Yorks: Hilyard Effigy, 59, **62**
Wingerworth, Derby, 177
Winscombe, Somerset: Stained Glass, **209**, 211
Winster, Derby: Font, 88, **89**
Winterbourne Abbas, Dorset, 242
Winthorpe, Lincs: Bench End, **108**, 109, 110
Wintringham, Yorks, 282, **284**
Wirksworth, Derbyshire: Saxon Tomb, **46**, 47, 48
Wistanton, Salop, 169
Witheredge, Devon: Stone Pulpit, **118**, 122
Witton, 287
Wivelsfield, Sussex, 275
Wolverhampton, St. Peter's: Pulpit, 122
Wolverton, Hants, 163
Woodcote, Hants: Churchyard Yew, 37
Wooden Effigies, **63**, 66, 67
—— Headposts, **34**, 35
Wool, Dorset: Bells, 79, **82**
—— —— Cresset Stone, 231
—— —— Embroidery, 296

Wootten-Wawen, Warwickshire, 196, 279
Worcester Cathedral, 269
—— St. Michael, 169
Worle, Somerset: Pulpit, 121
Wormingford, Essex: Wooden Effigies, **63**, 66
Wormleighton, Warwick: Altar Rails, **253**, 255
Worth, Sussex: Pulpit, 131
Wychling, Kent: Lead Font, **10**, 19
Wymondham, Norfolk: Candelabra, **227**, 229
—— —— Sedilia, 267, **270**

Y.

Yarnton, Oxon.: Jacobean Screen, 148, **150**
—— —— Stained Glass, **210**, 211
Yatton: Wardens' Accounts, 166
—— Keynell, Wilts.: Screen, 133
Yew, Ceremonial Use in Churches, 36, 37
York Minster: Stained Glass, 199
—— St. Denys, 199
—— St. Michael, 205
Youlgreave, Derbyshire, 240, 241, 295

www.ingramcontent.com/pod-product-compliance
Lightning Source LLC
Chambersburg PA
CBHW081346230426
43667CB00017B/2740